SalonOvations'
Marketing
and Advertising
for the Salon

Delmar Publishers' Online Services
To access Delmar on the World Wide Web, point your browser to:
http://www.delmar.com/delmar.html
To access through Gopher: gopher://gopher.delmar.com
(Delmar Online is part of "thomson.com", an internet site with information on
more than 30 publishers of the International Thomson Publishing organization.)
For information on our products and services:
email: info@delmar.com
or call 800-347-7707

SalonOvations'
Marketing
and Advertising
for the Salon

Dr. Henry J. Gambino

Milady Publishing Company
(a division of Delmar Publishers)

3 Columbia Circle, Box 12519
Albany, New York 12212-2519

Notice to the Reader

Publisher does not warrant or guarantee any of the products described herein or perform any independent analysis in connection with any of the product information contained herein. Publisher does not assume, and expressly disclaims, any obligation to obtain and include information other than that provided to it by the manufacturer.

The reader is expressly warned to consider and adopt all safety precautions that might be indicated by the activities described herein and to avoid all potential hazards. By following the instructions contained herein, the reader willingly assumes all risks in connection with such instructions.

The publisher makes no representations or warranties of any kind, including but not limited to, the warranties of fitness for particular purpose or merchantability, nor are any such representations implied with respect to the material set forth herein, and the publisher takes no responsibility with respect to such material. The publisher shall not be liable for any special, consequential or exemplary damages resulting, in whole or in part, from the readers' use of, or reliance upon, this material.

Cover Design: Suzanne McCarron
Cover Photo: Michael Dzaman

Milady Staff:
Publisher: Catherine Frangie
Acquisitions Editor: Marlene McHugh Pratt
Production Manager: Brian Yacur
Project Editor: Annette Downs Danaher
Production Art/Design Coordinator: Suzanne McCarron

Printed in the United States of America
Printed and distributed simultaneously in Canada

For more information, contact:
SalonOvations
Milady Publishing Company
3 Columbia Circle, Box 12519
Albany, New York 12212-2519

1 2 3 4 5 6 7 8 9 10 XXX 01 00 99 98 97 96

Library of Congress Cataloging-in-Publication Data

Gambino, Henry J.
    SalonOvations' marketing and advertising for the salon / by Henry J. Gambino.
        p.   cm.
    ISBN 1-56253-262-6
    1. Beauty shops—Management.   2. Beauty shops—Marketing.
3. Advertising.   I. Title.
TT965.G37   1996
646.7'2'0688—dc20   95-13216
                                                                CIP

Contents

Foreword   ix
Acknowledgments   xi

Chapter 1—Marketing Basics   **1**

Marketing: A Description   1
Overview of Marketing Principles   2
The Marketing Environments   5
Marketing Planning   19
Trends in Marketing   20

Chapter 2—Marketing Information   **31**

The Value of Information and Knowledge   31
Information Needs   32
Know Your Customers   34
Know Your Competition   40
Know the Market Situation   42
Know Yourself   43
Market Research   44
Data Analysis   57
Sources of Information   58
Summary   65

Chapter 3—The Marketing Plan   **69**

Marketing Plan Structure   69
The Marketing Planning Process   78
Marketing Communications   79
Summary   79

Chapter 4—Computerizing the Salon   **81**

Uses of the Computer   81
Marketing Communications with the Computer   89
Computer Equipment   89

Choosing Your Computer System and Software   99
Using Your Computer Properly   99
Summary   100

Chapter 5—Product   **101**

The Importance of Image   102
Establishing Your Image   102
Salon Services   110
Salon Retail Operations   125
The Market for Retail Sales   125
Products for Retail Sales   126
Retail Selling   128
Summary   130

Chapter 6—Pricing   **133**

Factors in Pricing Decisions   133
Cost   136
Demand   137
Competition   139
Goals   140
Cash and Expense Management   140
Pricing Policies   143
Raising Prices   144
Retail Product Pricing   146
Summary   148

Chapter 7—Place   **151**

The Channels of Distribution   151
Retailer Utility   155
Availability   155
Concepts in Retailing   156
The Retail Sales Area   170
Summary   171

Chapter 8—Promotion   **173**

A Brief Theory of Communication   174
Marketing Communications   176
Legal and Ethical Issues in Promotion   180
Trademarks, Patents, and Copyrights   186

Model and Property Releases 188
Summary 189

Chapter 9—Marketing Communications **191**

Objectives 193
Strategy 195
Tactics 200
Measuring Communications Effectiveness 200
Marketing Communications Budgets 201
Creative Agencies 202
Client/Agency Relationship 207
Finding a Creative Agency 208
Summary 209

Chapter 10—Fundamentals of Design **211**

Importance of Design 211
Principles of Design 211
Layout 215
Copy 219
Typography 222
Graphics 230
Color 235
Size and Shape 237
Summary 238

Chapter 11—Fundamentals of Production **241**

The Production Process 241
Printing Processes 244
Alternative Production Processes 246
Reproducing Photographs and Graphics 248
Color 249
Paper 251
Choosing and Working with a Printer 254
Summary 256

Chapter 12—Advertising **259**

Overview of Advertising 259
Advertising Objectives 261
Advertising Effectiveness 263

Advertising Media   267
Measuring Advertising Effectiveness   285
Anatomy of a Print Advertisement   287
Anatomy of a Radio Commercial   291
Summary   294

Chapter 13—Direct Marketing   **297**

Direct Marketing and Advertising Comparison   297
Direct Marketing Lists   300
Direct Marketing Vehicles   302
Direct Mailers   302
Sales Letters   310
Brochures and Catalogs   312
Circulars   314
Cooperative Mailings   316
Newsletters   316
Annual Reports   319
Video Mailings   320
Telemarketing   320
For the Future   322
Measuring Direct Marketing Effectiveness   323
Summary   323

Chapter 14—Sales Promotion and Public Relations   **327**

Personal Selling   328
The Salon   329
Displays   329
Sales   333
Special Events   333
Open Houses and Demonstrations   336
Tie-In Promotions   336
Other Promotion Strategies   337
Public Relations   341
Publicity   341
Personal Appearances   345
Sponsorships   345
Community Service   345
Summary   346

Glossary/Index   349

Foreword

You've already read the statistics somewhere. They're published and updated every so often in magazines, newspapers, and books. I'm talking about the very high rate of new business failures. The U.S. Small Business Administration says that over 50 percent of all new businesses fail within the first two years. These statistics are believable because you've seen the evidence in your own home town. A new business, store, or restaurant opens up. Announcements are placed in the local paper. "Grand Opening" banners are hung. The owner is interviewed on TV. Six months later, the business is having a "Going-Out-Of-Business" sale. Then the space is vacated and a "For Lease" sign is hung in the window. It's a shame because these owners invested time, energy, spirit, and a lot of money (sometimes their entire life savings) in their business. The real shame is that the business didn't *have* to fail.

I've been a business consultant for more than 10 years, and in my experience, more than 85 percent of all small business failures are caused by poor marketing. Ask the former owners of any failed business why it closed and they'll give you a variety of reasons—lack of profits, poor cash flow, high expenses, partnership disputes. They still don't have a clue! If you investigate further and ask them some pointed questions, you'll find that the business wasn't profitable because it couldn't bring in customers. Poor cash flow meant that the sales were so poor that there wasn't enough flow of money to support a viable business. High expenses? The owners weren't buying Cadillacs and taking weekend trips to Saint Thomas. They had reasonable and normal expenses. They just didn't have enough monthly business income to support them. Partnership disputes? If the partners were busy and the place was making money, they wouldn't have the time or inclination to fight. But sales are poor and they're sitting around in the salon all day waiting for a paying customer to show up. And when few do, the partners spend their spare time blaming each other for their lack of success.

This doesn't have to happen. You are holding in your hands the best failure-prevention method available—knowledge and

expertise. This book contains all the information you need to create a successful marketing program for your salon. It will show you
how to bring in customers who will pay you the prices you require
to be a profitable and successful business. The writer is an expert.
Do not be misled by Dr. Gambino's Ph.D. This is not a theoretical
textbook. Dr. Gambino has not only studied small businesses, he
has owned several, including a beauty salon. He didn't just study
the small business world. He lived in it. He had to make payroll
every week, just like you do. He had to set and live by an operating budget, just like you'll be doing. He had limited resources to
spend on advertising and, therefore, had to get the most bang for
his buck—just like you need to. Dr. Gambino writes from experience. This book is about hard, cold reality. It states problems, offers
suggestions, and proposes solutions.

You need to read this book in a special way. Devour it. Mark
relevant passages with a highlighter marker. Make notes to yourself in the margins. Make lists of things to do as you are inspired by
the book's ideas. And when you're done, read it again. Don't con-
sign this book to a bookshelf for the rest of its life. Pull it out and
read it as you need to. It will help you make advertising and marketing decisions as your salon grows and prospers.

Marketing is a lifetime task. You can't just formulate a strategy
and forget it. You must change and evolve your marketing strategy
and promotional methods as your salon grows, as the demographics
of your town shift, and as your competition changes. Make this book
your friend for life.

JOSEPH M. SHERLOCK

*Joseph M. Sherlock is the president of Sherlock Strategies, in Vancouver, Wash-
ington. Sherlock Strategies is a management consulting firm that specializes in
small to midsize businesses. Mr. Sherlock has been a contributor to several business magazines and is the author of a newspaper column, "Doing Business."*

Acknowledgments

It takes a lot of people to make a book. This book is no exception. I would like to thank all those people who helped turn this book from an idea into a reality. Very special thanks go to Joseph M. Sherlock, president of Sherlock Strategies and an expert in marketing for small businesses, and to Clifford W. Keevan, an expert in advertising and promotion. They are both good friends whose suggestions and encouragement have helped make this a better book.

Special thanks to the following professionals for their expertise and helpful input while reviewing this manuscript: Ken Young, Oklahoma City, Oklahoma; Don Osborne, Costa Mesa, California; Barbara Horvath, Little Canada, Minnesota; Nancy Phillips, Tolono, Illinois; Margaret Cipolla, Hathorne, Massachusetts; and Tom Sollock, Oklahoma City, Oklahoma.

Thanks also go to the many people who have reviewed individual chapters and who have graciously consented to let me use their materials to illustrate parts of the book. These include Joseph W. Rizzuto, for his insights into design and production; and William Silva, owner and operator of Silva Hair Works in Doylestown, PA for permission to use his ad. Thanks also to Dee Levin, owner of Salon Norman Dee, for the use of her salon newsletter.

Mary Ann Trainor, of McGraw-Hill, Inc., granted permission to use her company's famous "Man-in-the-Chair" ad. Suzi Weiss–Fischmann of OPI Products and Peter Samerjan supplied photographs of counter displays. Janine Allegretto of Clairol Professional let me use the Clairol ad. And Joanne Kuchera of Telephone Concepts let me use photos of focus groups and telephone surveys. To all of these people, thank you.

Thanks also go to the entire staff of Aeone Communications, especially Quentin, Petunia, Sammy, Erika, Frederika, and LC, for creating a number of original marketing communications pieces specifically to illustrate this book. Finally, very special thanks to the person without whom this book probably wouldn't have gotten finished: my wife Maureen, who patiently proofread, corrected, and suggested, and who supported and encouraged me through every page.

CHAPTER 1

Marketing Basics

Recognize one fact right from the beginning: Marketing is the most important factor you'll face if you want your salon business to be successful and prosper. Marketing drives business. It steers your salon in the proper direction and keeps you from getting lost. Pay attention to marketing and follow sound marketing principles, and you should do well. As marketing guru Joseph M. Sherlock, president of the West Coast–based marketing consulting firm, Sherlock Strategies, says, "In all my years of experience in counseling and advising business clients, I've found that 85 percent of all client problems are marketing related."

Marketing is not a concept only for big business. It is as vital to the small, one-person salon as it is to General Motors Corporation. You can't do business and survive in today's marketplace unless you are aware of and practice good marketing principles. The only difference between the small salon and the major multinational corporation is one of scale.

Sounds daunting, doesn't it? But don't worry. Marketing is not as complicated or as dreadful as you might think at first glance. In fact, a lot of good marketing practice is just plain old common sense, coupled with a thorough knowledge of your business and your customers.

MARKETING: A DESCRIPTION

Just what is marketing? The American Marketing Association has defined it as "the process of planning the conception, pricing, promotion, and distribution of goods and services to create exchanges that satisfy individual and organizational objectives." That's a wordy way to say that marketing is that series of actions you take to develop your products and services, ensure their quality and value to the customer, set their prices, make them available, identify to whom you want to sell them, inform consumers of them, persuade prospects to come into your salon, satisfy clients' needs, *and*

1

get them to come back, again and again. In short, marketing comprises virtually everything you do to run your business.

THE IMPORTANCE OF MARKETING TO BUSINESS SUCCESS

Why is marketing essential to your business? It is essential simply because consumers have a choice of where they will purchase their goods. As long as they have a choice, marketing will drive business. Remember, people don't buy things. They buy solutions to their problems, even if they're not consciously aware of what the problems are. Marketing, with the help of your marketing communications, tells them what those solutions are and helps them make the right choice.

In its most simple terms marketing is "demand creation." Simply put, this means just what it says—you have to create a demand for your product or service in the mind of the customer. In today's highly competitive business climate, however, marketing is really much more. It is the sum total of all you do to satisfy your customers' needs.

Marketing is a different way of thinking. It is a way of looking at your business that you may not be used to. It's knowing just what business you're actually in and knowing how to reach your customers. No doubt you are an accomplished practitioner of your craft. You can be a wizard when it comes to cutting and styling hair. You can be a genius in caring for your clients' skin. You can be an artist in applying makeup. But that, in itself, isn't enough to succeed. No matter how good your services are, if you don't recognize exactly what you are selling, your marketing efforts will fail. You have to sell the benefits of the service, not its features. That's what the customer really wants.

OVERVIEW OF MARKETING PRINCIPLES

THE MARKETING MIX

The marketing process traditionally starts with the marketing mix, commonly referred to as the four P's—product, price, place, and promotion. These are the foundation on which the marketing structure is built. Current marketing thought adds two additional factors to those four—quality and customer service. Not one of these six elements is more important than any other. They are all equally

---

- **PRODUCT**
  The products and services you offer for sale, as well as your salon and yourself

- **PRICE**
  The amount of money the customer gives you in return for the value he or she receives

- **PLACE**
  The distribution channels for the products and the methods by which you get your products in the hands of the client

- **PROMOTION**
  Marketing communications and the steps you take to inform and persuade your customers

---

Figure 1-1. The four P's are the cornerstone of marketing.

vital. Your marketing efforts can be as good only as the weakest element in the structure. The four P's are outlined in Figure 1-1.

Quality and customer service must be a high priority in your operations. They should pervade everything you do. These two elements are not something extra you provide to your customer. They are the elements that get you into the game. Without them, you won't be able to compete effectively.

Product refers to your services and to the products you sell at retail, those items you offer to your customers in exchange for money. It also includes the image you project to your customers, which is a reflection of your own vision of your business and your goals. When you choose your product mix, make sure to pick those that meet your customers' needs and wants. Then make sure you can deliver them to the best of your ability. Treat each service or product line as a separate profit center. Keep careful records of each and retain only those that meet your goals and the customers' expectations. Remember, like people, products have a life cycle—birth, growth, maturity, old age, and death. Be aware of these cycles and know where your products are in their evolution. This topic is discussed thoroughly in Chapter 5.

Price is also important. How accurately you set the prices for your services will play a large role in your success. Pricing is more complicated than you might think. It goes well beyond establishing your costs and then adding for profit. You must also consider competition, the economy, your customers' ability to pay, and the overall image of your salon. Price is covered in Chapter 6.

Place covers the distribution channels for your products. It describes how you get your goods and services into the hands of your customers, and the channels through which you get your products. This element is no less important than price. It is a major part of your reliability. You must give your customers the confidence that they will be able to receive the services when and where they want them. This element largely determines your hours of operation, your scheduling, and your purchases of materials. Place is covered in Chapter 7.

Promotion includes all of the steps you take to inform customers of your products, persuade them to purchase them, and foster satisfaction with them. It covers the marketing communications tools available to you. These tools include personal selling, advertising, direct marketing, sales promotion, and publicity. These tools are described in Chapter 8 and covered in detail in the second half of this book.

MARKETING INFORMATION

To plan your marketing and carry out the strategies effectively, you need a lot of information. First, you have to know yourself.

- What are your strengths and weaknesses?
- How do you view your business?
- Do you know exactly what business you're in?

You also need information about your market.

- What is the total size of the available market in the area you cover?
- What share of that market can you reach?
- Who are your potential customers?
- What are their demographics?
- What motivates them to buy?

You need to know your competition, as well.

- Who are your competitors?
- How many of them are there?
- Where are they located?

- What services and products do they offer?
- What are their price structures?
- Who are their customers?
- How do you stack up against them?
- What can you offer that they can't?
- What can they offer that you can't?

What external factors do you face? The state of the economy plays a large part in determining whether your prospects will be willing to part with the sums of money you charge for your services. Population shifts in your area of interest may cause changes in your marketing plans. Trends in fashion will affect how your services may be received. Advances in technology are also important. They will determine what products and services you might add or delete.

Remember, however, that information is not knowledge. It is one thing to gather the data. It's another to analyze the data and draw conclusions. Analyze the information carefully. This is the basis for forecasting your business—that is, making an estimate of what business you are likely to attain as a result of your efforts.

The information you gather will also form the basis for your marketing communications. It will determine your positioning and your strategy for creating the demand for your services in the minds of your customers. The data will identify the "hot buttons" that will spur customers to act. Marketing information is covered in Chapter 2.

One of your most valuable tools in business today is the personal computer. It will help you analyze the information you gather and keep the data handy, ready to use. It will also do much more. There are few aspects of your business you won't be able to do quicker and more efficiently with the computer. Although it's possible to conduct your business without a computer, you will soon find the computer to be invaluable. Prices for computer hardware have reached a point at which computers are very affordable. They are also getting easier to use as business software becomes more user friendly. Consider adding a computer to your salon. What you can do with the proper equipment and software will astound you. The computer and its uses are discussed in Chapter 4.

THE MARKETING ENVIRONMENTS

It is necessary to be aware of the various environments in which you work. These are the market forces that shape your market and, therefore, determine how you approach it. There are quite a few of these forces, and they all can affect your business.

Although each is discussed here independently, keep in mind that they all interact. We all live in and are affected by multiple environments. You can't divorce the effects of one from any of the others. So you have to consider the effects of all the environments when you develop your marketing plan. The environments are summarized in Figure 1-2.

- **THE ECONOMIC ENVIRONMENT**
  State of the economy
  Clients' discretionary funds
  Clients' employment

- **THE SOCIAL ENVIRONMENT**
  Clients' lifestyles
  Age
  Ethnic and racial mix
  Education
  Gender
  Family trends

- **THE TECHNOLOGICAL ENVIRONMENT**
  Advances in technology
  Computerization
  Explosion of information
  New products and processes

- **THE POLITICAL ENVIRONMENT**
  Federal government regulations
  State and local government regulations
  Consumer movements

- **THE NATURAL ENVIRONMENT**
  Environmental protection
  Recycling
  Green products
  Health and safety issues

- **THE COMPETITIVE ENVIRONMENT**
  Competitive intelligence
  Differentiating your salon from others

Figure 1-2. Characteristics of marketing environments.

THE ECONOMIC ENVIRONMENT

The economic environment determines how much your customers may be willing or able to pay for services. It affects their receptivity to the services as well. Is the economy in recession or in a boom? You have to be aware of economic conditions in the area from which you draw your clientele and how those conditions are affecting your customers. Consider the employment statistics for the area. These should be available through your local Chamber of Commerce. If unemployment is high, there will be less discretionary income available for many salon services. If employment is high, people will have more money to spend and will be more inclined to spend it.

Also be aware of what kinds of jobs your clientele have. This will help you determine their income levels. In the case of two-wage-earner families, add both incomes to arrive at a family income. Remember, you're looking for averages you can use to characterize the population. The income level of any individual family is not important, and your clients are unlikely to tell you this information. Knowing about your clients' jobs will help you decide which services you can offer profitably and which won't sell.

You have to consider more than just the local economy. In many ways, the entire global economy has an effect on your business, at least indirectly. The value of the dollar rises and falls in relation to other currencies as the global economy changes. The exchange rate can affect the prices you pay for materials and products that are imported. When the dollar is high relative to foreign currency, prices of imported goods tend to be low. When the dollar is low, prices of imported goods tend to be high. Whether you pay more or less for the goods you buy affects your profit margin.

Many practitioners believe that the salon business is recession proof. In a sense, two factors make this partly true. First, people require some services, such as haircuts, no matter what the state of the economy. Your hair grows whether you're out of work or not. Second, compared with other luxury items, many salon services are relatively inexpensive. In poor economic times, therefore, a woman looking for some respite from her economic miseries is more likely to treat herself to a manicure than she is to buy a new outfit.

Don't be lulled into a false sense of security by these factors, however. They hold only to a point. Although it's true that people will still get haircuts, they won't get them as often and many will start doing them at home. Price will become a factor more than

quality. The same holds true for the luxury services. So recession-
ary times will determine how you will conduct your business.
Never underestimate the power of poor economic conditions to
destroy your business.

The good news is that you can survive a recession with smart
marketing. Adjust your prices. Offer specials such as family discounts or a free manicure with a haircut. Use your imagination to
keep people coming into the salon. And remember, the economy is
cyclic. Bad times don't last forever. Good times always follow. Survive the bad times and maintain your customer base, and you'll
prosper when good times come again. Good economic times,
though, don't mean you can forget marketing. You will have to
adjust the way you market your services. You will have more flexibility, but marketing will be just as important.

THE SOCIAL ENVIRONMENT

Since the middle of the twentieth century, there has been a
tremendous change in our lifestyles—the way we live and how we
perceive our existences. Social patterns have changed along with
our mores and ethics see (Figure 1-3). There have been a number
of reasons for this phenomenon, ranging from technological
advances in communications and in medicine to the influences of
multiculturalism. Lifestyles evolve. We no longer think and feel the
way our grandparents, or even our parents, did. Our children and
grandchildren won't think and feel the way we do.

These changes in lifestyles—that is, the social environment—
will also affect your market. People are mobile and move often,
changing regional trends in the process (Figure 1-4). People are
living longer. There is less emphasis on family ties and there are
more people living alone. The population is aging. Ethnic and
racial mixes are changing. More women are working. All of these
factors will enter into the marketing decisions you will make.

The general population can be classified in a number of different ways, depending on the social characteristics you want to consider. These include age, economic status, ethnic background,
education, and gender or sexual orientation. How you classify your
potential clients will determine what marketing approach you take.

Consider aging. The population can be ordered by age ranges:

- children, birth through age 9
- preteens, 10 through 12

- teenagers, 13 through 19
- young adults or "generation-X'rs," 19 through 29
- adult, 30 through 50
- middle age, 51-65
- elderly, 66 and older

Each of these age groups has different needs and different social mores. Children and preteens, for example, have little say about the services they need. The decisions and payments are made by their parents. Teenagers tend to have more freedom to make purchasing decisions, but the money may still come from the parents. Young adults and adults are generally in the striving stage. They are establishing careers and building equity in the future. Time is important to them, and although they may have considerable discretionary income, they also tend to have higher expenses while raising their families. Middle-agers tend to be more settled and be

---

- **Average Size of Household—Down 5%**
  Decreased from an average of 2.76 persons in 1980 to 2.63 persons in 1991

- **Number of One-Person Households—Up 29%**
  Increased from 18.3 million in 1980 to 23.6 million in 1991

- **Number of Women in the Labor Force—Up 25%**
  Increased from 45.5 million to 56.9 million during the 1980–1991 period

- **Households with Both Spouses Working—Up 23%**
  Increased from 23.5 million households in 1980 to 28.9 million in 1991

- **Number of College Graduates—Up 53%**
  Increased from 22.2 million in 1980 (17% of the population aged 25+) to 34.0 million in 1991 (21% of the population aged 25+)

- **Per Capita Disposable Personal Income—Up 15%**
  Increased from $14,430 (1991 dollars) in 1980 to $16,658 in 1991

Figure 1-3.   Changes in American consumer characteristics. The consumer today is better educated, has more real disposable income, and is typically in a smaller family. (Data from Cahners Advertising Research Report No. 701.3B. Reprinted with permission from Cahners Publishing Company.)

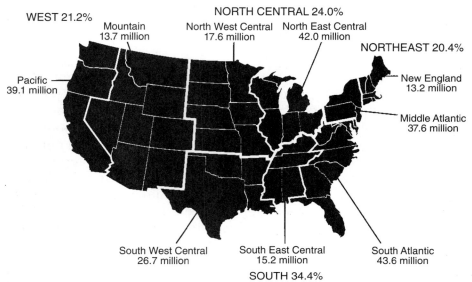

POPULATION BY REGION
April, 1990

WEST 21.2%   NORTH CENTRAL 24.0%
        Mountain   North West Central   North East Central
        13.7 million   17.6 million   42.0 million
                                                      NORTHEAST 20.4%

Pacific   New England
39.1 million   13.2 million

                                                      Middle Atlantic
                                                      37.6 million

South West Central   South East Central   South Atlantic
26.7 million   15.2 million   43.6 million
                        SOUTH 34.4%

Figure 1-4.   Regional distribution of American population. The South
is the most heavily populated region, with 34.4 percent of
the total U.S. population. The Northeast, with a population
representing 20.4 percent of the total, is now the smallest.
(Data from Cahners Advertising Research Report No.
701.1B. Reprinted with permission from Cahners Publishing Company.)

more conservative in their tastes. They have established themselves and have more discretionary income because the hardest
part of raising a family is behind them. As a result, they tend to
pamper themselves more. The elderly tend to have more leisure
time, but discretionary income may be limited by living on a fixed
income. Health problems increase with age, leading to more concern about health-related matters.

These comments refer to general trends that apply to the population as a whole. They do not necessarily apply to individuals
within the age group. Individuals are individuals, after all, and
each person has his or her own needs. Each group has different
needs and responds to different stimuli. One set of differences is
neither better nor worse than any other. There is an unfortunate
tendency among some marketers to look down on some of the age
groups, especially the young and the elderly. This is not only
wrong from a common-sense viewpoint. It is shortsighted from a

marketing perspective. All age groups are important and deserve the same respect and care.

As a marketing target, the elderly are becoming especially important. Statistics show that the population is aging. If the trend continues (and there is no reason to believe it won't), the population over 50 will increase by almost 75 percent in the next 25 years, whereas the under 50 population will increase by only 1 percent.

It is also necessary to consider the ethnic grouping of the population. We are a true multicultural population, made up of diverse origins and backgrounds. Each group has its own particular sense of self, which determines the needs and wants of its members. Again, you have to know from which groups your client base comes. Marketing opportunities come from all groups—whether African American, Asian, Hispanic, or Caucasian—as long as you are aware of how to reach them. Learn the different needs of each group and the subgroups within each. An ethnic group is not necessarily homogenous within itself. Asians, for example, consist of Chinese, Japanese, Koreans, Vietnamese, Thais, etc., each of which has its own particular culture. You have to approach each one differently.

Family trends are also important. The family is becoming less of a factor for social norms than in the past. People are getting married later or not getting married at all. More people are living alone or living together without being married. Families are having fewer children. And in fewer of the families with children does the mother stay at home. Recent statistics show that both parents work in almost 85 percent of families with children.

This increase in working mothers brings its own set of problems and marketing opportunities. Working mothers tend to have their own needs and wants, and you should cater to these if there are significant numbers of working mothers in your client base. Don't limit your thinking to working mothers, however. Consider all working women. There are currently about 57 million of them in the United States. Determine how to reach them most effectively. But be careful in your approach to them. Consider how your marketing efforts might affect the marketing you do for your male clients. The appeals you use to persuade one may not persuade the other.

You need to know from which groups your clients come and then find out what they need and want. Don't make assumptions based on what you might think. Make decisions based only on facts that are provable. Then plan your marketing strategy accordingly. Pay attention to statistics. They can tell you a lot. Especially

follow trends. Always know how the social environment is changing, and change with it as necessary.

THE TECHNOLOGICAL ENVIRONMENT

The technological environment will shape your business, too, both
indirectly and directly. New frontiers in medicine, for example,
have eliminated some diseases and extended life spans and have
shifted the population in a more elderly direction.

We are also in the midst of an information explosion, a factor
that is both an advantage and a disadvantage. More people have
more access to information today than at any time in the history of
humankind. All the communications media are growing at a staggering pace. More television channels are becoming available.
The proliferation of cellular telephones and pagers has let people
stay in closer contact with one another. Fax machines are virtually
everywhere. Electronic mail is an everyday fact of life. Many
homes now have personal computers. As a result, people are more
aware of what is going on around them than ever before.

The disadvantage of this information explosion is that consumers are inundated with messages, which often conflict. This
causes confusion and uncertainty. It makes your marketing communications more difficult because you have to cut through the
clutter and the noise to make yourself heard, let alone have your
message understood.

Businesses also are more and more computerized, and they
can reach their customers in ways never imagined before. The
computer has made possible the compilation of vast databases,
which give marketers all the information they need to target individuals with appeals specifically aimed at them. The computer also
lets the government compile more accurate statistics on the population and to publish those statistics more rapidly.

In addition, new products and new processes are being
invented and marketed with ever more rapidity. Advances in the
technology of the beauty industry, whether in new cosmetics or
new equipment, can alter your product and service mix. Some of
these advances spark new trends in consumer thinking, which will
move you in new directions. An example is the introduction and
proliferation of thigh creams based on the chemical aminophylline,
originally introduced as an antiasthmatic medical compound.
These products purportedly reduce cellulitic fat deposits on thighs
and other fatty areas. You might consider expanding your skin and

Figure 1-5. A typical beauty show crowd. (Photography by Steven Landis, with direction from Vincent and Alfred Nardi at Nardi Salon, New York City, New York.)

body care business to include these treatments. The products you use can also be sold at retail to complement the service.

Stay aware of technological advances in the beauty industry. Read the trade magazines and attend beauty trade shows, either regional or national, as shown in Figure 1-5. Read the consumer magazines and listen to your customers. Often they will have read about a new development and will ask you about it. When you find something new, get all the information you can about it, and then consider whether it will fit into your product line. Don't forget to poll your customers. Get an idea of what they think of the idea before you make a commitment. Then determine the competitive situation and other factors that may make or break sales of the service. Don't add anything new to your line just because it's new. Do the research on it so that you're reasonably sure you can create a market for it.

THE POLITICAL ENVIRONMENT

The political environment has a tremendous effect on business. Government agencies, such as the Food and Drug Administration and the Federal Trade Commission as well as many others on the federal, state, and local levels, exert considerable regulatory pressure on the conduct of business. These pressures are not limited to government agencies. The consumer movement is a big part of this, as well. Consumers are demanding more and more information and more proof of value for their dollars.

The two major federal agencies that affect the salon business are the Food and Drug Administration (FDA) and the Federal Trade Commission (FTC). The FDA is the regulatory agency responsible for making sure that a wide range of products—from medical devices, drugs, and food to cosmetics—meet the standards of the Food, Drug and Cosmetic Act, and that these products are both safe and effective. The agency tests and approves products and has the authority to remove from the marketplace products that don't meet standards. It can also refer cases to the Justice Department for prosecution in instances of fraud.

Many ingredients used in foods, drugs and cosmetics must go through a rigorous certification process before the FDA will allow their use. For example, colorants fall into this category. Colorants give a product its characteristic color. Vegetable, mineral, or animal dyes or pigments may be used without specific government approval. These compounds and chemicals usually fall under an FDA classification known as GRAS, Generally Recognized As Safe. Coal tar derivative dyes, however, must undergo a long and expensive certification process before they can go into skin care products. Certified colorants are listed as FD&C (Food, Drug and Cosmetic) colors, D&C colors or ext. D&C colors. FD&C colors can be used in food, drugs and cosmetics. D&C colors may only be used in drugs and cosmetics. Ext. D&C colors are for external use only in drugs and cosmetics.

The FDA has the legal authority to challenge claims made for products under its jurisdiction and to require substantiation for those claims. For example, the FDA is actively disputing the assertions some manufacturers of skin care products are making about the antiaging capabilities of their products. If these manufacturers cannot prove their claims to the FDA's satisfaction, they will be forced to withdraw the products. If they do not withdraw the products voluntarily, the FDA has the authority to seize the products and bring the manufacturers into court.

The FDA can also regulate equipment, such as tanning booths, and set conditions for their operation and use. If you offer such a service, you must comply with all of the relevant regulations.

By law, the FDA also has jurisdiction over packaging and labeling. Packaging cannot contain unsubstantiated claims about the product's effectiveness. Any information contained on the package must be factual. In addition, all cosmetic products must list all ingredients on the label.

The FDA also provides materials for consumer education, which are designed to keep consumers aware of the safety of the products they purchase. The agency's monthly magazine, *FDA Consumer*, available by subscription from the FDA, is an excellent source of consumer information (Figure 1-6). In addition, the agency distributes a wide range of consumer-oriented pamphlets through government bookstores.

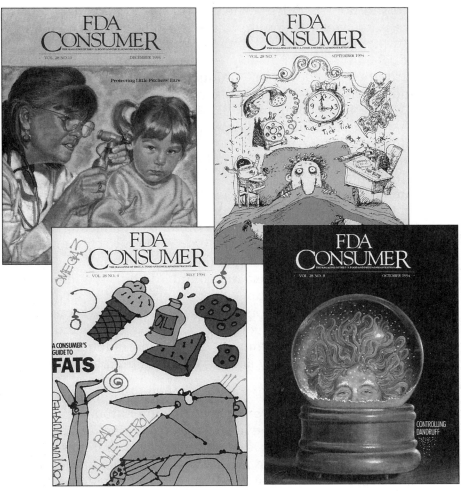

Figure 1-6. *FDA Consumer* magazine.

The Federal Trade Commission (FTC), the other major consumer watchdog agency, regulates commerce in the United States. This agency is responsible for enforcing laws that prevent unfair competitive practices. The agency helps maintain a level playing field so businesses can compete fairly. The FTC has little direct influence on the cosmetology business, but its rulings can have a significant indirect bearing.

As a general rule, you won't be involved with the FTC, although there are two areas in which you may have dealings with the agency. The first involves franchises. The agency sets rules for the sale of franchise operations. All franchise operators must abide by a set of comprehensive reporting regulations when they promote and sell the franchises. These laws were enacted to protect franchise purchasers. If you are a franchised operation, both you and the franchiser are subject to the agency's regulations.

The FTC is also responsible for preventing the manufacture and distribution of counterfeit products, a major problem in the salon industry. Many well-known national brands of cosmetic products have been counterfeited. Although these fakes are less expensive than the legitimate item, in many cases they are of inferior quality and may be unsafe to use. Moreover, it is illegal to purchase counterfeit products knowingly and sell them in your salon as the real thing.

State and local regulatory agencies will probably have more effect on your business than the federal agencies, however. Zoning laws, for example, may regulate your signage, which can affect the image you want to project. Since you are probably not engaged in interstate commerce, your business practices may not be subject to FTC regulations. But you must still comply with the regulations of your state Consumer Protection Agency, especially if either your customers or your competitors complain about your actions. So know which agencies can affect your marketing. Know and understand the regulations. Ignorance of them is no defense. If you're not sure of the legality of any action you're contemplating, consult with your attorney.

Government regulations are not your only concern with respect to the political environment. Consumers today recognize their collective power and have become more demanding about the quality of the products and services they purchase. They demand honesty, fairness, and integrity in exchange for their loyalty. So make sure to be open and honest with your customers. Give them fair value for their dollars. Be free with information. Know what ingredients are in the products you use on them and be able to impart that knowledge to them.

You must also be concerned with the causes your customers espouse and, insofar as possible, incorporate those into your marketing plans. For example, many consumers object to products that have been tested on animals. So you might consider using only products that have not been tested on animals, as far as possible. Then promote that fact. Support other causes that you and your clients believe in. Just make sure that your clients don't perceive that you're supporting the cause just for the sake of business.

THE NATURAL ENVIRONMENT

You can't ignore the natural environment, either. Environmental concerns affect what products you use, how they are packaged, and how you dispose of your wastes. Some of these concerns are regulated by the government. Others are enforced by consumers.

As its name implies, the Environmental Protection Agency (EPA) is responsible for protecting the environment. One of the EPA's major concerns currently is the emission of volatile organic compounds (VOCs). These are the vapors released into the atmosphere when products made with petroleum-based solvents are used. Although the EPA is mostly concerned with VOC control in manufacturing industries at present, be aware that some of the products you use in your salon emit VOCs as well. These include nail polishes and nail polish removers. If the agency decides to issue rules regulating the use of such salon products in the future, you will have to be aware of and follow them.

Among its other duties, the EPA also establishes rules for handling and disposing of hazardous waste materials. Many of the materials you handle in the salon can be considered hazardous. These include a variety of solvents, disinfectants, and sanitary chemicals. Your concern with the EPA will pertain to how you dispose of these.

Safe handling of hazardous waste products in the salon is a concern of the Occupational Safety and Health Administration (OSHA). This agency is responsible for ensuring safety in the workplace. You will have to be concerned with OSHA regulations in the conduct of your business, but they have little bearing on your marketing efforts.

Most of the waste products you generate in the salon will not be considered hazardous. Some, however, such as alcohol and acetone, are classed as hazardous wastes. Be careful how you dispose of these. Do not pour them down the sink, where they can enter the sewer system and contaminate the water supply. Similarly, in skin care service departments, used lancets and cotton and gauze that have been in contact with a client's blood or other body fluids may be considered as hazardous and should be disposed of according to EPA guidelines. Check with your local EPA office to see which of the agency's provisions apply to your salon. Then follow those provisions.

Proper waste disposal procedures are important whether or not the waste is considered hazardous. During the course of a day's operations, the salon generates a considerable amount of waste, both reusable and disposable. These must be handled safely and efficiently to avoid risk of contamination. Trash should not be allowed to accumulate in the salon, but should be periodically bagged in heavy-duty plastic trash bags, tightly sealed, and disposed of according to local ordinances, either through municipal or private trash collection services, or disposed of in legal land fills.

It is good marketing as well as good citizenship to practice environmental safety. Do it as a matter of course, not because it's good business. But don't be afraid to let your customers know you're doing it.

THE COMPETITIVE ENVIRONMENT

The competitive environment will play a major role in your decision making. Although competition shouldn't drive your marketing, you can't ignore it. What your competitors do will have a definite bearing on your business. You need to be aware of how they do business, their pricing strategies, their product mixes, and their approaches to the markets. You have to see where their markets overlap yours or differ from yours.

A lot of your decisions will depend to an extent on what your competition is doing. You can't, for example, charge considerably more for a service similar to what your competitors offer. Nor do you want to charge considerably less. In addition, knowing what services your competitors offer may point the way to similar or different services that you can offer. The key is to differentiate your services from theirs. Look for the value you add to a service that they don't. Then capitalize on that.

Gather all the competitive intelligence you can. Then analyze it to determine how to differentiate your products. Just don't worry too much about what the competition does. If you focus too heavily on meeting the competition, you will become a follower, not an innovator. You want to put yourself in a position in which you are the leader. Let the competition follow you.

MARKETING PLANNING

There's an old adage in business: To fail to plan is to plan to fail. And it's true. You may feel your whole business has been nothing but planning. Just as you generated a comprehensive business plan (or should have) when you started your salon, you will have to plan your marketing as well. Your marketing plan will include your goals and objectives, which may be derived from your overall business plan. It will progress to your strategies and tactics and include your marketing communications plan. Don't skip this step. Give it a lot of careful thought. The plan is your basic guide to your marketing efforts. It is the light that keeps you from groping in the dark and stumbling over hidden obstacles. Marketing and marketing communications planning are discussed in Chapter 3.

Does marketing sound like a tall order? It is. But it's what you've been doing all along, whether you realize it or not. You started the marketing process when you began to develop your business plan. You continued it as you made decisions about the services and products you would offer and gathered information about your potential customers, and then utilized that demographic data plus analyses of all internal and external factors that would affect your salon to make forecasts about the share of the potential market you could capture. Now you must consider how you're going to reach those potential customers, convince them to try your salon, and turn them into clients. That requires you to develop your marketing communications plan, which includes all the communications tools you will utilize. These tools are key parts of your overall marketing strategy.

As the owner or manager of your salon, marketing is your responsibility. But you can, and should, also make it the responsibility of each and every employee. Involve them in the marketing process. Solicit their ideas. Train them to think about the business the same way you do. Above all, instill in them the desire to give each customer full value and more.

TRENDS IN MARKETING

The face of marketing has changed over the past few years. Once, marketing was considered a separate function of business, different from sales, manufacturing, administration, and so forth. In large businesses, the marketing department was a separate entity, manned by specialists in their field. Their purview was primarily demand creation. Their job was to gather data on the company's various markets and provide information to manufacturing and to sales that let those people determine what products to manufacture and where to sell them. The marketing departments also drove advertising and promotion. They were not concerned, however, with costs, pricing, or product quality. Those factors were the concern of other groups within the company. This older concept has been supplanted by a more integrated marketing approach. Now, marketing is seen as everyone's job. All aspects of business are concerned with marketing. In addition, marketing has been expanded to include quality and customer service.

A NEW EMPHASIS ON QUALITY AND SERVICE

In the past, marketing focused on the product. All the efforts of marketing were geared to moving the product. The customer was merely someone to whom the product could be sold and was not important in his or her own right.

Now, the customer is seen as the most important part of the business. Everything starts with the customer. No longer do marketing personnel try to force the product to fit the customer. Rather, the process consists of determining the customer's needs and then sculpting the product to meet them. It's a whole new thought process for business. Every aspect of the business is viewed through the customer's eyes. There is a new emphasis on quality—with the realization that quality is determined by the customer. Only the customer can decide whether he or she has received value for the money.

The key principle here is, "Satisfy the customers' needs." The marketing principles you adhere to in your salon, which include all of the policies and practices you follow in operating your business every day, will make or break your business. It is impossible to overstate the necessity for keeping your customers satisfied. Without following this one not-so-simple principle, you have no business, and nothing else you do will matter.

Recognize the importance of your customers. You will be successful only if you satisfy them. Business is an exchange. You give the customer something—the product or service. The customer gives you something in return—money. That exchange must be worthwhile for both parties. It is marketing's task to make that so. Make sure you give quality, service, and value for the dollars the customers give you. Build a loyal customer base so your clients will return again and again and recommend the business to their friends and neighbors. It is cheaper to keep a satisfied customer than it is to get a new customer or to get a dissatisfied customer to return. Remember, too, that a dissatisfied customer might not always tell you there's a problem. But he or she will certainly tell at least 10 other people. And you'll have little chance of converting those people into customers.

You can't rest on your existing customer base, either. You have to expand it constantly and bring new clients into the business. That takes marketing communications (i.e., advertising and sales promotion) to keep your name in front of existing and future customers. It is much easier to do this if you understand the most important principle of marketing: Businesses exist to meet customer needs. Customers buy product or service benefits, not the product or service features. Know what your customers want. And do everything you can to satisfy those wants.

How do you satisfy your customers? It's easy. All you have to do is give them what they want at a price they're willing to pay in a comfortable setting in a manner that makes them feel they've been treated honestly and fairly and have received an outstanding value.

First, you have to know what customers want, even though they may not know themselves. That means you have to know what you're selling. Understand the differences between the features and the benefits of your services. The service is what you offer. Its features are its identifiable attributes. Its benefits are what it does for the client. There is a definite distinction here. You may think you're selling the features. You're not. The clients may think they're buying the service. They're not. They are buying the benefits of that service, whether they realize it or not. That's what you should be selling.

For example, consider a basic haircut and styling. That is the service you are offering. The features of that service include cutting the hair to a suitable length and styling it into an attractive configuration. The benefit of the service is that it makes the client look and feel good. When your client comes into the salon, she doesn't want a haircut. She wants to look and feel better. If you don't understand that difference, you'll have a hard time satisfying her. If she believes she looks and feels better when she leaves your salon, she'll come back. If she doesn't, she won't, no matter how technically perfect the haircut and styling may have been.

There are other factors to consider in customer satisfaction as well. You have to treat the client with courtesy and appreciation. Every client is a guest in your salon. You have to provide surroundings that make the client feel comfortable and confident. It is important to establish an ambiance in your salon that reinforces the trust and confidence you expect your clients to have in your business. A beauty salon, more than most businesses, relies on a bond of trust between the client and the people who provide those services. Without that bond, the clients will never feel as though they've been really satisfied.

Your objective is to build customer loyalty to your salon and to have repeat business. You need to keep those customers coming to you over and over again. It is easier and less expensive to keep a customer than it is to find new ones continually. Building a solid base of satisfied clients is the key to your business success. And you want them to be loyal to the salon, not necessarily to any particular operator. You want the customer to stay, even if the stylist he or she always patronizes leaves. This is extremely difficult. The beauty business is very personal and intimate, and clients build close relationships with their stylists. You have to offer them a reason to stay with you. That reason starts with the way they are treated in your salon and the degree of satisfaction you provide.

Pay attention to the three C's of successful salon management: competency, consistency, and consideration. From your customers' point of view, competency means that the services and products you provide are of the highest quality. The services are performed quickly and efficiently and are done to the customers' complete satisfaction. Clients feel they have received the best value for the money they spend. Remember, your customer determines quality, you don't. However, from your point of view, competency also means that you handle all the aspects of your business to the best of your ability.

Consistency means that your customers know they can rely on you and your employees to do the job right every time they patronize your salon. It means you are open when you're supposed to be open; you have the services available when they're supposed to be available; you keep your appointments; and you never let your salon waver in the quality of the services you provide. In short, it means you are reliable.

Consideration means that you treat everyone with respect—your customers, your employees, and the people with whom you do business. Your honesty is above reproach. You operate your salon under the most stringent ethical standards. You recognize the value of a good reputation and do what you must to earn it and keep it. You understand that your customers are the reason for your business, and you pass that understanding along to your employees. You go out of your way to make the customer feel appreciated. You earn your customers' respect and patronage.

MASS VERSUS MICRO MARKETING

The concept of mass marketing is being replaced by the idea of micro marketing. In the past, the customer base was viewed as a large monolith that could be served by a limited number of products. Every member of the perceived market was treated exactly the same. They got the same advertising messages with the same positioning. They were sold virtually the same products, though not always at the same prices. Sales and marketing made few, if any, distinctions among their customers. It was a one-size-fits-all approach that matched the view that the product was more important than the customer.

Micro marketing, on the other hand, recognizes that there are differences among customers. The overall market can be segmented, broken into smaller niche markets, each with its own strategy and its own marketing communications approaches. Micro marketing puts more emphasis on the customer's needs and desires and less focus on the product and, as such, recognizes the need for customer service. In this concept, products are geared to smaller, more tightly defined groups of customers.

There is some disadvantage to this approach, for large companies at least. By operating in smaller niches, manufacturers can lose some of their economies of scale. As a result, their products may cost more to make. However, it is usually possible to offset increased manufacturing costs by controlling other costs and working more effectively.

For the salon, there should be no disadvantage to niche marketing. You will probably find you're segmenting your markets anyway. At least you are if you consider the customers interested in facials as one segment, those interested in hair cuts and styling as another, and so on. You can do this even though the same customers may be purchasing more than one kind of service. Remember, you're using different messages and different positioning for each service, even if they are directed at the same people.

DIRECT MARKETING

As a result of the shift from mass to micro marketing, direct marketing has become more widespread as businesses have attempted to segment their customers more closely and then tried to reach them on a more individual level. Technology has been an important contributor to this trend, cutting costs and making segmentation easier.

To a large extent, people's buying habits have changed as their lifestyles have changed, creating a new environment for marketing. People are busier than ever and have less time to shop. More and more, therefore, they are shopping from home and are more predisposed to be swayed by direct marketing efforts.

Direct mail marketing—that, is sending printed sales solicitations through the mail—has long been a major weapon in the marketers' arsenal. It takes many forms, ranging from a simple black and white postcard to a lavishly illustrated, multipage, four-color brochure. What has changed is the ease with which direct mail can be accomplished. Technology has been a key factor here. Computerization has made production and printing of these pieces cheaper, especially for producing relatively short runs, so that it is economical to print hundreds of copies as opposed to thousands. This, coupled with the availability of computerized databases that allow the marketer to segment prospects more closely, makes it less expensive to target smaller audiences with appeals developed specifically to reach them.

Telemarketing has also come of age. In this form of direct marketing, sellers use the telephone to reach potential customers. Customized databases allow these consumers to be segmented so that a targeted sales pitch can be delivered. The advantages of this type of direct marketing are immediacy and personal contact. The salesperson talks directly to the prospect and can elicit a response quickly. The disadvantage is that this technique is intrusive. When the phone rings, the prospect has to drop whatever he or she is doing to answer it. If the interruption comes at the wrong time, the caller will only alienate the prospect. In addition, some unscrupulous practitioners disguise the fact that they're making a sales pitch by representing themselves as taking a survey. This is a highly unethical practice.

LIFESTYLE MARKETING

People are living longer. As stated earlier, there is less emphasis on family ties and there are more people living alone. The population is aging. Ethnic and racial mixes are changing. More women are working. There are ever more factors affecting the way we live. Successful marketers have learned to take lifestyle factors into consideration when developing marketing strategies. Those who tap into changes in lifestyles will succeed. Those who don't will fail.

Lifestyle marketing is nothing more than knowing and understanding how people live and how their lifestyles affect their buying habits. It goes far beyond changes in fashions and styles. Of course, you have to be aware of trends that affect the salon business, such as hair lengths and colors. That's part of the technical aspects of marketing your product mix. These changes in lifestyle will also affect your market.

You have to consider those changes, all of which will enter into the marketing decisions you will make. You have to be in tune with your customers' needs every bit as much as their tastes and adjust your practices accordingly. For example, over the last few years, there has been a tremendous increase in the number of working women. Statistics show that there are more than 57 million women in the American labor market today. Suppose the demographic analysis of your customers and potential prospects shows that you have a large percentage of working women in your area of operations. Analyze their needs. What approaches will appeal to them? You can assume that they are all very busy people who need flexibility in the hours they can purchase services. Smart marketing, then, may dictate that you open the salon at 5:00 A.M. to serve women who want to come in early. Or you might extend your hours later in the evening or on weekends. If you're located in a business area, you might want to have more staff on hand between 11:00 A.M. and 2:00 P.M. so those women can come in during their lunch periods. If you do this, you'll also have to guarantee to perform the services in the time they have to spend.

There's no rule that says you have to be open from 9 to 5 on weekdays. You adjust your hours to meet the needs of your customers. That's an example of lifestyle marketing. If you analyze your market they way you should, you'll find many other ways to tap into your customers' lifestyles.

ENVIRONMENTAL MARKETING

The one thing we all have in common is that we live in the same natural environment. The planet Earth is all we have, so we have to take care of it. Fortunately, there is an ever-growing awareness of this simple but basic fact as people realize it is necessary to conserve resources, limit waste, and curb pollution. Environmentalism is here to stay.

Environmentalism has also become good marketing. More and more, marketers are learning that utilizing environmentally safe practices is good business. Many consumers are consciously looking for products and services that meet environmental standards. And they're taking their sales dollars to those businesses who share their concerns and do something about them.

All businesses can benefit from a concern for the environment, the small salon no less than the large manufacturing industries. Compliance with government regulations is a start, but that's only a beginning. There is no marketing advantage, since everyone has to comply with the laws. Environmental marketing goes far beyond that. It includes those measures you take that are in step with your customers' beliefs and that demonstrate your concern for the environment. These measures can be as simple as replacing disposable styrofoam coffee cups with ceramic cups or as complex as installing filtered ventilation systems to take care of emissions from sprays and other chemicals you use.

Even seemingly unimportant measures count. For example, how does switching to ceramic coffee cups help? It means more work, since someone will have to wash and sterilize the cups. But it reduces non-biodegradable waste that would clog a landfill. And you can turn this change into a marketing plus by giving your regular customers their own mugs, imprinted with their names and your salon name. This is a simple step, perhaps, but one that can go a long way toward building customer loyalty. It reinforces customers' feelings of belonging and makes them more comfortable doing business with you.

ADVOCACY MARKETING

We live in an era of causes, those beliefs that move consumers to passionate action. Causes abound in our fragmented society, with the result that almost everyone is caught up in some movement or another. Some marketers have found that they can tap into the minds and hearts of activist consumers by taking up the cause themselves.

One well-known clothing manufacturer, for example, promotes causes ranging from racial equality to helping the homeless in its advertising. A noted cosmetics manufacturer does the same thing, expanding the concept to include the types of products the stores carry, such as no products tested on animals and products made only from natural ingredients. The approach works for these companies because they are committed to the causes. Part of the proceeds from their sales goes to help finance the causes. Some companies spend advertising dollars to promote awareness for specific causes, as shown in Figure 1-7. In this ad, Clairol has promoted national Color Can Make A Difference Day to raise money in support of AIDS research.

Marketing in support of a cause works, as these companies, as well as many others, have learned. People respond to causes. Advocacy marketing gives companies an easy, pain-free way to become involved. At the same time, it helps the company's bottom line.

There are two important cautions to advocacy marketing, however. The first is that it will work only if the marketer is truly committed to the cause. If consumers perceive that the company is taking that approach only to increase business, the strategy will probably backfire. The second is that the marketer must be aware that he or she may alienate some potential customers who do not share the belief in the cause. Generally, the more controversial the cause, the more danger there is in this respect.

Advocacy marketing can work for the small salon just as it can for large businesses—if you're careful. Don't go into it blindly. Choose a cause wisely and make sure it's one you can support conscientiously. Investigate the cause thoroughly. Contact the sponsors of the cause and volunteer your help. Then solicit the administrators' suggestions as to how you and your salon can help.

Help can take many forms, from distributing informational literature in your salon to donating a part of your proceeds for a certain service or length of time. It can also take a more proactive

Figure 1-7.   Advocacy marketing example. (Reprinted courtesy of Clairol Professional.)

form—for example, using only products not tested on animals in support of the animal rights movement.

Then consider your customers. Is the cause one they are likely to support? To do this, you have to know their likes and dislikes. Demographics are important in making this decision. For example, you wouldn't be wise to support abortion rights if your customers are staunch antiabortionists. Don't promote a cause in your salon that will alienate a majority of your customers. Of course, you can support the cause if you truly believe in it; just do it privately.

Remember, if you are not truly passionate about the cause you choose, stay away from advocacy marketing. There are plenty of other ways to market your services.

"IN-YOUR-FACE" MARKETING

Over the past few years, there has been growth in a type of marketing that has disturbing overtones: "in-your-face" marketing, a confrontational approach that some marketers have found necessary to reach their customers. Messages tend to be loud and raucous and focus more on style than substance. Or they stress the disadvantages of the competition. Rarely is anything said about the benefits of the product.

At its worst, this form of marketing is typified by political campaigns, in which the politician spends all the time and effort telling you how crooked his opponent is while never telling you what he stands for. A lot of large companies take the same approach, usually because the products they market offer few, if any, benefits or they can't be differentiated from the competitive products.

It's hard to believe that this kind of marketing can work. It is condescending and it probably does more to alienate customers than to attract them. It should not have a place in your salon. Concentrate on the benefits you provide, not the shortcomings of your competition. Don't be condescending or offensive. Never talk down to your customers or scream at them. They'll know it when you do, and they will resent it.

CHAPTER 2

Marketing Information

Successful marketing relies on information and knowledge. The more you know about the situation you face, the better you'll be able to plan and implement your strategies. Knowledge is your most valuable asset. You can never know too much about any factor that can help, or hurt, your business. It is only through knowing as much as possible that you can make sound marketing decisions. To get that knowledge, you need to amass large amounts of information about your customers, your competition, your environment, and yourself. Then you need to analyze every bit of that information to turn it into knowledge.

THE VALUE OF INFORMATION AND KNOWLEDGE

Don't confuse information with knowledge. There is a difference. Information refers to the facts, the data you gather that tell you how many, who, what, where, and when. They are the raw ingredients of the mix. Knowledge refers to the awareness and understanding that come about from studying the facts and making inferences about what they mean based on your experience and learning. It tells you why and how and lets you make decisions. Knowledge is the finished dish that results from combining and cooking the ingredients.

You need both knowledge and information. Information by itself is like having the pieces to a jigsaw puzzle. It doesn't form a picture until you put it together. And like a jigsaw puzzle, it takes a lot of trial and error and moving pieces around before you see the pattern. Information and knowledge don't just happen. They take a lot of work.

When you start gathering information, you'll find that you are collecting vast amounts of data. Some facts will be useful; many will not be. It takes attention to detail and a focus on your goals to separate the important facts from the unimportant. You have to know what your objective is to determine what kind of information you need to gather.

There are two types of information, hard and soft. Both are important, and you have to recognize which is which. Hard information is quantitative. It is the data you can measure and tends to be objective in nature. It answers the questions how many, where, when, and who. Statistics are examples of hard data. Soft data is qualitative. It is anecdotal rather than measurable and intuitive rather than statistical. This type tends to be subjective in nature. It answers the questions why and how.

INFORMATION NEEDS

You need many different categories of information, gathered from a variety of sources, as summarized in Figure 2-1. Even though you might place the information into categories, it is important to remember that no single category is more important than any other. Each category just provides different pieces of the puzzle.

Information starts with your target audience. Know your audience. There is no more fundamental precept in marketing.

- Who are you trying to reach?
- How many of them are there?
- Where are they?
- What motivates them?

You need the quantitative, or hard, information, the demographic data that describe the characteristics of your potential customers. And you need the qualitative, or soft, information, the psychographic data that describe the motivations that get customers to buy products and services.

Knowing your target audience is one category of information. The competitive situation is another.

- How many other salons are in your area?
- What services do they offer?
- What prices do they charge?
- Which are trying to reach the same audience that you are?
- What are their positive features?
- What are their negatives?

Competitive intelligence is no less valuable than knowing your customers.

- **TARGET AUDIENCE**—Demographic and Psychographic Data
  Who are you trying to reach?
  How many of them are there?
  Where are they?
  What motivates them?

- **COMPETITIVE SITUATION**
  How many other salonsare there in your area?
  What services do they offer?
  What prices do they charge?
  Which overlap your audience?
  What are their positive features?
  What are their negative features?

- **MARKETING ENVIRONMENTS**
  What is happening in the world around you?
  What are the trends?
  What situations do you face?

- **INFORMATION ABOUT YOURSELF**
  What is your internal situation?
  What are your strengths?
  What are your weaknesses?
  How are you unique?
  What are your advantages?
  What do you have to offer that others don't?

Figure 2-1. Checklist of information needs.

Information about the various marketing environments in which you operate is also important. You have to be aware of the world around you and the different trends and situations that are developing. Competitive intelligence can also help you gather some information about these factors.

Just as important as any other data is information about yourself. Analyze your internal situation (those personal and business factors within your own salon that can affect how you conduct your business).

- What are your strengths and weaknesses?
- What do you offer that is unique?
- How good are your services?
- What advantages do you have in terms of what you offer, your skill, your location, etc.?

- Why should anyone patronize your salon?
- What will customers gain from your salon that they won't get elsewhere?

Be honest with yourself.

The information you gather helps you understand the composition of your market and make a reasonable estimate of its size. This estimate lets you forecast—that is, determine how much of the available business you are likely to get—and establish a goal, the percentage of the available business you are trying to get. Your objectives, coupled with the analyses of the competitive situation, the marketing environments, and your internal factors, help you set sales objectives and formulate your overall marketing plan.

KNOW YOUR CUSTOMERS

It might sound trite, but it is true: Customers are your most important asset. If you don't have customers, nothing else you do in your business will matter. It's a simple axiom. You need to have people who will patronize your salon and give you money in return for the services and products you offer. And you need to have enough of them to generate the cash you need to operate your business and provide you with a reasonable income. You face two issues. First, you have to find customers. Second, once you have customers, you have to keep them. At the same time, you have to keep finding new customers. You may have to market your services to each of these groups differently. So you have to consider that in your marketing plan.

To market your services properly, you have to know everything possible about your customers, both potential clients and current clients. You need to know the demographics of your service area to be able to identify customers. And you need to know the psychographics that motivate customers to buy. Demographic data quantify your target audience; psychographic data qualify it.

DEMOGRAPHIC DATA

Demographic data describe the characteristics of the people living and working in the area from which you draw business. They chart population growth or decline and track the trends in population changes, such as age groups or family structure. They tell you who your potential customers are, how many of them there are, and what they want or need in the way of your services.

- How many people are in the area?
- Where do they live?
- What kind of houses do they live in?
- What are their ages?
- Are they male or female?
- Are they married or single?
- How many children do they have?
- What are their occupations?
- What are their economic situations?
- What are their tastes?

This type of information is available from a number of sources. The U. S. Government Census Bureau provides population breakdowns by age, sex, and households. Some of the data are available in your local library or from the Government Printing Office bookstores. Trade associations can provide demographic data specific to your business. You can find much demographic information through your computer, by subscribing to a service such as America On Line or CompuServe. Local newspapers and real estate offices also are good sources of demographic data in specific localities, as are local merchants' associations. You can also learn much about the demographics of your area through observation—for example, by visiting local shopping malls and supermarkets or taking walks through the neighborhoods in your service area.

Your demographic data form the principal base for your decision making. The accuracy of this information is crucial to your planning.

- Who are the people you want to reach?
- What are their characteristics?
- How many of them are there in the area you will cover?
- What activities do they take part in?
- What do they like to do?
- Where do they shop?

You should have identified the kinds of customers you want to service when you developed the mission statement in your original business plan. Now you have to characterize them. Who is going to patronize your salon and give you money in exchange for the services you plan to offer? Create a profile of your model customer. The profile should incorporate all of the characteristics you would like to see in your clients. For example, let's say you feel your ideal customer should be a female, 24 to 38 years old, a white-collar worker who dresses well and is interested in her appearance. She may be either single or married. She earns enough money to afford the wide range of services you will offer at the prices you will charge. Now, based on the demographic data you've gathered, how many people either living or working in the area fit that profile? How many of them can you reasonably expect to patronize your salon? Are there enough potential customers to let you earn enough profit to keep your business in operation?

You may find that there are not enough customers in the area to support your operation. In that case, you will either have to expand the area in which you intend to operate or widen your customer profile to include more people. Or you might discover that the people living and working in your area of operations don't have the economic resources to purchase your services. That might lead you to change the mix of services you plan to offer and to lower your price expectations. As with most parts of your marketing plan, this information may lead you to revise your original projections.

PSYCHOGRAPHIC DATA

The demographic data, however, provide only the quantitative information. You also need psychographic data to provide the qualitative information, which tells you why these people should patronize your business.

- What will you offer that the competition doesn't?
- How will you reach these people?
- What message will you use to convince them to try your services, especially if they are satisfied with the services they're getting elsewhere?
- What motivates them to buy?
- What do your services mean to your customers?

You have to understand why consumers buy products. What influences their decisions? What are the "hot buttons" that prod them to action? This information is harder to get than the demographic data. It is more qualitative than quantitative and is, therefore, harder to measure.

Your potential customer has to meet two basic criteria to reach the purchasing decision. First, he or she has to have the willingness to purchase the goods and second, he or she must have the ability to purchase them. Ability to purchase depends on income. There has to be enough discretionary income to let him or her afford the services. Discretionary income is that amount of money over and above what is needed for essential goods and services (i.e., food and shelter). In other words, your clients have to have enough extra money that they can afford the services. This is relatively easy to measure.

Keep in mind though, that as a rule, income is a function of education and occupation. In general, better educated people have better paying jobs and, thus, have higher incomes with more discretionary income. In addition, they are usually more sophisticated in their buying behavior. They have more flexibility to pick and choose their suppliers. The amount of discretionary income available, however, even among the more affluent, depends on the economic climate.

Willingness to purchase depends on the customer's motivations and is much harder to judge. It is a difficult factor to measure since it is qualitative and relies on an understanding of human behavior.

Motivation is driven by needs and desires on both physiological and emotional levels. The noted psychologist Abraham Maslow identified a hierarchy of needs starting at the physiological level and progressing through safety to social to esteem and ending at self-actualization. One level of need must be satisfied before a person can be concerned with the next level. At the lowest, or physiological, level, it is necessary to satisfy hunger and provide shelter, those things necessary for survival. The second level, safety, satisfies the need for security and freedom from injury. At the social level, people satisfy their need to interact with other people. The next level, esteem, satisfies the need to be liked and to be accepted by one's peers. The highest level, self-actualization, satisfies the need to achieve one's goals, to become everything one wants to be.

When you interact with your customers, they will most likely be operating at the level of esteem or self-actualization. So these are the levels at which you should direct your marketing activities.

ROLE THEORY

You must also understand the various roles your customers play. According to role theory, each person fills a number of roles in his or her life. Thus, your customer might, at one time of the day or another, be a wife, a mother, a sibling, a business executive, a shopper, or a nurse. Each of these roles has an acceptable or desired mode of behavior, and each requires a different mind set. The differences among those various roles will affect your marketing decisions.

SELF-IMAGE

Just as important as the roles your customers play is their self-image. This is an important part of their need for esteem and is a major factor in your interactions with them. There are three sides to self-image. One is the person's ideal image, how he or she views him or herself. Then there is the real image, who he or she actually is. Finally, there is the image others see in him or her. The three seldom match. The Scottish poet Robert Burns said it most succinctly: "Oh would the power God had given us, to see ourselves as others see us." Your job is to make the three images match as closely as possible.

NORMS AND VALUES

The norms and values of the customers' culture also impact on their mind set. Just as you must understand the other aspects, so you must also recognize these factors. This can be especially difficult because we are a multicultural society, and norms and values change. Sexual mores, for example, are constantly changing. Behavior that was considered shocking as recently as 10 years ago is taken as almost normal today. Fewer people are getting married, but more are living together. Homosexuality is more open and accepted as an alternative lifestyle. More people are living alone.

SOCIAL CLASS

Even though we live in a supposedly class-free society, the concept of social class is important to your marketing efforts. There is a definite class structure in our American society, although it is defined by education and income rather than by legal right or birth. Sociologists recognize four basic classes: an upper class of owners and managers, an upper-middle class of white-collar workers and entrepreneurs, a lower-middle class of manual workers, and a lower class consisting of the poor and underemployed. The class distinctions, however, are fuzzy and there is considerable overlap among them as well as ample opportunity for mobility from lower to upper.

How you market your services will depend on which of the social classes you perceive that your target audience resides in. Your marketing communications to members of the lower-middle class will differ from those directed to members of the upper class. You have to consider two factors here. One is income level and, thus, the amount of discretionary income available. The other is the audience's self-image and need for esteem.

REFERENCE GROUPS

The customers' reference groups also affect your marketing efforts. Everyone belongs to one or more reference groups as an aspect of the human need for social interaction. Membership in some groups is a fact of birth, as with ethnic or racial groups. In some, it is a fact of occupation, as with doctors or cosmetologists, or of education, as with college graduates. And in some, it is a fact of social preference, as with a sorority or health club.

The reference groups are important to a person's self-image. They provide a sense of belonging and friendship. They also affect the mind set and are, therefore, important to the psychology of buying.

All of these factors influence the customer's wants and needs. You have to be able to determine what those wants and needs are before you can market your services effectively. But you have to know what the customer really wants, even though he or she may not be totally aware of that. You can't sell services. You have to sell benefits. Your customer doesn't want a haircut. He or she wants to look good. He or she's not interested in getting a facial. He or she wants healthier, better looking skin. He or she is not purchasing cosmetics. He or she is buying knockout good looks. He or she is looking to fulfill the need for self-image and esteem, not for the service itself.

The customer may not even recognize the difference. But you must. If you don't understand this distinction, subtle though it may be, you won't be able to sell your customer a thing. You have to look at your products, which are the services you provide as well as the accessories you sell at retail, the same way the customer sees them— from the benefits they give, not the features they have. Once you understand this concept and take this view, that knowledge will drive your marketing efforts and help keep you on the road to success.

KNOW YOUR COMPETITION

It is also important to know and understand the competitive situation in the area in which you intend to operate.

- Survey the area.
- Count how many salons are there.
- Look at the services they offer and the prices they charge.
- Look at their clientele.
- Check if the salons seem busy and if the work they do is adequate.
- If possible, talk to some of the owners.
- Talk to some of the customers. Get as much information as you can.

There's nothing illegal or unethical about gathering competitive intelligence. It's a necessary step in the marketing process. But it's a step that requires considerable effort. You'll have to go and look at the situation. The information you obtain will tell you a lot and will help you make informed decisions. You may find out, for example, that all of the salons in the area are performing one type of service you will offer, but only a few offer other types you're planning. That may give you a competitive edge in those services. But be aware that it may also mean there's no call for those services in your area.

Knowing the prices other salons charge will give you some idea of how much you'll be able to charge. The average prices of services will show you what the clientele in the neighborhood is accustomed to paying. That doesn't mean you can't charge more. But you will need a good reason to get the higher dollars. It also doesn't mean you can't charge less. But if you do, you may be throwing earnings away.

Having an idea of the general traffic flow of the other salons will give you an idea of the level of business they enjoy. Although it will tell you whether the salons are busy or not, it won't necessarily tell you how profitable they are. It is possible to be busy and not make any money, although busy salons do generally make a profit. What the information will really tell you is the overall level of business available in the area. It should also give you an idea of the types of customers available, their age groups, their tastes, and what kinds of services they prefer. This information is important when you gather your demographic data.

Determine also the population-per-salon norm for the area in which you intend to operate by counting the number of salons in your operations area and dividing that into the population in your operating area. Then establish an average norm for comparison purposes. You can establish that by counting the number of salons listed in the Yellow Pages and dividing that number into the overall population served. Do this for a number of areas by checking Yellow Pages directories in your local library. Average the norm to get a working number. Then compare the average with the norm for your operating area. Is it higher or lower? If you are in an area where the population-to-salon ratio is higher than average and the population is stagnant or declining, you might consider opening your salon somewhere else (see Figure 2-2).

Norm for My Area:

No. of salons:	14
Population:	9,000
Area norm:	
(9,000 divided by 14 = 642.9)	

Comparison Norms:

Area A (similar size community):

No. of salons:	18
Population:	8,500
Area norm:	472.2

Area B (small city):

No. of salons:	246
Population:	78,380
Area norm:	318.2

Area C (medium size city):

No. of salons:	387
Population:	182,044
Area norm:	470.4

Area D (major metropolitan area):

No. of salons:	1,086
Population:	1,585,577
Area norm:	1,460.0

Average norm: 680.2
(excluding major metropolitan area: 420.3)

Figure 2-2. Population-per-salon norm. Conclusions: The population norm for my area is close to average. Excluding the major metropolitan area, it is significantly above the average norm. This suggests that there is probably enough potential business to support the salon.

The competitive intelligence you gather, once analyzed, should provide you with a wide range of insights on business possibilities in your area of interest. If you note that a few salons are doing well and others are doing poorly, examine what the successful ones are doing. Look at their location, their services, and their prices. Try to identify the reasons for their success. Conversely, look at the less successful salons. Analyze what they're doing and try to identify the reasons for their failure. Learn as much as you can from other people's accomplishments and mistakes. Keep an open mind and look for opportunities you may not have thought of before.

The competitive situation provides a good benchmark for your salon. It gives you another standard for measuring your position in the marketplace. Although the competitive situation is important, don't put more emphasis on it than it deserves. You need to spend more time and effort working on what you're doing rather than reacting to what your competitors are doing. Don't follow them. Become the leader in your market and let them follow you.

KNOW THE MARKET SITUATION

The market situation you face will have a direct bearing on your marketing efforts as well. There are two aspects to market situation: the overall or global view—the big picture, as it were—and the local view. You have to be aware of what's going on the world and what's happening in your own neighborhood.

Chapter 1 discussed the various marketing environments in which you operate. These cover the economic, social, technological, political, and natural factors, as well as the competitive factors, and they define the playing field on which you find yourself. The national picture gives you the trend and helps you forecast what may happen in the future. The local picture gives you the situation around you and lets you make immediate decisions.

Technology is changing at an almost blinding pace. We're adopting new methods of communication, inventing new products, and developing new techniques. You have to stay abreast of changes in your field and in the ways you communicate with your target audience. How do members of your audience receive and respond to information? What new products or techniques will you have to incorporate into your business? How will you get people to try something new?

A word of caution, though. Just because something is new doesn't automatically mean you should adopt it. Don't become so mesmerized by new technology that you lose sight of your goals.

The more you are aware of the world around you and how the environments affect your customers, the better able you will be to react to the situations in which you find yourself working. Pay attention to these factors and use the information to your best advantage when you formulate your marketing plans.

KNOW YOURSELF

Know yourself. This is another fundamental principle without which you cannot be successful, yet it is one that many business owners and managers forget. You have to know who you are and what business you're in. You have to know your strengths and weaknesses. And you have to have goals and a strategic vision that will let you reach them.

The strategic vision describes the business you're in and how you plan to conduct it. It starts with a mission statement. This is a declaration that describes what type of business you envision. Keep it brief, but clearly state the purpose of your salon. What type of salon do you anticipate operating? It's not enough to say, for example, "The mission of this salon is to provide hair styling services." Rather, a more accurate mission statement would say something like, "The mission of this salon is to provide a full range of professional cosmetology services, including hair cutting and styling, manicuring, and skin care services to women within a 10-mile radius of the salon." This is short and to the point, but it clearly and concisely sets the parameters of your business and focuses your attention on the details that will help make your salon a success.

Let's examine what the mission statement for this hypothetical salon has accomplished. First, it has described the kind of salon the owner wishes to operate. She wants to cut and style hair and give manicures and facials. Next, it has indicated her customer base. She wants to offer these services primarily to women. Finally, it delimits the area of her business. Those women will be found mostly within a 10-mile radius of the salon.

Now, state your goals. The goals are different from your mission statement. That is a declaration of purpose. Your goals are a declaration of measurable accomplishment, both in the short term and the long term. Simply put, where do you want to be one year from now? Five years from now? Ten years from now? It is vitally necessary to consider these goals. How can you plan on reaching your destination if you don't know where you're going? This is the place to state your dreams and aspirations, especially for the long-term goals. Your short-term goals should be somewhat more realistic than the long-term goals. Both, however, should be specific, be attainable, and be measurable. That is, you should have a definite outcome in mind and it should be possible to reach that outcome. And there should be some way to measure when you've reached it.

A poor short-term goal might be stated as follows: "By next year, I want to service a lot of customers and make $500,000 a year." This statement is not specific. What constitutes a lot of customers? How do you measure it? Nor is the goal attainable. It is highly unrealistic to expect such a high return after only one year of operation. An example of a good short-term goal, however, might be stated as follows: "One year from opening the salon, I expect to have gross revenues of $100,000 per year, based on an average gross of $38.50 per client visit, and to earn a net profit of $6,000 after paying all expenses, including my salary." A long-term goal might state the following: "Ten years from opening, I want to have a chain of three salons offering a full range of services. I expect to employ a total of 25 people. I expect each salon to earn $125,000 a year in gross revenues." These goals are specific. They can be attained. And they can be measured.

Will the goals be reached? There's no guarantee of that. Success depends on a combination of hard work, perseverance, good management, and a measure of luck. Are they worthwhile? That's strictly a matter of judgment. Goals will differ among individuals. What is a valid goal for one person will not be to another. But no matter what your goals are, they give you something to reach for.

Take the time to analyze your operation. Know what you do best and what you don't do well. Look at your business from your customers' point of view. It's an ongoing process. You can't just analyze your business once and then forget about it. You have to do it constantly. Always be alert to changes in the marketplace and be ready to adapt your business to meet those challenges.

MARKET RESEARCH

Knowledge and its management can be approached in logical steps as a process.

1. You have to know what information you need.
2. You have to gather and collate data that provide that information.
3. You have to analyze the data to draw conclusions and make forecasts.
4. You have to make decisions that lead to your marketing plan.

There are many ways to acquire facts and information. All involve some form of market research, which can be as simple as reading current trade magazines or as complex as extensive mail or telephone surveys. Some you can do yourself, either formally or informally. Some methods are better left to trained professionals. The most appropriate method for you will depend on what information you are trying to get and on how accurate and reliable it has to be. Whichever research methods you utilize to get the information, however, you must be totally objective. You cannot have preconceived ideas about the results; nor can you let your personal biases interfere with the process. You must be willing to accept the findings of the research, even if they are not what you expect or want. Your business decisions have to be based on reality, not on desire.

Research methods differ widely in their execution, but there are elements common to all of them. Regardless of the research method you utilize, the results have to be valid and reliable. Validity means that the data measure what they are supposed to measure and are suitable for your needs. Reliability means that the data are accurate and can be relied on in making decisions. Although all data are important, not all carry the same weight in decision making, so the standards for validity and reliability can vary, depending on how the information will be used and how critical it is in your decision-making process.

All research methods require careful thought and design to assure that they will do what they are supposed to do. You start with a hypothesis, a statement of the problem that poses what you want to find out. Then you gather data that either confirm or disprove that hypothesis. Once you've formulated the problem, you have to determine what sources you can use to get the data. This can take a variety of forms, ranging from library research, to observation, or to any of a number of survey techniques. Generally, you can gather demographic or other statistical data through library research or observation. Attitude research into such things as buyer motivations usually requires some kind of survey technique.

Once you've gathered the information, you have to process it—that is, put it into some sort of order so you can work with it. Then you have to analyze it to determine what it means and whether it answers your questions.

LIBRARY RESEARCH

You can get a lot of information just by reading. Your local library is a good source of data, especially for demographics and statistics. The library generally has a wide range of materials of interest to business. And it has trained people to help you find the information you are looking for.

The Government Printing Office publishes a wide range of pamphlets and books on demographic trends and other business topics. If you have a government bookstore in your area, pay it a visit. If not, write for the free catalog and order what you find of interest.

Newspapers are a good source for keeping track of what is going on in the world around you. But read more than one. A national daily newspaper such as *USA Today* will give you more global information than your local daily. The local daily will give you more news about the community. Don't overlook smaller community weeklies, either. They contain a wealth of information about your neighborhood. You might also read specialized business newspapers like the *Wall Street Journal*. When you read a newspaper, however, keep your research objectives in mind and look specifically for information that benefits your business.

Trade and consumer magazines are also good sources of information. Trade magazines, such as *American Salon*, often feature articles on industry happenings and trends. Consumer magazines often do the same, but they cover the topics from the point of view your customers are most likely to hold.

Many organizations and suppliers publish newsletters that talk about business and industry trends. These are also an excellent source of information. Subscribe to as many of these as you can comfortably read.

Read as much as you can. It is about the least expensive form of research you can conduct. But read with your marketing objectives in mind. Glean nuggets of information from any written source you can get your hands on. Keep files for any interesting bit of information, even if you don't have an immediate use for it. Sooner or later, it will come in handy.

If you don't have time to read everything you should, assign some of the reading to members of your staff. Remember, marketing is everybody's responsibility. So spread the research load around. Make each employee responsible for a certain segment of information, and then discuss their findings at regular staff meetings.

OBSERVATION

You can gather a lot of information just by being observant. See what's going on around you. Walk through the neighborhoods in your area of operation and from which you expect to draw your clientele. Take a look at the way people live.

- What kinds of shops are in the areas?
- Are they high-end boutiques or low-end discount stores?
- What kind of traffic goes through them? How many people? How are they dressed?
- What kinds of housing are in the area? Are they single-family dwellings or apartments?
- Are a lot of children in the area?
- What kinds of cars are parked in parking lots or on the streets?
- Where are the schools?
- What kinds of schools are there? Are they grade schools, high schools, or college campuses?
- Are there businesses in the area that would have large numbers of employees, such as factories or office complexes?
- Are there retirement homes or hospitals in the area?
- What about theaters and restaurants?
- Are the restaurants fast-food types?
- Are the restaurants in the area white-tablecloth types?

Set up a schedule for taking walks. Revisit areas at regular intervals so you can monitor changes that are taking place. When you go out, have a clear idea of the kind of information you're looking for. Take notes so you won't forget. The notes will also serve as your records for comparison.

Don't just look. Talk to people. Ask questions. Stop in some of the shops and businesses and talk to the owners or managers. Get their impressions of business in the area.

The information you'll get in this way will amaze you. Demographic data you get from government publications or other sources will tell you the makeup of the community as a whole. Careful observation will give you the demographic data for the areas that interest you the most.

Think about what you see. Consider the marketing opportunities that suggest themselves. For example, if there are retirement homes in the area, you might offer senior citizen specials. If there are schools nearby, you might have back-to-school specials for the students. You might also offer discounts to the teachers. If there are churches around, there might be a chance for wedding specials. The list of possibilities is endless. It just depends on your imagination and being aware of what you see around you.

SURVEYS

Reading and observation can provide valuable demographic data. But they will tell you only how many people are in the area and whether or not they can afford your services. These data won't tell you whether any of those people would be likely to patronize your salon. To get that kind of attitude information, you need to use other methods. One of the best research methods for gathering information on consumer attitudes is the survey.

Surveys take many forms and cover a broad spectrum of complexity, ranging from simple informal surveys to complicated mail or telephone surveys. How complex or extensive any survey you conduct should be depends on the kind of information you're looking for. Figure 2-3 shows a sample survey form.

Informal surveys are relatively simple and straightforward. They consist of asking questions of a limited number of people, usually whom you know, to get general opinions on whatever subject you're asking about. These are limited in scope and in reliability, however, so the information may be of limited use in making marketing decisions. This is the type of survey you conduct when you ask your clients for their opinions. Just because an informal survey is simple and the results are limited, don't discount their value. Your customers can provide valuable insights that indicate the directions further research should take. Even an informal survey should have some structure, though. So think your questions out thoroughly before you ask.

TESS'S TRESSES TELEPHONE SURVEY

Call to be made between 7:00 P.M. and 9:00 P.M.. If no answer on call, call back twice more before listing interviewee as "no response."

Script:

Hello, my name is_____(interviewer name). I represent Aeone Communication Company, and we're conducting a survey for a local beauty salon. Would you please answer a few questions for us? The interview will take approximately five minutes.

(If interviewee refuses, thank the interviewee. Hang up and list as "unresponsive.")

(If interviewee accepts, begin questioning.)

1. Have you patronized a beauty salon within the last three months?

(If answer is "no," thank the interviewee and hang up. If answer is "yes," continue with question 2.)

2. What service or services did you purchase?

_____

3. Were you satisfied with the service?

_____Yes. Why?_____

_____No. Why not?_____

4. On a scale of 1 to 5, with 1 being the highest, how important are these qualities in a salon?

Ambience_____   Staff demeanor_____

Honoring appointment time_____   Quality of the service_____

Price of the service_____

Thank you for your time.

Figure 2-3. Sample survey form.

Face-to-face surveys represent a considerable step up from informal surveys. In this type, the person conducting the survey stops people at random and asks questions from a prepared list. This is the type of survey you often find conducted in shopping malls. Results from this kind of survey are usually accurate. The face-to-face contact allows a trained interviewer to gauge people's reactions to the questions, not only by what they say but by their body language as well. In addition, answers to particular questions can often open the way to questions in other areas of interest.

Surveys can also be conducted by telephone and by mail. In a telephone survey, an interviewer calls people at random and asks questions (see Figure 2-4). Although not quite as effective as face-to-face interviews, telephone interviews have the advantage of personal contact. The disadvantage is that telephone calls are intrusive and may annoy the person called if the timing is bad.

In a mail survey, questionnaires are sent to a selection of respondents who fill them out and mail them back. This type of survey is less intrusive on the respondents' time than the other types and is usually reliable. However, response is often low, so a lot of people have to get the questionnaires to ensure a response that will be large enough to be statistically significant. In many mail surveys, some kind of inexpensive premium is included to boost the response rate.

Although surveys may look simple, they are not. Survey research requires a lot of thought and effort to generate valid and reliable information. The questionnaire has to be designed careful-

Figure 2-4.   Telephone surveys can be an effective marketing tool. (Photograph courtesy of Telephone Concepts.)

ly so that it asks the right questions and elicits honest responses. The sample audience has to be chosen carefully. If you choose the wrong people, the results can be biased. Ideally, all the respondents should be chosen at random to minimize bias in the results. Results have to be analyzed carefully. It takes a lot of training on the part of the interviewers to get accurate response. You may be able to conduct your own informal surveys, but for more formal surveys you should consult with professionals. They are trained in survey design, execution, and analysis. Also be aware that although reading and observation may be relatively inexpensive, surveys can be very costly. A properly designed and executed survey can cost thousands of dollars.

Costly though they may be, surveys may be the only way to get some of the information you need about consumer attitudes. But you may be able to get survey data from sources other than conducting your own survey. Ask your suppliers for results of surveys they have conducted. Use that data to zero in on your own information needs. Ask your trade association as well. Trade associations often conduct surveys to help their members. And check with your merchant's association and your local Chamber of Commerce. These organizations often conduct surveys of business in their operating areas. If they are planning to conduct a survey among local consumers, you may be able to add a few questions of your own.

FOCUS GROUPS

Focus groups offer in-depth observations of consumer opinions. A small group of people, chosen from the target audience, is put in a room. A moderator asks questions of the group, allowing them to express their views. Often, the person sponsoring the focus group is in an adjoining room, watching the proceedings through a one-way mirror. The process is normally videotaped so the proceedings can be analyzed (see Figure 2-5).

This is a very effective way of gathering information about consumer opinions. The members of the group are encouraged to express themselves fully, far more so than they would be in responding to a questionnaire. Many focus groups become lively affairs. Like surveys, however, focus group research is complicated and requires trained moderators and researchers. Focus groups are also very expensive, running into the thousands of dollars.

Figure 2-5. Focus group. (Photography courtesy of Telephone Concepts.)

EXPERT PANELS

You may not be able to afford focus group research, but you can probably afford an expert panel. Expert panels are like an in-house focus group in that a group of people sits in a room and gives opinions on the subject being researched. The difference is that these people, rather than being invited at random, are people you know and trust.

Form an expert panel that meets at regular intervals, perhaps quarterly, to discuss ideas and problems you're having. Choose members from customers, employees, or friends whose opinions you value. Hold the meeting at a time and place convenient for everyone. You might consider hosting lunch or dinner. Give careful thought to the topic to be discussed. Encourage everyone to give his or her honest opinion, but keep the discussion focused on the topic under consideration. It is very easy to lose control of such a group and have the talk go off on tangents.

Expert panels are far less expensive than focus groups. But the results may not be as valid, since the respondents may be biased toward giving you the information they think you may want to hear rather than telling you their honest opinions.

RECORDS ANALYSIS

It is impossible to overstate the need for good recordkeeping in your salon. Analyzing the records of your day-to-day operations is also a form of market research, one that can give you a lot of important information.

Most market research methods are predictive. The information gathered lets you forecast, or predict, what is likely to happen to your market in the future. Your records show you what is happening in your market right now. That information, coupled with the predictive information from other research methods, can give you a better picture of where you stand and where you have to go.

Accurate records do much more than let your accountant figure out how much you owe in taxes or whether you're operating at a profit or a loss. From a marketing point of view, they tell you which services are profitable and which are not, and they help you in both your short-range and long-range planning for the future. Complete and accurate records are the scorecard by which you measure your current success in business and the road map that helps point your way to future success.

Proper recordkeeping starts with the sale. Give each operator a supply of sales slips. Stock forms are available from stationery stores, or you can design your own and have them printed, as shown in Figure 2-6. Every transaction must be recorded on a sales slip. When an operator performs a service or sells a product, the name of the client, the services or products purchased, and the prices should be itemized on the sales slip, which should be turned in with the cash. Each operator should initial the slip. These sales slips will become an integral part of your recordkeeping, so be thorough with them. They are your primary record of who did what, to whom, when, and for how much.

By the same token, record every cash disbursement on a debit slip. Note the amount and the reason. Keep these with the sales slips. At the end of the day, both will be part of your daily reconciliation procedure.

Don't think that records are only for financial purposes. You also need employee records, records of supply inventories and pur-

TESS'S TRESSES©

SALES RECORD

DATE _____

NAME _____

ADDRESS _____

TELEPHONE NO. _____

OPERATOR _____

SERVICES/PRODUCTS	PRICE

COMMENTS	TOTAL:

Figure 2-6. Sample sales slip. (Copyright 1995, Aeone Communications Co., Dublin, Pennsylvania.)

chases, as well as customer records. Establish and maintain a complete customer database, as shown in Figure 2-7. Make a file on every client who comes into your salon. The file should contain the following customer information:

- name
- address
- telephone number (both home and work)

- birthday (but not necessarily age)
- preferences
- any personal items that may be pertinent.

Itemize all services and products the client purchases, along with the dates and any comments about the service—that is, its success, what problems the operator may have encountered, etc. Also record any comments and suggestions the customer offers. With a new client, ask why he or she left the salon patronized before. Was he or she dissatisfied with something there? If so, make sure you don't make the same mistake. Learn from other salons' experiences. Make sure all entries are legible. Keep them current. Update them as needed.

The information contained in the customer file will enable you to do a better job of satisfying your clients. It will also give you valuable data about your services. Don't be afraid to ask the clients for the information. Every part of it is useful. The address lets you make mailings to your customer base. You might use this to send Christmas or Chanukah cards, use it to announce specials, or use it to mail your own newsletter. The telephone number is important so

TESS'S TRESSES©

CUSTOMER DATA RECORD

NAME ______________________________

ADDRESS ______________________________

CITY ____________ STATE ____________ ZIP ____________

TELEPHONE NUMBER ____________ BIRTH DATE ____________

SERVICE RECORD

DATE	SERVICE	PRICE

REMARKS

____

____

____

Figure 2-7. Sample customer database entry. (Copyright 1995, Aeone Communications Co., Dublin, Pennsylvania.)

you can reach the client if there is a delay in his or her appointment or if you want to conduct a telephone survey.

Knowing the birthdate is valuable if you want to send each client a card on his or her birthday. This is a very nice but often overlooked touch that builds customer good will. Knowing the client's preferences in styles, colors, products, etc. lets you more readily tailor the services to meet his or her needs.

If you have some personal information about the customer, you can handle conversations better and give friendlier and more personal service. For example, if you know that the customer has children, you'll be able to inquire about their health when the client comes in. You don't have to ask specific personal questions to get this information, however. As you talk to the client, much of this information will surface. Just write it down when you learn it. Be careful not to intrude on the client's privacy or seem to pry by asking too many questions of a personal nature. And make sure you keep all such information confidential.

By keeping a record of the client's purchases of services, you can establish patterns in his or her patronage of your salon. This lets you make some predictions about future business, which is necessary for your long-range planning, and it helps you keep track of your repeat business. If you know the customer's pattern, you can send out timely reminder cards as the time for another service approaches. The information may also be a good indicator of when you are losing repeat business.

For example, suppose your records show that for the past year, Mrs. Jones has come in for a haircut every third week and has gotten a permanent every four months. As the time for the next permanent approaches, you can remind her of it, either by sending a card or by bringing it to her attention when she next comes in for a haircut. Suppose, though, that Mrs. Jones hasn't come in for eight weeks. This break in the pattern might tell you something. You may want to call Mrs. Jones and ask if there is a problem with your service. She may have been on vacation, or she may have been ill, or she may have been dissatisfied with the service she received the last time she was in. You won't know, however, unless you ask. Don't worry about annoying her with the call. In all likelihood, she will appreciate your concern and the fact that you consider her patronage important. Just be careful not to overdo calling.

Each time a customer makes an appointment, pull up his or her file and review the information on it. Be ready for the client when he or she comes in. Know your clients.

The point is that unless you are aware of your customers' patterns of patronage, you'll never be aware of problems early enough to do something about them. You cannot have too much information on which to make business decisions. Get that information whenever you can.

But remember, it is not enough just to gather the information. You also have to analyze it. Take time to review the data you've collected and make inferences about your business. Do this on a regular basis. Look for the patterns that develop and adjust your marketing as needed, according to what the data tell you. Pay special attention to your clients' comments and suggestions. You can learn a lot about your business by listening carefully.

It's important to develop a system for recording and accessing the information you gather. It is no good to you if you can't find it when you need it. Although it is possible to do a good, accurate job of information handling without a computer, it is far more efficient to employ one. In this day and age, you will find that installing a computer and learning how to use it can give you a definite competitive edge. This topic is covered in Chapter 4, "Computerizing The Salon." If you choose not to computerize, though, at least make sure your files are orderly and legible.

DATA ANALYSIS

Once you've finished gathering data, you have to analyze the facts so they will be useful to you. The raw data won't tell you much. You have to sort out the facts, group them into categories, count what needs to be counted, and work out the relationships among the numbers.

Before you can analyze the data, you have to process them. This involves deciding which data answer your questions—that is, those facts that support or disprove your working hypothesis—and which are irrelevant—those facts that have no bearing on your hypothesis. So your first step is sorting through the mass of facts in front of you. Keep your hypothesis in mind. What is it you were trying to find out? Put all of the facts dealing with that hypothesis into one category and put anything else aside. Don't discard any data, however. Although some facts may not be important to the questions you've been trying to answer, they may be important for answering questions you may have later.

After you've grouped the facts into categories, you can begin to quantify them—that is, count how many fit your hypothesis and, just as importantly, how many don't. For example, suppose you were trying to find out how many people in your operating area meet the criteria for your ideal customer. If you've gathered the data correctly, you should be able to get the number easily by counting how many of those people you found. Then determine the percentage of the population that meets those criteria.

Quantifying the data is one aspect. You should also look for trends, especially in attitude research. For example, do your expected customers come from one part of your operating area? What common threads have you found that you can generalize across the population you've tested?

When you have the data sorted, counted, and categorized, you can start drawing conclusions. What do the figures mean? How can they support or disprove your hypothesis? Now that you know the number of people in your area who are potential customers, for example, you can conclude whether there are enough of them to support your business. If the numbers are high enough, you can proceed with your plans. If they are not, you'll have to rethink your plans and work out new criteria.

Analyze the data dispassionately and objectively and draw conclusions that are not colored by your expectations. It is very easy and tempting to disregard data that disprove what you believe. Resist the temptation. Base your marketing decisions on the realities of the situation, not on your wishes. That approach is crucial to your success in business.

SOURCES OF INFORMATION

The amount of information you need to gather may seem overwhelming. How will you get the information you need? When you get all the data, you're faced with analyzing them and using them to make decisions.

Fortunately, there is a lot of help available to you—if you know where to look for it. Virtually everyone you do business with, including the government, can provide some kind of information or help in analyzing data. So don't overlook any possibility.

RESEARCH AND READING

You can get a lot of information on your own just from reading and doing your own research. Books and magazines covering almost every imaginable subject are readily available to you. Take advantage of them.

THE LIBRARY

Your first stop should be your local library. Get to know the librarian. He or she can point you in the right direction to find critical information. Do you need to know the address and phone number of a trade association? Look it up in the *Encyclopedia of Trade Associations*. The list could go on and on. You just have to do your homework.

BOOKS AND MAGAZINES

Build your own reference library. In your office, you should keep a shelf of basic books to which you can refer when you need fast or recurring information. These can include almanacs and statistical abstracts. Just be sure to use the latest editions.

Don't forget magazines. There are a number of consumer and trade magazines that offer demographic and statistical data and that discuss trends. Again, look through the periodicals index in the library. Ask the librarian for suggestions. Browse through your local bookstore. Pick up and examine some of the magazines that cover the information you need. Choose the best ones, and subscribe to them.

Don't limit yourself to magazines directed to general business subjects. The trade magazines that cater to the salon industry often offer information on trends and statistics.

When you see a book or magazine that has information of value, buy it. And read it. Make notes. Underline relevant passages. Mark the passages so you can find them quickly. Make the reference work for you. Remember, all the information contained inside the book or magazine is useless to you if you never look at it.

Start a clippings file. When you read a newspaper or magazine article that has relevance to your business, cut it out and file it away for future reference. If you have any doubt about whether or not to keep an article, keep it. It's likely you'll need the information it contains at some point in the future.

NEWSLETTERS

Newsletters are an increasingly important method of communication in business. There is a wide variety of newsletters available, covering a wide range of topics, and coming from an equally wide variety of sponsors, from manufacturers to advocacy groups.

Some manufacturers of hair and skin care products publish newsletters that describe new products and applications, industry news, as well as salon management tips and recommendations. The information they provide, though often slanted toward their products, can be very helpful. Some of these are free. Others may be sold by subscription. Newsletters from advocacy groups, such as some health care providers, also provide a wide range of information relating to specific fields of interest. These publications can also contain many helpful tidbits of information that may be useful to you in your business.

Newsletters range in size from four pages to many times that amount and in frequency from weekly, monthly, and quarterly to whenever the publisher manages to get an issue out. Many are sold on a subscription basis, with costs varying from a few dollars to many hundreds of dollars. In many cases, the information you'll glean from the publication will repay its cost many times over. Remember that the publications you buy (books, magazines, etc.) are deductible as business expenses.

To get information on manufacturers' newsletters, call or write to the manufacturers of the products you use, or ask the distributors of those products about the availability of newsletters. For information on advocacy group or other newsletters, check with your librarian and look through a current directory of newsletters in the library's reference section. With any newsletter, ask for sample copies before you subscribe.

GOVERNMENT PRINTING OFFICE

One of your best sources of printed information is the Government Printing Office (GPO). This arm of the federal government offers a wide range of books, booklets, and pamphlets. Some are free. Some have a modest cost. You can also get census data from the GPO.

If you have a Government Printing Office bookstore in your city, pay it a visit and see what it has to offer. In addition, the GPO has a free catalog of books. Write to: Free Catalog, Government Printing Office, P.O. Box 37000, Washington, D C 20013-7000.

ASSOCIATIONS AND ORGANIZATIONS

Like minds working together can accomplish many things that can't be accomplished by one person working alone. Since the beginning of time, people have been banding together to provide themselves with mutual protection and collective advantage. Businesses are no different. Virtually every industry, whether manufacturing or service, is represented by a trade association. Many retail and commercial areas are represented by a merchant's association. And there are countless fraternal and business organizations that cross industry and business lines to help give a voice to the concerns of individual members of various groups. Such associations and organizations can be a tremendous aid to you and your salon, providing you with information and advice.

Trade associations are organizations established to serve the collective needs of member businesses in a given industry. They are typically financed by dues and fees paid by the members and run by a salaried professional staff, governed by an executive board made up of elected representatives from the businesses. They are usually national in scope, with a number of state and local branches. There can be more than one trade association for any industry. The current edition of the *Encyclopedia of Trade Associations*, for example, lists nine trade associations under the heading of Cosmetology (see Figure 2-8).

These organizations offer an impressive array of services to their members. They keep members up to date on industry trends. They conduct educational and public relations programs and promote industry standards. In addition, they monitor legislative activity and lobby on behalf of the industry. They also provide for group health and liability insurance coverage for member businesses. Some also offer assistance in finding financing.

Some associations publish newsletters and magazines. These are slanted toward the industry and contain many articles about salon management. Many associations also conduct an annual convention, complete with trade show exhibits, seminars, and training courses. These are excellent opportunities for a salon owner or manager to keep up with industry trends and to increase knowledge about the field.

If you are in business, you may find it worthwhile to join a trade association. It should provide services and advice that you will find invaluable. Get the information from all the associations that service the beauty industry. Study the literature. Then join the one that offers the most benefit to you, and become active in the organization. Attend local monthly meetings and the national convention. Remember, dues and expenses you incur attending the meetings are usually deductible as business expenses.

- **AESTHETICIANS INTERNATIONAL ASSOCIATION**
  4447 McKinney Ave.
  Dallas, TX 75205
  Telephone: (214)526-0752

- **AMERICAN BEAUTY ASSOCIATION**
  401 N. Michigan Ave.
  Chicago, IL 60611
  Telephone: (312)644-6610

- **ASSOCIATION OF COSMETOLOGISTS AND HAIRDRESSERS**
  1811 Monroe
  Dearborn, MI 48124
  Telephone: (313)563-0360

- **HAIR INTERNATIONAL/ASSOCIATED MASTER BARBERS AND BEAUTICIANS OF AMERICA**
  124-B E. Main St.
  P.O. Box 273
  Palmyra, PA 17078
  Telephone: (717)838-0795

- **INTERCOIFFURE AMERICA**
  540 Robert E. Lee
  New Orleans, LA 70124
  Telephone: (504)282-4907

- **INTERNATIONAL CHAIN SALON ASSOCIATION**
  661 E. Olive Way
  Seattle, WA 98102
  Telephone: (206)323-7773

- **NAIL MANUFACTURERS COUNCIL**
  c/o American Beauty Association
  401 N. Michigan Ave.
  Chicago, IL 60611
  Telephone: (312)644-6610

- **NATIONAL BEAUTY CULTURISTS' LEAGUE**
  25 Logan Cir. NW
  Washington, DC 20005
  Telephone: (202)332-2695

- **NATIONAL COSMETOLOGY ASSOCIATION**
  3510 Olive St.
  St. Louis, MO 63103
  Telephone: (314)534-7980

- **WORLD INTERNATIONAL NAIL AND BEAUTY ASSOCIATION**
  1221 N. Lake View
  Anaheim, CA 92807
  Telephone: (714)779-9883

Figure 2-8.   Cosmetology trade associations.

Merchant associations, in contrast with trade associations, are small, local groups, usually consisting of small retail and service business owners in a given area. They are formed by the merchants in a neighborhood or shopping area and limit their activities to that area. They are not allied with any given industry. Like trade associations, merchant associations look after the interests of their members. They are not usually managed by a paid staff, but are run by committees elected from the membership.

Merchant associations offer a number of activities. They can provide support in tenant-landlord negotiations. They lobby at the local government level. They keep members informed about pending legislation that may affect small business operations in the area. They may also organize neighborhood clean-up campaigns and other programs to make sure the merchants are good neighbors in the locality. Join your local merchant association, and take an active part in its activities. The rewards can be substantial.

There are any number of fraternal and service organizations that can provide help to your salon. These are organizations made up of people who share common interests and are not related to any industry. Some can give direct aid (for example, the National Association for Female Executives can provide financing to women who meet certain credit requirements).

Most of these organizations, however (such as service organizations like the Kiwanis or Rotary), provide indirect help. They are ideal avenues for networking—that is, establishing those informal relationships that you can call on for help. Don't discount the value of networking. The people you meet and the contacts you make can pay great dividends. By investing your time and effort in a fraternal or service organization, you will develop a fertile source you can mine for information and assistance. You'll also be helping to better your community. This is a good way for you to give something back the community in which you work.

THE GOVERNMENT

There are many people who feel that government help is a contradiction in terms. And it is true that dealing with a government agency, on any level, can sometimes be a frustrating experience. The government is more than just a body that promulgates laws, regulations, and requirements, however. Through its various agencies, it is also a great compiler of information. More important to the business owner, though, is that government agencies, especially at the federal level, will share much of that information willingly and freely—if you know where and who to ask for it.

At the federal level, you can get information and advice from a number of agencies. The Government Printing Office discussed earlier is just one example. Other agencies that can give you help include the following:

- The Small Business Administration (SBA) offers a number of programs to assist small businesses. It publishes a vast array of pamphlets and books on business subjects. These are available at little or no cost. The SBA also operates loan guarantee programs to help small businesses get financing. Contact your local SBA office and find out what programs they offer that can help you.
- The Department of Labor can provide you with statistical information about the cosmetology industry and can keep you abreast of the laws governing employment.
- The Food and Drug Administration (FDA) is your best source to answer questions about the safety and efficacy of beauty care products and equipment. The agency publishes a monthly magazine, *FDA Consumer*, which contains articles about a number of health and safety issues. The magazine provides valuable information and is a worthwhile addition to your library. It would also make interesting reading for your clients.
- The Federal Trade Commission (FTC) can give you information about business and industry practices. This agency is a good source for information about the rules and regulations that govern franchise operations.
- The Internal Revenue Service (IRS) can keep you up to date on the tax laws that govern your salon. The agency publishes a number of informational pamphlets that explain the tax laws and regulations. These are free.

Most states have similar agencies that can provide the same type of information and help, although on a more limited basis. At the state level, your most important agency will be your local State Board of Cosmetology, which can apprise you of the laws and regulations governing salons in the state. It can also answer your questions and provide guidelines for your operation.

Regardless of the level of the government agency, however, keep in mind that it exists to help you. Don't be hesitant to ask for help and information when you need it. Your taxes pay for these services. It's up to you to utilize them. All of these government agencies are listed in major city telephone books. Look them up and make a file of those you are likely to call.

SCORE

You can get free advice and counsel on business matters from SCORE, the Service Corps of Retired Executives. This is a volunteer counseling group made up of experienced business executives who are either retired or still active in business but donate their time to provide advice and guidance to small business owners. The group is sponsored by the SBA, and its services are free.

There are SCORE branches in all major cities. They are listed in the telephone book, or you can call your local SBA field office for the location of the branch nearest to you. This is an excellent source of help for you. It can give you one-on-one guidance that you would be hard pressed to find anywhere else. If you do nothing else, you should take advantage of this service.

SUMMARY

- Information is just the facts, the raw data. Knowledge is the understanding that comes from analyzing the facts. You need both. Information is the pieces of the jigsaw puzzle. Knowledge is the total picture.
- Information is either hard or soft—that is, quantitative or qualitative. Hard data, such as statistics, are measurable. Soft data, such as opinions, are subjective. To market successfully, you need both types.
- To market your services, you have to know everything possible about your customers. That includes both demographics and psychographics.
- Demographics describe the characteristics of the people that you want to make up your target audience. They tell you who those people are, where they are, how many of them there are, and what they may need in the way of services. Demographic data form the principal base for your decision making.
- Psychographic data are qualitative and harder to measure. They are the kind of data that tell you about consumer attitudes and what "hot buttons" you need to push to get con-

sumers to respond. Psychographic data describe the customer's motivations.

- To understand consumer behavior, you have to understand consumers' physiological and emotional levels. You also have to understand the various roles your customers play. It is also necessary to be aware of their self-image, their norms and values, social class, and the reference groups to which they belong.

- You have to know your competition. Find out the location of other salons, what they offer in the way of services, their pricing structures, their traffic flow, and anything else you can. Look for the edge that will let you differentiate your salon from theirs.

- The market situation is also important. Be aware of what is going on in your area. But don't limit your view to your area. Look at the global picture, too. Be aware of the various environments in which you operate.

- Look inward, also. It is just as important to know yourself as it is to know the external situation. Know who you are and what business you're in. Develop a strategic vision, reflected by a strong and accurate mission statement. Establish long-term and short-term goals for your salon. Make them realistic and attainable.

- There are many research methods you can use to gather information. Whichever type of research you conduct, however, make sure the results are valid and reliable. You can get information from sources such as the Government Printing Office, newspapers, trade and consumer magazines, and newsletters published by many organizations and suppliers. Read as much as you can. This is about the most inexpensive form of research you can conduct.

- Get information through observation. Be alert to what's going on around you. Walk through the areas you service and look at the way people live. Take notes so you won't forget. Talk to people in the area. Ask questions.

- Surveys give you information about attitudes. They are actually sophisticated research tools that require a lot of thought and planning. They are best conducted by experts in the field of consumer research, and they can be costly.

- Focus groups offer in-depth observations of consumer opinions. Like surveys, focus groups are costly and should be conducted by trained experts.

- A less costly form of focus group that you can conduct yourself is the expert panel. Although not as scientific as focus groups, expert panels can often provide valuable insights.
- Don't overlook the wealth of information contained in your own records. If you keep records properly, you can glean a wealth of data about your operations and trends.
- Turn gathered information into knowledge. This requires analysis of the data. When you analyze the data, be dispassionate and objective. Don't color your conclusions by your expectations.
- There is a lot of help available to you, starting with your local librarian. In addition to the materials available in the library, start your own reference library. Also, join relevant associations and organizations. Build up a network of friends and associates you can count on for help. Don't overlook the help you can get from the government.

CHAPTER 3

The Marketing Plan

Marketing is not a haphazard undertaking. Like every other aspect of your business, your marketing programs must be planned. Without a comprehensive, well-thought-out plan based on your goals and objectives, you will not enjoy much success. You can't just "wing it" and expect to get positive results.

The marketing plan is an outgrowth of your business plan, and it starts with the assumptions you made in that document. It considers your corporate vision and mission statement and then your company goals. It describes the internal and external environments in which you operate, utilizes the marketing information you gathered, and sets strategies and tactics for attaining the goals. It provides for measurement and analysis and is flexible enough to let you make adjustments based on your analysis of the measured results.

It takes time to work out a marketing plan. Take the time and do it right. Put the plan in writing. Consider all the factors carefully. Remember, it is the blueprint that helps you reach your marketing goals. It is the guide that helps you make use of your information, analyze your markets, and develop strategies and tactics that you will use to capture your share of the business.

The marketing plan gives you a structure to direct and control your marketing programs. It gives you a means of coordinating the various activities you'll need to administer, and it provides a way of controlling them to get the results you expect.

MARKETING PLAN STRUCTURE

A marketing plan has a definite structure. Like a good story, it has a beginning, a middle, and an end (Figure 3-1). Hopefully, it has a happy ending. Unlike the characters in a story, however, at the end your marketing plan won't ride off happily into the sunset. Rather, it will lead you back to the beginning, providing you with new information and new insights so you can keep your business dynamic.

PART 1—BEGINNING

- Corporate mission statement
    Declaration of purpose
- Corporate goals
    Declaration of measurable accomplishment
- Market assumptions
- Market information

PART 2—MIDDLE

- Objectives for each service
    Short term
    Specific
- Strategy
    Overall game plan
- Tactics
    Steps to implement strategy
- Budget

PART 3—END

- Measurement
    Results of marketing programs
    Quantifiable change
- Analysis
    What worked?
      Why?
    What didn't?
      Why?
- Feedback
- Continuation of planning

Figure 3-1.   Structure of a marketing plan.

The marketing plan starts with a statement of your corporate mission, your vision for your business. It moves from that to a statement of your company goals. Your mission and goals guide the plan. Review the discussions on mission and goals in Chapter 2, "Marketing Information."

MISSION AND GOALS

To recap the discussions of Chapter 2, your vision describes the business you're in and how you plan to conduct it. The mission statement clearly and concisely sets the parameters of your business and focuses your attention on the details that will help make your salon a success. Your goals are different from your mission statement, which is a declaration of purpose. Your goals are a declaration of measurable accomplishment for your business as a whole, both in the short term and the long term. In short, how do you expect your business to grow in the future? Your goals have to be attainable. That is, you have to have a reasonable expectation that they can be reached. If you set goals you can't reach, you're not planning. You're merely dreaming.

OBJECTIVES

The material that follows these statements works to implement the plan. This part of the plan, corresponding to the middle of the story, begins with a statement of objectives. Don't confuse objectives with goals. According to the dictionary, *goal* and *objective* are synonyms that can be used interchangeably (*Concise American Heritage Dictionary, Revised Edition.* Boston: Houghton-Mifflin, 1987). In a business context, however, they are quite different. The difference is one of scope. Whereas goals are long term and more general, objectives are short term and specific.

You can have more than one objective. In fact, if you are treating each service (including retail sales) as a separate profit center, you should have at least one objective for each. The sum total of your objectives should lead you toward your goal.

Like your goals, your objectives should be attainable. If they can't possibly be reached, they are simply not reasonable. And they must be measurable. If you can't measure the results, you'll never know if you've reached them.

STRATEGY AND TACTICS

Your goals and objectives tell you where you want to go. Strategy and tactics tell you how to get there. Your strategy is your overall game plan, which outlines the means you will use to get to your objectives. Your tactics are the detailed steps you will take to implement the strategy. Tactics have the same relationship to strategy as objectives have to goals. The difference is more one of scope than of kind.

A strategy for meeting an objective of increasing permanent wave services by 10 percent might be to increase awareness of the availability of the service among the people living in your area and to demonstrate the benefits of the service. There might be several tactics you use to do this. For example, you might

1. distribute flyers to all of the residences in your target neighborhood announcing the availability of the service
2. have an article on the benefits of permanent waving published in the local newspaper
3. offer a special sale on permanents.

Your strategies, and the subsequent tactics you use to implement them, are affected by two factors. One is your image. The strategies and tactics must be consistent with the image you've established for your salon. You can't offer the lowest prices in town, for example, if you've set your image as an upscale salon, just as you wouldn't promote the ultimate in personal pampering if your salon is a high-volume, low-price shop.

The other is where the particular service fits into your overall business—that is, what role it plays in your product mix. As discussed earlier, for purposes of planning, you should treat each service as its own business. Make each service a strategic business unit (SBU), responsible for generating its own revenues, paying its own costs, and contributing its share to your overall profit picture. It takes time, good recordkeeping, and constant analysis to do this properly.

Each SBU will have its own needs, which may require its own part of the marketing plan, with its own marketing and marketing communications approaches. And each will occupy its own niche and make its own contributions to your business as a whole. Analyze each SBU carefully. Know how each fits your overall mission and what it brings to your business.

STRATEGIC BUSINESS UNIT THEORY

According to a marketing theory promulgated by the prestigious Boston Consulting Group (BCG), you can categorize each SBU as either a star, a cash cow, a question mark, or a dog, depending on its place in generating cash flow for your business, your market share for the segment, the segment's potential for growth, and the amount of marketing funds you should allocate to its promotion. Although the concept was developed for big business, it has application even for small businesses (see Figure 3-2).

The stars are those services for which you have good market share. They generate significant cash flow and have good growth potential. They will also require spending a good portion of your marketing dollars to promote their growth. Suppose, for example, that you enjoy a good business in hair coloring, and that business generates a lot of cash. Your marketing information indicates that

CATEGORY	MARKET SHARE	CASH FLOW	GROWTH POTENTIAL	PROMOTION NEED	STRATEGY
 ★	HIGH	HIGH	HIGH	HIGH	BUILD (Rising Star) HOLD (Falling Star)
 (cow)	HIGH	HIGH	LOW	MODERATE TO LOW	HOLD
?	LOW	LOW	UNKNOWN	UNKNOWN	BUILD OR HARVEST
 (dog)	LOW	LOW	LOW	NONE	HARVEST OR DIVEST

Figure 3-2. SBU theory.

you are only selling your hair coloring services to a relatively small segment of your target audience, so there is ample room for this SBU to grow. This is one of your stars. But to make it grow, you'll have to spend a significant part of your budget to promote it.

As long as you spend the money and the effort to make it grow, your sales of hair coloring services will increase until you reach a point at which no further growth is possible, at least among your current target audience. At that point, hair coloring services will become a cash cow.

The cash cows are those services for which you have a high market share and generate significant cash flow, but for which there is little prospect for further growth. In other words, sales of these services are about as high as they will ever get. Unlike stars, however, these services don't require as much promotion, so you can spend correspondingly less to keep them going.

Suppose you have a very good business in basic cutting and styling. You're keeping your staff busy with the service, and they are generating a substantial part of your revenues. But your marketing information shows that you can't expect to increase your sales of these services by any great amount. This service is a cash cow and won't require as much money or time to promote.

The question marks are those services for which you have a low market share and which generate little cash flow, but which have the potential to become stars. These services require a major decision on your part. You can either spend the considerable resources needed to promote them into stardom, or you can decide they're not worth the effort and do nothing. Suppose that you have recently introduced facial services. You don't have a lot of business at this point, and the services are not bringing in much money. But you think there is a good likelihood that this business will increase. (Hopefully, you have done your homework and have gathered market research data before you instituted the service.) To make the business grow, however, you will have to spend a lot of money and effort to promote facials and create a demand for the service. You have to decide whether it is worth allocating the resources necessary to turn the service into a star.

The dogs are those services for which you have low market share and which generate little cash flow, but for which there is little or no growth potential. They don't bring in enough money to justify spending cash or making much effort to promote them. You might be breaking even on recouping their cost, but it is just as likely that they are costing you money. Suppose, for instance, you offer pedicures as one of your services. You don't sell many of them and there is not much demand for the service, and your research shows that you would not be able to increase the demand. The pedicure service, then, is a dog in your product mix. You have to decide whether to keep it in the mix or get rid of it. Although this may seem to be an easy decision, it is not so simple to make. You have to determine what resources the service takes in terms of staff, equipment, space, and supplies, and you must weigh that against its value as part of your product line. You may, for example, need to keep pedicures in your product line to buttress your sales of manicures. You may want to get rid of dogs so that you have more time to nurture stars.

Why is this concept important in your overall business picture? Simply, categorizing your various services in this way will help you decide on the basic strategy to use in marketing them. The BCG theory recognizes four basic marketing strategies, which can be to build, hold, harvest, or divest. Which is appropriate for any one of your services is a function of which category the SBU fits into.

You would use a build strategy for promising question marks and rising stars. Here, you make the effort and spend the resources necessary to promote the service and improve it. With a build strategy, you are attempting to expand market share and increase customer loyalty.

A hold strategy, however, is more appropriate for cash cows and fading stars. In this case, you are trying to maintain your market share and hold onto customer loyalty. You may have to spend some effort and money to do this, but not nearly as much as you would in a build strategy.

You would use a harvest strategy with dogs, uncertain question marks, and cash cows that are drying up. The object in these cases is to milk them for as much cash as possible before they collapse. With this strategy, you spend as little time, effort, and money as possible, and you reduce the costs of providing the services as drastically as you can. You are not concerned with keeping market share or customer loyalty.

When you can no longer harvest cash from a dog or question mark, it may be time for a divest strategy. Here, you drop the service from your product mix or, in the case of a service you need to keep to support another, more profitable service, you reduce spending to the absolute minimum required to keep that service from adversely affecting the profitable service it is supporting. Then you use that money to support more worthy services. Here, market share and customer loyalty are irrelevant. After all, if you enjoyed good market share for these services, they wouldn't be in this category.

BUDGETING

As you formulate your marketing plans, it won't take you long to realize that tactics cost money. To reach your objectives, you will have to spend some amount of cash. How much depends on the situation. Analyze your financial position. Do you have enough cash to pay for the tactics you need to employ? If not, where can you get the financing you need? Can you accomplish the same result in another, less costly way?

There's an old adage in business: "It takes money to make money." Money is a resource that you have to utilize to make your business grow. The amount of money you are willing and able to spend will determine the strategies and tactics you will use. Consider the category the particular service is in. You need to spend more on stars and questions marks than you do on cash cows.

When it comes to marketing communications, some methods cost more than others. Space and radio advertising, for example, are expensive. Direct mail or simple flyers are relatively cheap, and under some circumstances they may do a particular task for you just as well.

Just as you budget for supplies and equipment, so will you budget for marketing, especially for marketing communications. Don't be haphazard in this area. Know how much you'll have to spend to achieve an objective. Weigh the cost against the potential return. And keep your cash flow requirements in mind. Don't deplete the cash you need for other aspects of the business.

MEASUREMENT AND ANALYSIS

At the end of the marketing plan comes measurement and analysis. How much effect did your efforts have? What do the results mean for your business? How did the results influence your corporate goals? As with your overall goals, whatever strategies and tactics you employ, there has to be some way to measure their results within a given time frame. You have to be able to see a quantifiable change; otherwise, you can't possibly know whether your efforts have worked. You won't know if you wasted your time and money. Nor will you know if your business is growing or declining.

An integral part of any strategy or tactic you employ is a consideration of how you are going to measure its results. You must also plan on a length of time so the process has a beginning point and an end point. You can't measure a process that doesn't finish. You can only monitor its progress.

Measurement can take any form that helps you determine whether you met your objective. The analysis of the results lets you make decisions and plan further.

Your measuring device will be suggested by the objective, which should have been stated in quantifiable terms. Thus, using the example of an objective noted earlier, you can count the number of new permanent wave customers you've gained in the quarter the objective covers. Then you calculate the percentage by which your business grew. If it was 10 percent or more, your strategies and tactics were successful and you reached your objective. If the percentage was less, the opposite is true.

Either way, you will have to analyze the results so you have a clear idea of why the effort did or didn't work. Admittedly, analysis is easier when you've been successful than when you've failed. If you didn't meet your objective, it is vital that you find out why not. You may have to go all the way back to your original assumptions and recheck your marketing information. Are the demographics correct? Did your market research really support the need for a particular service? Or were you letting your heart overrule your head? Be ruthless in your assessments. It's your business that will suffer if you're not.

Feedback is important whether you've reached your objectives or not. Talk to your new customers. What tactic did they respond to? What approach attracted them? What didn't work for them? Talk to your employees, too. Involve them in the process and solicit their ideas. Use that feedback when you formulate plans in the future.

Measurement and analysis may be the end of a particular plan, but they're not the end of the process. Marketing planning is a never-ending process. As long as you are in business, you will be doing marketing planning in one form or another, utilizing a constant flow of information you derive.

THE MARKETING PLANNING PROCESS

You start the marketing planning process by making a series of assumptions about your markets. For the assumptions to be valid, you need accurate marketing information and a comprehensive analysis of the situations you face. The more you know about the situation, the better your plan will be. Information starts with your target audience. Know your audience. There is no more fundamental precept. You'll hear this time and again. You should have gathered most of the information you'll need when you formulated your business plan. Here is the place you'll really use it.

Review the discussions in Chapter 2, "Marketing Information." Your demographic data form the principal base for your decision making. The accuracy of this information is crucial to your planning, because this information helps you determine the potential demand for your services.

In addition to knowing your target audience, you also have to know the competitive situation. This information helps you determine what market share you have and what you might expect to gain.

Also analyze your internal situation. Be honest with yourself. This information is important to your planning. It helps you determine if you have the resources and ability to carry out your marketing efforts.

The marketing information you gather helps you understand the composition of the market and make a reasonable forecast of its size. This forecast helps you determine market share potential (i.e., how much of the available business you are likely to get). Your analysis of the situation helps you categorize your services into their proper place in your product mix. All of this information helps you make assumptions about the market, which help you formulate your objectives.

Your objectives for each SBU should be specific, reasonably attainable, and measurable within a reasonable time span. Collectively, all the objectives should move your overall business toward its goals. The strategies and tactics you devise should be chosen to meet the objectives. They should be targeted to your particular audiences, they should be affordable, and they should be consistent with the image of your salon.

The results should be measured and analyzed. Get feedback from customers and employees. Recheck your information, and use the new insights you receive to reformulate your original assumptions as the situation demands. Then start the process all over again.

MARKETING COMMUNICATIONS

Marketing communications are those devices that further your marketing objectives by providing information to your customers and prospects. Simply put, they encompass all the efforts you make in promoting your services and your salon. The communications aspects of marketing are an important part of your strategies and tactics. Like your overall marketing plans, your marketing communications have to be planned. This topic is covered in detail in Chapter 9, "Marketing Communications."

In essence, you plan your marketing communications by considering your objectives and then working out strategies and tactics to achieve those objectives. Like elements of the marketing plan, you have to consider how you will measure the effectiveness of your marketing communications, and you have to decide how you will pay for them. Your marketing communications plan is a subset of your overall marketing plan, and it is just as important as any other aspect of your business. In some ways, it is the most important part because it is the most visible part of your plan. Your marketing communications are what your customers see first. And as the old adage says, you never get a second chance to make a first impression.

SUMMARY

- Marketing must be planned, just like every other aspect of your business. Without a comprehensive plan, you will probably not be successful. The marketing plan grows from your overall business plan, and it provides you with a structure for conducting your marketing programs.
- The marketing plan has a structure. In the beginning, you review your mission and goals. In the middle of the plan, you set objectives, which differ in scope from your goals. You then proceed to set your strategy and tactics, the overall game plan and the detailed steps that let you reach your objectives and lead ultimately to your goals.

- An important concept in marketing planning is the strategic business unit theory, in which you treat each service you offer as a separate business. Thinking of services in this way helps you decide on the basic strategies to use in marketing them.
- According to the SBU theory, there are four strategies: a build strategy for some question marks and rising stars, a hold strategy for cash cows and fading stars, a harvest strategy for dogs and some question marks, and a divest strategy for dogs and unprofitable segments.
- Budgeting is an important consideration in marketing planning. You have to allocate money to perform the tactics you'll utilize.
- It is important to measure the results of your actions and analyze them so you can make sound, prudent business decisions.
- Marketing communications are an important part of the marketing process. You have to plan how you are going to communicate with your audiences, just as you have to plan for everything else.
- The marketing process doesn't end once you've analyzed the results. It is a continuing effort. You will be planning your marketing efforts as long as you remain in business.

CHAPTER 4

Computerizing the Salon

Although it's possible to conduct your business without a computer, today's business climate makes it almost mandatory to have one. A computer can make virtually any task in your business a whole lot easier, from helping you manage your customer base, to generating financial reports, to handling a variety of communications options. The uses you'll find for a computer in your salon are limited only by your imagination.

In the past few years, the number of computer manufacturers has increased greatly and machines have gotten smaller, easier to use, and far less expensive. At the same time, many relatively low-cost programs have been written to make the computer an effective tool for business. Because of these developments, a computer system is a very practical and cost-effective acquisition for small businesses. Salons are no exception. In fact, computer use has become so pervasive in business that you will probably be hard pressed to compete without one.

USES OF THE COMPUTER

The computer can handle a wide variety of tasks in your salon ranging from database management to publishing your own newsletter. You can use a computer to:

- keep your records
- schedule appointments
- write letters
- keep track of your inventory
- compute your taxes
- entertain your customers
- educate your customers.

As you start using a computer in your salon, you'll find more and more ways it can help you. Figure 4-1 lists the ways a computer can help you run your salon more effectively.

DATABASE MANAGEMENT

- Customer lists
- Customer service records
- Employee records
- Scheduling and appointments

BUSINESS DATA MANAGEMENT

- Data compilation and analysis
- Accounting and bookkeeping
- Inventory control

COMMUNICATIONS MANAGEMENT

- Word processing
- Graphics
- Video
- Networking

Figure 4-1.   Uses of the computer in the salon.

You have to remember, though, that your computer is a tool, not a miracle worker. It doesn't replace common sense and thought on your part. A computer does exactly what you tell it to do. If you give it a wrong instruction, it will carry it out. It doesn't think or make decisions for you. It is just a machine that is only as good as the information you put into it. There is a word for this in computer circles—GIGO (Garbage In, Garbage Out). So if you use a computer in your salon, make sure you know how to use it properly.

DATABASE MANAGEMENT

Computers are at their best in handling data. Look at your office now. Chances are there are filing cabinets full of papers, files stuffed to overflowing, and notes and bits of information scattered all over the desk. A database management program is like an electronic file clerk who organizes all that information, sorts it out, and makes it accessible to you when you need it. Imagine having all that paper and all those files contained in a handful of small disks, ready for you at little more than the push of a button (Figure 4-2).

It's not quite that simple, of course. Even the best database management programs require that you enter the data correctly.

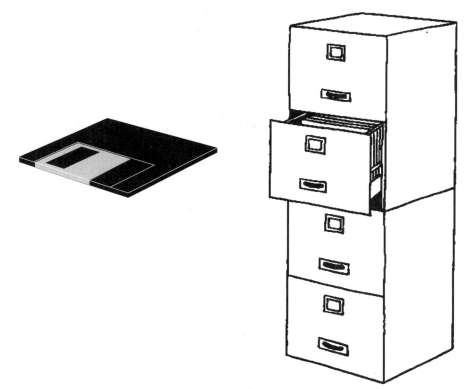

Figure 4-2.   Computer disk versus file cabinet. One 3.5-inch high-den-
             sity floppy disk holds 1.44 megabytes of information. This is
             the equivalent of 300 pages of text.

But if you take the time to learn how to get the maximum use from
the program and take the time and effort to put the information
into the computer, you will reap the electronic rewards in terms of
prompt access and efficiency. If you don't have the time or inclination to set up your database, you can hire freelancers who specialize in this work to set up your database at the start.

   Once you have your database management program in operation, there are many tasks you can ask it to help you with.

CUSTOMER LISTS

Your up-to-date customer list is your most important treasure. It is
your primary record of who your customers are, their preferences,
and their buying habits. You can keep your customer list on file,

with the ability to access any customer by name, address, telephone number, preferences, frequency of patronage, birthday, personal information, and any other information that might be useful. This becomes your basic mailing list that lets you send special notices, holiday greetings, and birthday cards to each customer.

CUSTOMER SERVICE RECORDS

Closely allied with your customer lists are your customer service records. Use the computer to keep a record of customer purchases of services, such as facials, hair coloring, and permanents, with a notation when the next service is due so you can send a reminder card to the customer. It also lets you know the results of all services performed and lets you keep track of specific information, such as skin care products used or the formula for the hair coloring. Figure 4-3 shows an example.

CUSTOMER SERVICE RECORD

Last Name: Moore   **First Name:** Maureen
Address: 161 N. Broadway Ave.
City: Doylestown   **State:** PA   **Zip:** 18901
Telephone No: (215)555-4411   **Birthday:** April 4

Preferences:
Use hair color number 33. Does not like mousse on hair. Sensitive skin. Use hypoallergenic makeup.

Service History

Date	Service	Operator	Cost	Remarks
1/4/94	Hair cut	Cindy	$28	New style for client
2/7/94	Color & style	Cindy	$44	Changed color to red
4/1/94	Hair cut	Cindy	$28	
4/1/94	Manicure	Laurie	$15	
4/12/94	Perm	Olivia	$38	Perm special
5/15/94	Facial	Catherine	$60	
5/15/94	Makeup app.	Barbara	$20	

Figure 4-3.   A sample customer computer service record.

EMPLOYEE RECORDS

Just as you should keep records on your customers, so is it important to keep records of your employees. You need these records for the government, but also for business reasons. The computer lets you keep all of your employee information on file, with the ability to call up any information you might need, from attendance records to pay data.

Properly kept, current employee records provide the information necessary to meet government regulations for withholding taxes and to generate data for unemployment compensation and workers' compensation programs, among others. They are also vital as records in cases of employment disputes, for insurance purposes, or for keeping track of which employees are trained on which skills. You can also use them to keep track of sales by employee, which is important if you pay on a commission basis.

SCHEDULING AND APPOINTMENTS

Making and keeping customer appointments is a vital part of salon business. You can use the computer to establish a calendar to let you keep track of appointments, as well as to schedule employee work hours and vacation times. This can help you adjust operator schedules to meet customer demand. In addition, you can use the calendar to list dates of trade shows and industry meetings you might attend.

BUSINESS DATA MANAGEMENT AND ANALYSIS

You can use the computer to help you compile and analyze information that lets you see how well your business is doing. This gives you the data you need to make prudent decisions about your salon. By tracking sales of services and products, you can see which are profitable and which are not. You can also see which operators are generating income and which may not be. This information lets you adjust schedules or add or subtract services.

ACCOUNTING AND BOOKKEEPING

You can keep all accounting records and financial data on the computer and use the information to generate financial reports for the bank when you apply for a loan. You can also generate profit and loss reports for tax purposes or for the use of your partners, if you have any. You can even use the computer to print checks, pay your bills, and pay your employees.

INVENTORY CONTROL

You can keep track of your inventory of products that you use in the salon as well as those you stock for retail sales. In addition, you can use inventory information to monitor the sales, use, and reordering of products.

Just as you keep meticulous records on your sales of services, so should you keep them for all your retail sales. Enter all sales into the computer. Know where and when each item went and for how much it sold. Gather all the data you can, and analyze the data regularly. Look for information that tells you which products sell best and how long it takes each product to sell. These data will help you when it comes to deciding which products to keep or which to discontinue and what quantities of each product you should stock. Also keep records on which products you have to discard because they have become outdated. The price data let you figure the profitability of each product.

You can also use inventory information to keep track of quantities of various products and automate your reordering, to make sure you always have enough product on hand, either for use in the salon or for retail sale.

COMMUNICATIONS MANAGEMENT

In addition to managing your data, the computer can let you manage your communications. Word processing and graphics programs give you great flexibility in generating reports, letters, and various marketing communications vehicles. Various on-line services give you access to vast quantities of information and e-mail networks. You can even use the computer to send and receive faxes.

WORD PROCESSING

A good word processing program turns your computer into much more than just a substitute for a typewriter. It gives you the capability to write letters and memos as well as generate complete documents, including your Employee Handbook, Salon Procedure Manual, or customer newsletter. The computer lets you write the original document and make revisions easily. And it stores the document so you can reprint or make revisions as needed, without needing to retype the entire manuscript.

GRAPHICS

Some word processing programs have graphics capabilities that let you import pictures and tables from other programs and incorporate them into the document you're preparing, as illustrated in Figure 4-4. These capabilities can be somewhat limited. Dedicated painting and drawing programs are much more powerful for generating graphics, however. Programs are available that let you retouch and crop photographs and create original drawings and illustrations. Other programs let you create and publish your own documents, incorporating text from your word processing program with graphics from your painting or drawing program.

VIDEO

Your computer can give you immediate access to the video explosion through its capacity for multimedia. This capacity lets you create presentations for your clients, which can even include movies that show the latest in hair styles. With the proper software and hardware, you can hook up a video camera or a still digital video camera to your computer.

NETWORKING

Most computers either have built-in networking capability or it can be added relatively inexpensively. Networking allows communication between computers, either in your salon if you have more than one computer or with other computers anywhere in the world.

Networking capability gives you access to a wide range of information and talk through on-line networks. This is the widely touted Information Superhighway. With the proper equipment, you can also send and receive faxes and other electronic mail.

TESS'S
TRESSES®

1616 W. Main St. Doylestown, PA 18901
(215)555-1000

March 10, 1995

Dear Valued Customer:

St. Patrick's Day will soon be here and it's a time for everyone to be Irish. We're certainly no exception. Join us on March 17 as we celebrate this happy holiday with refreshments, fun, door prizes, and **great values.** Take advantage of our Shamrock Specials:

- Free manicure with any hair service
- Free makeover with any facial
- 25% off permanent wave or hair color services
- 10% off all retail merchandise

Our little leprechauns are waiting to work their magic on you. So call today for an appointment and come to the party. **The number to call is (215)555-1000.**

Hope we see you on the 17th!
Erin Go Bragh!

Tess

Figure 4-4. A sample computer sales letter with graphics.

MARKETING COMMUNICATIONS WITH THE COMPUTER

Given the right computer hardware, software programs, and the talent and experience to use them well, you can generate many of the marketing communications you will need right from your desktop. The capabilities the computer gives you are virtually limitless. You can write sales letters, advertisements, flyers, brochures, and mailers, marrying text with graphics that you draw, clip art, or photographs. You can work in black and white or in color. And you can use your database management systems to personalize the pieces and to print mailing labels.

There is much more you can do. Specific types of projects will be covered in depth in succeeding chapters. But all of these capabilities will be yours only if you get the right computer and software and learn to use them properly. They can be one of the best investments you'll make in your business.

COMPUTER EQUIPMENT

A computer system consists of a combination of hardware and software. The term *hardware* refers to the machinery. The term *software* refers to the programs, or instructions that tell the machinery what to do. To be functional, the system requires both. It also requires that both be compatible—that is, that they work together. Figure 4-5 shows a typical system.

The computer's operating system is the hardware manufacturer's program that is built into the computer and organizes and manages all of the internal functions of the computer and its various parts. Hardware and software will be compatible only when they utilize the same operating system. As a general rule, if the operating systems are different, the machinery and programs won't be able to work together.

COMPUTER HARDWARE

Computer hardware consists of the basic computing unit and related peripherals, as well as its related input and output devices. Input devices are those that let you put information into the computer. Output devices are those that let you get information out of the computer. The minimum hardware required is the basic computing unit and monitor, a hard disk drive for storing data, a key-

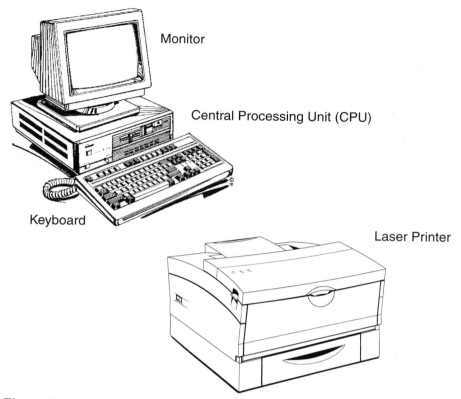

Monitor

Central Processing Unit (CPU)

Keyboard

Laser Printer

Figure 4-5. A typical computer system.

board for data input, and a printer for data output. The hard disk drive can be built in or external. You can add other input and output devices as you need them. Some will be more useful in the salon than others.

BASIC COMPUTING UNITS

The basic computing unit is the heart of the system. It is the box that contains the central processing unit, the memory, and, in most modern computers, one or more disk drives. It also has a series of connectors that allow you to plug in the peripherals and a cooling fan to keep the various electronic components from overheating. The brain of the system is the central processing unit (CPU), a microprocessor that performs all of the analytical and computational functions of the computer. The CPU is usually housed on the main logic board, a circuit board that holds the microprocessor as well as the *random access memory* (RAM) and *read-only memory* (ROM) memory and other circuits that let the computer perform its many functions.

The computer's memory capacity is an important feature. It determines how much information the unit can hold and process. In general, the more memory your computer has, the better off you are. There are two types of memory: read-only memory (ROM), and random access memory (RAM). Both types store information for later use. ROM can't be changed. You can read the data in the memory, but you can't alter it in any way. It is the memory built into the computer by the manufacturer, and it contains the instructions that let the computer start up when you turn it on and run the basic functions of the computer. The contents of the read-only memory stay in place even when there is no power going into the computer. RAM is the internal memory that takes the information fed into the computer from disks or other input devices and stores it so it can be used. This memory is also built into the machine but can be both read and changed. When you turn the computer off, either deliberately or by accident, this memory is lost, along with any information you haven't saved to a data storage device.

Computers are supplied with different amounts of random access memory. The more application programs you intend to run, the more you will need. Memory is measured in units called bytes. One byte generally represents one character—either a letter, number, space, or punctuation mark. Your computer's RAM will be rated in kilobytes or megabytes. One kilobyte equals 1,024 bytes. One megabyte equals 1,024 kilobytes, or 1,048,576 bytes. So if you have a machine with four megabytes of RAM, you can store 4,194,304 characters worth of information. This amount is sufficient to handle simple word processing and database management programs. If you are going to use more sophisticated programs or use graphics, you should get a machine with a minimum of 8 megabytes of RAM.

Many computers can have additional RAM memory installed through the addition of SIMMs (single in-line memory modules), so if you find you need more RAM, you can add it if your machine can be upgraded. In addition, there are programs available that increase the effective RAM of the computer without physically adding more. In essence, these programs fool the computer into thinking it has more RAM by setting aside parts of the hard disk for use as virtual memory.

MONITORS

Monitors are the eyes of the computer. They are similar to small
television sets and display the information contained in the computer. Some relatively simple computers have monitors built in. For
most computers, however, the monitor is separate. The standard
size monitor for most computers is 14 inches, although they are
available in sizes up to 21 inches. The larger monitors are useful
for desktop publishing and graphics, where it is desirable to see a
whole page at once. The smaller monitors are adequate for normal
database and word processing uses.

Monitors are available in black and white, monochrome, or in
color. Black-and-white monitors are useful for word processing or
database applications. Monochrome monitors, since they can handle up to 256 shades of gray, are useful for graphics applications in
which color isn't necessary. Color monitors display from 256 to over
16 million colors on their screens and are used for generating and
working with information that has to be in color. To generate high-
quality color, it may be necessary to add a color accelerator card to
the computer's CPU.

DATA STORAGE DEVICES

Disk drives are devices for storing and accessing additional information. They let you use memory that is not built into the computer—that is, memory other than RAM—by writing information onto
or reading information from a diskette. There are two types of disk
drives in common use. Fixed, or hard, disk drives contain a metal
disk that is sealed permanently into the drive. These are very fast
and hold a lot of information, typically ranging from 40 to 230
megabytes, although they are available with capacities of more
than 1 gigabyte (1,000 megabytes).

Floppy drives utilize plastic diskettes to read or write information. Floppy disks hold much less information than hard disks
but have the advantage of being portable. The two most commonly used sizes of floppy disks are 3.5-inch and 5¼ inch,
although the 3.5-inch disks have mostly supplanted the larger
size. The 3.5 inch floppy disks have a storage capacity of up to
1.44 megabytes. The information is actually stored on the
diskette, so it is not lost when the computer is turned off, as is the
case with information in random access memory. Floppy disks are

magnetic and should be stored away from magnets and telephones and handled carefully.

Other types of data storage devices include removable cartridge drives, optical drives, and tape cartridge drives. These are
generally high-capacity external storage devices used for handling
large amounts of data or for backing up data contained on the hard
drive. Removable cartridge drives are the most common types and
are available in capacities of 44, 88, 105, and 270 megabytes. Optical drives are available in capacities up to 150 megabytes. Both
types feature random accessibility—that is, you can access the data
at random. They are used for transferring large amounts of data
from one computer to another and for back up.

Tape cartridge drives, on the other hand, which look and
operate like a conventional tape cassette, offer only linear access.
You have to play the whole tape to find the information you're
looking for. These are most commonly used for back-up purposes.

INPUT DEVICES

KEYBOARDS

The keyboard is the primary input device for the computer. Keyboards generally resemble typewriter keyboards and function in
much the same way, although they also contain a number of specialized keys.

MICE AND TRACKBALLS

In addition to the keyboard, there are other devices for entering
information into the computer. The most common of these is the
mouse. A mouse is a small, hand-held device that lets you point to
specific locations on the screen and, by pressing the mouse button,
enter certain commands. A trackball is a type of inverted mouse,
which operates by manipulating the ball directly.

DIGITIZING TABLETS

Digitizing tablets are like drawing boards for the computer. They
provide a flat surface on which you can draw pictures with a stylus.
You draw on the tablet surface, but you see the result on the com-

puter monitor screen. Some tablets have a clear acetate overlay that lets you slide in artwork to be traced. Others have pressure-sensitive styluses that let you vary the width of the line by the amount of pressure you use, just as though you were using a brush. Some styluses have programmable keys on the barrel that let you assign specific functions to the tablet. The tablets are available in a variety of sizes from drawing surfaces of 4 inches by 6 inches to 24 inches by 36 inches.

SCANNERS

A scanner is a device that translates images—that is, photographs and drawings—into digital information that can be handled by the computer. This lets you add pictures to your documents. This kind of device may be useful if you are an experienced computer user and are producing newsletters or other documents that contain pictures as well as words. Scanners are very expensive, although, like other computer peripherals, their prices are coming down rapidly.

CD-ROM PLAYERS

Another input peripheral for the computer is the CD-ROM player, a device that takes data from a laser disk and inputs it into the computer. The laser disks hold a staggering amount of information that can be accessed very quickly. One CD-ROM disk can hold as much as 500 high-density floppy disks. Other CD-ROM disks contain volumes of clip art, royalty-free predrawn images you can use in your documents. Although the CD-ROM disks hold an extremely large amount of data, it is only possible to read from the disks. You can't add to them or change any of the data.

DIGITAL STILL CAMERAS

One of the newest input peripherals available for the computer is the digital still camera, which takes pictures like a regular camera but puts them on a tiny floppy disk built into the device instead of on regular film. The image quality is not as good as film, but it is adequate for many applications.

One potential use for a digital still camera in your salon is to record clients' hair styles and insert the photo into the customer record database. When you print out the record the next time the customer comes in, you'll also have a photo of the finished style.

OUTPUT DEVICES

PRINTERS

A printer is a device that lets you produce hard copy from the information you've entered into the computer. There are a number of different kinds of computer printers.

- Dot matrix printers can print copy and some limited graphics.
- Daisy wheel printers work like automatic typewriters. They produce letter quality print with copy but can't reproduce graphics.
- Ink jet printers work much the same as dot matrix printers; they can print both copy and graphics and their print quality is better than dot matrix printers. Some ink jet printers can print in different colors by using different color inks. In some cases, it is necessary to use special paper with these printers to prevent ink smearing.
- Laser printers offer the best quality of printing. They can handle both copy and graphics.
- Color printers and black-and-white printers are available. A number of inexpensive color ink jet printers are on the market that give good-quality color reproduction at a relatively low price.

Choose your printer based on the quality of output you need and consider what you are going to use it for. In addition to print quality, look at features such as resolution, speed, and paper feed.

- Resolution is a measure of print quality and is measured in dots per inch (DPI). The higher the DPI, the better the quality of the print.
- Speed is measured in pages per minute. Check how fast the printer will turn out copy. This is usually rated in pages per minute (ppm), although the actual speed depends on the content of the page. Graphics take longer to print than plain text.
- Computers generally use either continuous form paper or single sheets. Continuous form paper must be separated into individual sheets by hand after printing. There is a greater variety of paper grades and colors available in single sheets.

OTHER PERIPHERALS

MODEMS

A modem is a device that lets your computer communicate with other computers by telephone. You will need a modem to use any of the on-line services. Modems may be either internal—that is, built into the computer—or external—that is, attached to the computer as a separate accessory.

Modem performance is measured in units called bauds, and the devices come in various baud ratings. The higher the baud rating, the faster the modem transmits and receives information. The faster your modem, the lower your telephone bill will be. Look for a modem with at least a 9,600 baud rating.

VOLTAGE SPIKE PROTECTORS

Computers are vulnerable to voltage surges coming through electric power lines. If a surge occurs while you are working on the computer, you can lose valuable data. For this reason, you should connect the computer and its peripherals to the electric power source through a specially designed voltage spike protector. This will prevent damage and loss of information in your system.

Some voltage spike protectors also function as control consoles. They let you plug all of your devices into the protector and give you the capability to turn them on and off with one master switch. Other protectors have batteries built into them that will keep power going to the CPU long enough to save whatever data you're working on in case of a power failure.

COMPUTER SOFTWARE

Computer software programs tell the computer what to do and how to do it. To make your computer work, you will need a number of software packages. These are available from a number of sources. The most widely used business software comes as proprietary packages from a number of vendors. You don't really buy this software. Rather, you purchase a license to use it. You may not lend or give it to someone else to use. Software publishers protect their rights vigorously. Misuse of such proprietary software can lead to serious penalties.

Some software is in the public domain and its use is free. Such software is available through computer user groups and on community bulletin boards and other on-line services. You will need a modem to access this type of software. You will also use a number of proprietary software packages. The software comes on one or more disks, or on a CD-ROM disk, which you load into your computer memory. Most software packages come with instruction manuals and tutorials, subprograms that teach you to use the program.

WORD PROCESSING PROGRAMS

Word processing programs let you write and edit documents. This is the type of program you would use to write customer letters, employee manuals, salon procedure guides, and the like. Most programs let you format copy—that is, set margins and columns—and most let you use a variety of type styles and sizes. Some let you draw simple graphics, such as borders and boxes, and import graphics from other programs.

DATABASE MANAGEMENT PROGRAMS

Database management programs organize and manage information. This is the type of program you would use to maintain your customer lists, your employee records, etc. These programs let you set up your data in fields, listing names, addresses, telephone numbers, and any other data you require. Once entered, you can search for any item using simple find commands. You can also have the program print reports in a wide variety of formats.

SPREADSHEET PROGRAMS

Spreadsheet programs are analysis tools for business. You set up your spreadsheet in a series of rows and columns. The programs also let you create mathematical formulas for manipulating the data. Many of the programs also let you generate reports in a variety of formats and use the data to create charts and graphs for use in presentations.

ACCOUNTING AND BOOKKEEPING PROGRAMS

There are a wide variety of accounting and bookkeeping programs available that will let you do everything from keeping your basic financial, sales, and expense records to printing out checks so you can pay bills. Some can even calculate your taxes. Like other types of computer programs, they are available with a variety of features, depending on the sophistication of the program.

DESKTOP PUBLISHING PROGRAMS

These programs let you publish your own brochures and documents by doing basic typesetting and design. With a desktop publishing program, you can integrate copy and graphics into one document. This is the type of program you would use, for example, if you published a salon newsletter for your customers.

GRAPHICS PROGRAMS

Graphics programs let you draw pictures and illustrations that you can use in other programs. Depending on the sophistication of the graphics program, you can create anything from a simple line drawing to a complicated painting. Some programs let you manipulate images and retouch photographs.

CALENDAR PROGRAMS

These programs let you make up a calendar to keep track of appointments, meetings, etc. They can serve as valuable time management tools by automating your customer appointments and employee work and vacation schedules.

VIRUS PROTECTION PROGRAMS

A computer virus is a destructive program introduced into a computer as a prank or with malicious intent. Virus protection programs seek out these viruses in your computer and erase them before they can do any damage.

SPECIALIZED SOFTWARE PACKAGES

Some manufacturers supply software packages designed to meet specific business needs. Some offer programs and equipment designed especially for salons.

UTILITY SOFTWARE PACKAGES

There are many utility programs available for computers. These perform a variety of maintenance and housekeeping functions that let your computer operate more efficiently. Some can detect and repair problems with hard disks; others segment your disk space more effectively.

CHOOSING YOUR COMPUTER SYSTEM AND SOFTWARE

When it comes to buying your system and software, you have a lot to choose from. Do it carefully.

- Take the time to think about your needs. Talk to other business computer users, get advice from your accountant, and read as much as you can on the subject.
- Start with the basic components and software and learn how to use them to their fullest. Then add to them as you need.
- Know exactly what you want the computer to do for you. Research your needs and have a good idea of your expectations.
- Shop for the best package you can get. Don't consider price only, however. Service is very important. Look for a computer vendor who is knowledgeable, who is willing to work with you, and who provides service.

USING YOUR COMPUTER PROPERLY

Once you have your computer, take the time to learn to use it properly.

- Read the instruction manuals.
- Take the tutorial subprograms that come as part of most software packages.
- Consider taking one or more courses in computer use.
- Consider who will use the computer in your salon. Limit access to it. Make sure anyone who is authorized to use the computer is fully trained in its use.
- Carefully consider the location of your computer. Make sure the location has adequate ventilation and does not get too hot.
- Security is also an important consideration. Your data are valuable; safeguard them. Keep disks locked when not in use.

- Utilize passwords to limit access to the data. Change your passwords on a regular basis.
- Enter data carefully. Make sure it is accurately put into the computer. As you enter data, save it often. Remember the discussion on RAM memory earlier. RAM memory is lost when the computer is off. If you have a power failure while you are entering data, anything you have not saved to the disk will be lost. So get into the habit of saving the data every few minutes.
- Back up your disks frequently, at least on a daily basis. (Backing up just means making copies of your disks so you have duplicates in case of emergency.)

SUMMARY

- In the salon, a computer can help you manage your database, keep your records, schedule appointments, manage your inventory, compute taxes, and even write a newsletter.
- Computers are at their best in handling data. That makes them ideal for recordkeeping of all types, from employee records to customer service records, customer lists, and appointment lists.
- You need hardware and software in a computer system. Hardware is the machinery. Software is the programs that tell the machinery what to do.
- A basic hardware package consists of the computer central processing unit to do the calculations, a monitor to let you see what's going on, a hard drive to store the data, a keyboard and a mouse to input data, and a printer to output data.
- Memory and storage capacity are two important parameters for making a choice when you purchase your computer.
- Other hardware you may find useful are scanners, CD-ROMs, digital still cameras, and modems
- Software packages are sold as proprietary programs, although some software is available as shareware or freeware through on-line databases.
- Do your homework before you shop for a computer. Know what you want to use it for before you make a decision, and then buy the computer system and software that will let you do what you want. Shop around, but don't buy based only on price. Service is an important factor. Learn how to use the computer properly.

CHAPTER 5

Product

Product is the first of the classic four P's of marketing. But the term *product* covers much more than the physical items you sell. Product is a comprehensive concept that includes the sum total of the services you provide and the items you offer at retail. Equally as important, product includes your entire business. You, your staff, your facilities, and your operations are just as much a part of your product offering as the services you provide and the retail items you sell. Every service you offer is a product, just the same as any physical item you sell at retail.

But your most important product is yourself—this is what you're really marketing in a service business. Your product mix—that is, the services and retail products you sell—supports the image you have created for your salon. It defines who you are.

Products (services) have both tangible and intangible attributes. You can't think of a product only as a generic product, defined in terms of its physical attributes—that is, the core idea of what that product or service is. For example, a haircut is a physical action consisting of wetting the hair, shearing it to a specific length and shape, drying it, and combing it into a preconceived style. These are the generic, or tangible, attributes of the service (product) the customer is purchasing.

But you also have to consider two very important intangible attributes of the product, which take it far beyond its generic nature. The first intangible is the expected product. What is the product the customer expects to get? Does the product meet all the requirements the customer has in his or her mind? In short, does it satisfy the customer? The second intangible is the augmented product. That includes whatever you do to make the generic product exceed your customer's expectations. Again, this deals with customer satisfaction, which is the keystone of contemporary marketing thought.

THE IMPORTANCE OF IMAGE

Before you determine your product mix, you have to establish your own identity. Determine the image you want to project, based on who you are and what you want to accomplish, and then make that image match the reality of your business. In short, market your image. Once you've done this, choose products and services that support your image. Then make sure that every aspect of your business plays its part.

No matter what image you choose, however, it is important that the image matches the reality of your business. To succeed in your business, you have to be true to the image. You can't promise something you don't deliver. For example, if you project an upscale image, the services and products you offer have to be of the highest quality. You can't afford to cut any corners. And you have to price those services and products accordingly. Your customers will expect and demand extra pampering.

On the other hand, if you've decided on a high-volume, low-price image, you will conduct your business differently. Quality is still important, but price and speed are paramount. Customers will still expect and demand that the services be performed well, but they won't expect the same level of service and pampering as they would in an upscale shop. In this case, though, you can give them more than they expect. In fact, you should always give customers more than they expect. You can never give them less.

Your image governs your customers' expectations. You have to live up to those expectations and exceed them when you can if you expect your customers to come back. Remember, customers also get their expectations from competitors who have set a standard for service in their minds.

The image you project should also differentiate your salon from your competitors. It should set you apart from them and give you a distinction in the marketplace that they don't have. The right image helps get the customer into your shop instead of the competition's.

ESTABLISHING YOUR IMAGE

Developing your image depends on a variety of factors and involves virtually every aspect of your business. It starts with your clientele and location, affects the decor and ambiance of the salon, and determines even your signage, business cards, and stationery. Even the name you choose for your salon affects your image. From the time you open for business until the day you close your doors for the last time, the image you've selected will drive your marketing efforts. Your product mix may change. Your staff may change. But your image will be a constant. So choose the image you want carefully. Once you've established an image, it can be very difficult to change.

CLIENTELE

Look at your business plan. What clientele did you target? Choosing and developing an image starts with the clientele you're looking to attract. Are they upscale businesspeople? Or are they college students? Or the elderly? Or do you want to be known as a high-volume, low-price shop? With what business are you most comfortable? What group fits into your business plan the best? The image you try to foster for the upscale businesspeople will be far different than the image you establish as a volume- and price-oriented business.

LOCATION

The location of your salon also affects your image. The neighborhood in which you set up shop can say volumes about the type of salon you operate. Your selected clientele also plays a part in your selection of location. In general, you will locate where your clientele is most apt to reach you. Thus, an upscale shop will locate in a posh neighborhood or in the downtown area, where other high-end shops do business. It would not open in a seedy, run-down area. Conversely, the high-volume shop would open in a more working class neighborhood, or perhaps, in a downtown area where the other shops match its image.

There is a lot of flexibility in this concept. Obviously, you don't always have the opportunity to choose the ideal location. There are times when you can get away with a lesser location, but you'll have to work even harder at marketing to do it.

NAME

What's in a name? Contrary to Shakespeare's oft-quoted maxim, a rose by any other name does not smell as sweet. The name you choose for your salon has as much of an effect on your clientele's perceptions of your shop as any other aspect of the image you've created.

Whatever name you choose, make it appropriate to your image. Keep it simple and descriptive so that customers have a good idea of what to expect when they see the name. Don't be afraid to use your own name in the name you give your salon. Your family name would be more appropriate for a high-end salon. Your given name might be better for a volume-price salon. Thus, "Johnson's Hair Works" may be more suitable for your intended image than "Happy Henrietta's Holistic Hair Emporium." However, temper the use of your family name with good judgment so there won't be any question of who you are and what you do. For example, if your name is Wendy McDonald, you probably wouldn't want to use your family name for your salon name.

Avoid bad puns, and don't be too cutesy. Be aware of undesirable connotations. For example, if you choose a name like "Hair Today," someone's next thought might be "gone tomorrow."

When you choose a name, test it by getting sample opinions from prospective clients. What are their reactions? Make sure it is not similar to the names of existing salons in your general area. Register the name with the state through the fictitious name registration procedure. In addition to protecting your rights to the name, the registration procedure will tell you if another business has been using that name.

DECOR

The way your salon looks also carries your image. Choose your look carefully, and then make sure your equipment and decorations match. Be careful that your color combinations match the image you're trying to project. For example, if you have a high-tech image, you might use a lot of white and chrome, with black accents. You probably would not use pastels or earth tones. Unless you are an expert, you would be well advised to hire a professional decorator. Image is such an important facet of the salon business that expert help is money well spent.

Don't stint on equipment or supplies. Get the best you can afford, as long as it is consistent with your image. Top-quality equipment looks more professional, works more efficiently, and lasts longer than cheap equipment. Your choice of equipment quality will tell your prospective clients a lot about the quality of your services. In the beginning, at least, get only the equipment you need. Idle equipment costs money. You want to maximize the use of the equipment you have. Keep it working for you, not against you. You can always add more equipment later, when business warrants it.

Signage is an important part of decor. Have your signs made professionally, with a design appropriate to the image. Make sure outdoor signs are well lighted, either with external fixtures or with internal back lighting. Check with your local code authority before installing outdoor signs.

Window signs may be painted or made of neon. Again, the design should be appropriate to the image. Don't let the signage clutter up the window. Allow plenty of visibility inside.

Hire a graphic artist to design your logo. It is an important part of your image. Use the logo on your business cards, stationery, etc. It makes a big difference, and it's worth the expense.

AMBIANCE

Salon ambiance is more than just the decor. It is the feeling the client gets when he or she walks into the salon. It is the atmosphere generated in the salon, and it should be one that fosters confidence and trust. Regardless of the decor, the salon should be bright, cheerful, clean, and inviting. The employees should be friendly and courteous. Everything about the facilities and staff should make the client feel both welcome and appreciated. Sounds, smells, and attitudes are every bit as important as colors.

With respect to sound, make sure there is no unnecessary noise in the salon. Choose the background music with care, according to the tastes of your clients, and appropriate to your salon's image, not the image of you or your staff. You may be the world's biggest fan of rap music. If your clientele wants opera, you play opera. If in doubt about the type of music to play, stick to middle-of-the-road music. Don't turn your nose up at what some people disparagingly call "elevator music." It may not inspire anyone, but it won't offend anyone either. Whatever you play, keep it low. It should remain in the background and not intrude into the activities in the salon. Its purpose is to soothe and calm, not to entertain.

Salons generate certain smells. Permanent wave lotions, manicuring supplies, etc. all have a distinct odor. You can't help that. But you should keep those odors to a minimum with proper ventilation. Use air fresheners where appropriate. Keep your salon smelling good. Bad smells turn off clients. Remember, you may be so used to the odors that you don't notice them. But your clients will.

Attitude starts in the reception area.

- Was the client met with a cheerful welcome and a smile from the receptionist?
- Does he or she have a comfortable place to sit?
- Is there fresh coffee or tea available?
- Do you have a good stock of current magazines? Make sure they're not dog-eared or torn!
- Are style books available so the client can get ideas?

Attitude continues in the working areas of the salon.

- Did the operators have a friendly greeting for the client?
- Did the service start within a few minutes of the appointment time?
- Was the client spared a long wait?
- Was the service done quickly, efficiently, and to the client's complete satisfaction?
- Did the operators thank the client after the service?

A lasting impression may be formed back at the reception area.

- Did the cashier thank the client?
- Did you thank the client for his or her patronage?
- Did you ask how he or she liked the service?
- Did you ask whether he or she was satisfied?
- Did you let the client leave without being satisfied?
- Did you invite the client back? Now is the perfect time to ask the client to schedule his or her next appointment.

EMPLOYEE DEMEANOR

You understand the importance of good customer relations. Make sure your employees understand that also. Your employees interact with your customers. Establish your rules of employee conduct, and make sure they are included in your Employee Handbook. Enforce those rules. Instill in your employees the necessity for courtesy and respect at all times. Your employees should be friendly with customers, but not familiar. It is up to you to set the example for your employees. If you don't practice what you preach, you can't expect them to pay attention to your rules.

Regardless of the image you want to establish, it is necessary to maintain a professional image for your salon. You and your employees should look and act the part of professional cosmetologists. Set a dress code, according to the image you want your salon to project. Will it be casual? Trendy? Formal? That's up to you. But make sure the employees dress accordingly. Have your employees wear the latest hair and nail styles, too. You are selling the concept of looking and feeling good. Demonstrate it in your salon. It's part of your marketing.

All of your employees should also respect each other and work together. They should be friendly toward each other and cooperate with each other. As long as they are in the public areas of the salon, they should work in harmony. Keep internal disputes among your staff off the salon floor. Good-natured banter among the employees should be encouraged. Horseplay, however, should not be tolerated. It degrades the salon image and is dangerous.

Employees should be in the public areas of the salon only while working. Breaks and meals should be in the break room. Don't allow eating in the public areas of the salon. Whether to allow employees to smoke in the public areas is a decision you'll have to make. Generally, they should not smoke while working on a client. Again, let the image you're projecting for your salon be your guide.

CUSTOMER SATISFACTION

Remember, the primary aim of marketing is to satisfy the customer. Conduct your salon affairs with that uppermost in mind. One important aspect of customer satisfaction is reliability. That includes being available when you're supposed to be and honoring your commitments, including keeping appointment times.

Have a definite schedule for your salon. Establish your opening and closing hours and days of operation and post them in a conspicuous place in the salon. Set your hours of operation to meet the needs of your market. If your market segment demographics indicate that you need to open at five o'clock in the morning, or that you need to be open late in the evening to satisfy working customers, then set those hours. Open for your customers' convenience, not your own.

Be consistent. Be open and ready for business when you're supposed to be. Your customers should be able to rely on those hours. If you are going to close the salon for vacation, make sure your customers know the dates far in advance. This might sound like a simple policy, but it is one that is often ignored. It can be hard to fight the temptation to close the salon early on a day that business may be light. Don't do this. If you deviate from your set and posted hours, you will develop a reputation for unreliability.

If you must close the salon for a short period of time because of some emergency, call all of your clients who have appointments and reschedule. Emergencies do happen, and you have to be flexible enough to handle them. But make sure you only close in a real emergency when there is no other alternative.

By the same token, entrust at least one employee with a key to the salon so the business can be opened when you might be unavoidably delayed. This is important. You can't let your patrons stand around outside because you overslept one morning.

Make appointments carefully, and then keep them scrupulously. Don't make clients wait to receive the services. Nothing will turn off your clients like waiting an unreasonable time for the service to begin. When a client makes an appointment for a certain time, he or she has the right to expect to be accommodated at that time. To do otherwise is simply bad business and bad marketing.

SERVICES

The type of salon you operate will depend on the services you want to offer, the clientele you want to serve, and the image you want to project. The services can be as varied or as specific as you desire and, to a large extent, will reflect your ability and your interests. So, for example, you may decide you want to offer a full range of hair, skin, and nail services. Or you may decide you want to offer only hair services, or skin and body care services only, or nail services only. You may wish to specialize even more narrowly and offer only hair coloring services, for example.

Full-service salons generally offer a complete range of basic hair, nail, and skin care services, although they may not offer more specialized services, such as electrolysis or full-body care. These salons are usually larger, require more equipment, and have larger staffs than salons that limit their services to one or more specialties. Regardless which combinations of services you choose to offer, any service you give in your salon should either make a profit or lead to sales of other, more profitable services.

The image you've established will also help determine what services you will offer. A high-tech salon, for example, will offer a wider, more varied range of services than a high-volume, low-price shop.

The services you offer will be built around your core specialties, which will set the tone for your salon. These are the services that best reflect your own interests and abilities and your view of what you want your salon to be. Build your services around what you do best. By all means, look for new services and add them as you expand and grow. But always be driven by what the customer needs and wants and not by technology. It is very easy to become enamored with new technology in the field. New products and uses are introduced constantly. Don't begin a service just because it's based on new technology.

Conversely, don't begin a new service just because your customers want it. That doesn't mean you should be the one to provide it. Whenever you start a new service, it should be because:

1. there is a customer demand for it
2. you can offer it profitably
3. it is a service that fits your interests and abilities
4. it is appropriate for the image of your salon

Similarly, you can define the clientele you want to service as widely or narrowly as you wish. Establish a profile of your primary intended clients. Do you wish to perform your services on women only? On men only? On children? Or do you expect to service any combination of these? What age range do you wish to service? The services you offer and the clientele you offer them to are interrelated, so you must consider both when you make your decisions. For example, you would probably not offer full-body waxing services if your intended customers were primarily men.

Your decision will also be determined, in part, by the demographics and needs of the area in which you locate. Your preliminary examinations of your intended area of operation should have revealed how many and what type of people who will make up your customer base live and work there. Your surveys of other salons in the area, along with talking to as many people as you could, should have given you a good idea of what services those people want and which services you can profitably offer. Remember, your object is to make a profit. It makes no sense to spend the money for equipment, facilities, and training to offer a service you can't sell. You are better served by using that money, time, and energy to establish popular services that will be profitable.

Each type of salon has its own set of needs with respect to facilities and equipment. And each type has its own requirements for talent, training, and cost to establish and operate. So base your decision on your personality, interests, ability, and pocketbook. Whichever type of salon you choose to operate, however, will have to generate a rate of return to fit the lifestyle you want. This means that you may have to offer some services that don't particularly interest you to generate sales of the services that do. So choose wisely and judiciously. Offer as many different services as you are comfortable with. Keep in mind that it is not necessary to offer every service that interests you at the beginning. You can add more services as your business grows. Concentrate on your basic, income-producing services first.

You can shape your salon as your abilities, interests, and pocketbook allow. But you have to consider your choices carefully, always keeping an eye to their profitability with your clientele in your area of operation.

SALON SERVICES

Today's salons offer an amazing variety of services, from the simple and traditional, such as haircutting, to the esoteric, such as body wraps and spa treatments. All of these services are designed to enhance the client's appearance and, in some cases, help him or her to achieve a healthier lifestyle.

All services, however, must be limited to application on the exterior of the head, hands, feet, or body. No service given may involve the internal application of any implement or substance. No service may be sold for anything more than improvement of appearance, even though there may be some health-giving aspect to the service. Remember, a salon is not a medical facility and may undertake no operation that impinges on medical services.

Cosmetology is a highly regulated profession. Most of the services offered may be given only by a properly licensed practitioner in a duly licensed salon. In virtually all states, all staff members must possess a valid license. Just about the only employees exempt from this stricture are shampoo people and receptionists. License requirements vary somewhat from state to state, so it is necessary to check with your state licensing board for the latest regulations.

There are five general categories of salon services:

1. the hair
2. the nails
3. the skin and body
4. makeup application and cosmetics
5. retail sales.

Each service in each category has its own special requirements with respect to training, licensing, and equipment and supplies needed. Keep in mind, however, that some equipment may be used for more than one type of service.

HAIR SERVICES

Services for hair care are the most commonly offered salon services and are representative of the basic services offered by the cosmetology industry. A salon may offer as many or as few of these services as the owner desires, although some of these services complement each other. The various services require specific training and equipment. In many cases, however, the same capital equipment is used for more than one type of service. Almost all services must be performed by a licensed operator, working in a licensed salon. Check with your state Board of Cosmetology for complete and current requirements in your state.

SHAMPOOING

Although discussed here as a separate service, shampooing is a prerequisite to performing all other hair services. No matter what type of hair service salon you operate, you will have to shampoo the client's hair first. Most state laws require that the client's hair be thoroughly washed before performing any other hair service. It is, however, one of the few services that may be performed by an unlicensed individual. Few states require that the shampoo person be a licensed beautician. It does require some on-the-job training to make sure the shampooist knows how to drape clients, wash their hair correctly, and keep them comfortable. He or she must also know how to choose the correct shampoo for the client's type of hair. Outside of this, the shampooist is a relatively unskilled position.

HAIRCUTTING

Haircutting is the most popular and arguably, most important, of all the hair services. It is a service used by men, women, and children alike, and it may be the most recession proof of all the services. People still need their hair cut and trimmed, no matter what the economic conditions are. Operators must be licensed beauticians or barbers. Training in haircutting is an integral part of the beauty or barber school curriculum, and basic skills must be demonstrated during the licensing examination. Operators should also undergo continuing training in current hair styling and cutting techniques (see Figure 5-1).

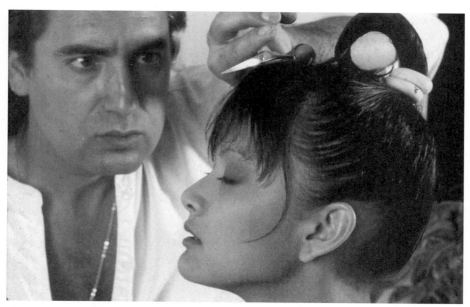

Figure 5-1.   Haircutting. (Photography by Steven Landis, with direction from Vincent and Alfred Nardi at Nardi Salon, New York City, New York.)

Figure 5-2. Hair styling.
(Photography by Steven
Landis, with direction
from Vincent and Alfred
Nardi at Nardi Salon,
New York City, New
York.)

HAIR STYLING

Most hair salons offer a range of wet and thermal styling services
along with cutting. Wet styling services involve the use of curlers
and a hot-air hair dryer. Thermal styling services include blow drying and the use of a curling iron. Styling services are most often
provided to women, although men's hair is sometimes blow dried
and styled after a haircut. Although hair can be styled without first
cutting it, styling, especially by thermal methods, is most often performed as an adjunct to the cut. Some salons cater to clients who
have their hair wet styled on a weekly basis (see Figure 5-2).

All states require stylists to be licensed beauticians. As with
cutting, styling by both wet and thermal methods is part of the
beauty school curriculum. Additional training is available through
supplier seminars and trade association meetings.

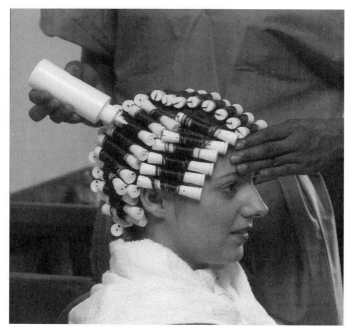

Figure 5-3. Performing a permanent wave. (Photography by Michael Gallitelli on location at Rielms Hair Salon. Latham, New York.)

PERMANENT WAVING

Permanent waving is a very popular and profitable chemical treatment that puts curls or body into hair. Although it is most often offered as a women's service, there are many men who get salon permanents. As with most other hair services, permanent waves may be given only by a licensed beautician. Training in permanent waving is part of the established curriculum in beauty schools and, like other services, proficiency must be demonstrated during the licensing examination. Additional training is available from supplier seminars and trade association meetings (see Figure 5-3).

SCALP TREATMENTS

Scalp treatments are designed to help alleviate various conditions of the hair and scalp and can be a profitable service. They are useful for both male and female customers and are not offered at all hair salons. Keep in mind, however, that all treatments are topical and are nonmedical. They cleanse and condition the hair and scalp and stimulate them to function more efficiently. You are not offering a cure for any specific condition. Scalp treatments must be given only by a licensed beautician. Some training in giving scalp treatments is given in beauty schools, but the operator should have additional training in trichology, which is the study of hair structure and function, including recognition of hair and scalp conditions.

HAIR STRAIGHTENING

Hair straightening services include chemical relaxing and pressing. These are very popular services, primarily among African American men and women. As usual, these services must be performed by a licensed beautician. Some training in these procedures is offered in beauty school, but additional on-the-job training or attendance at seminars may be advisable.

HAIR COLORING

Hair coloring can be a very profitable and popular service in the hair salon. These services range from single- and double-process coloring to highlighting and frosting. Like the other services, coloring may be done only by a licensed beautician. In many salons, hair coloring is a specialty and is performed by a highly trained and proficient colorist, who does nothing else. The colorist holds one of the most highly skilled positions in the hair salon. Although basic hair coloring is covered in the standard beauty school curriculum, true proficiency requires additional training and practice. Most manufacturers of colorants offer classroom study for aspiring colorists (see Figure 5-4).

WIG SALES AND MAINTENANCE

The popularity of wigs and hairpieces varies as fashions change. However, the sale and maintenance of these items can be a profitable adjunct to other services you might offer. The ephemeral popularity of wigs makes it somewhat risky to offer these services exclusively, but some people have operated successful wig salons. Wigs and hairpieces can be made of human hair or synthetic materials. They are available in a variety of hair colors, lengths, and basic styles.

Figure 5-4.   Colors are profitable services. (Photography by Michael Gallitelli on location at Rielms Hair Salon, Latham, New York.)

Not all states require that wigs and hairpieces be sold or maintained by a licensed beautician. The practitioner should be trained in fitting and adjusting them and should be able to wash, condition, and style them. Most beauty schools offer some training in the care of wigs.

NAIL SERVICES

Nail services are very popular and profitable and are most often offered in conjunction with hair services. They don't require as much space as hair services and are often sold as an additional service while the client's hair is being done. Although more popular among women, many men get basic manicures. Advanced nail techniques are usually offered to women only (see Figure 5-5).

It is also possible to offer only nail services. There are many successful salons of this type in operation. These services include manicures and pedicures. In addition to basic manicure services, you might also offer advanced services such as nail wrapping,

Figure 5-5. Nail services. (Photography by
Michael Gallitelli on location at
Rielms Hair Salon, Latham, New
York.)

sculptured nails, artificial nail application, nail painting, and nail
tipping.

Most states require that the practitioner hold either a mani-
curist license or a beautician license. Manicuring is covered as part
of the standard cosmetology curriculum or is offered as a separate
course in most beauty schools. Additional training in nail structure
and the recognition of nail disorders is advisable. Specialized
training in advanced manicuring techniques is available through
special classes offered by many suppliers.

HAIR REMOVAL SERVICES

The removal of excess or unwanted body and facial hair is a growing area for the modern salon. Offered as an adjunct to other hair
services, or offered as a specialty, these services can be profitable
and can bring considerable new and repeat business to your operation. There are four basic hair removal methods: shaving, chemical depilation, waxing, and electrolysis. Generally, only waxing
and electrolysis are offered as salon services.

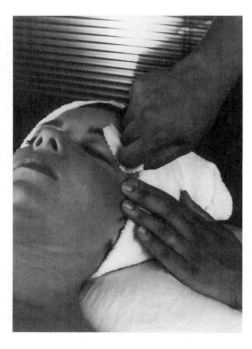

Figure 5-6. Waxing.

WAXING

Waxing is a relatively simple and efficient method for temporarily removing hair from the face and body. It requires a minimum of equipment and is relatively inexpensive for the client, yet it provides a good source of revenue. It can be offered to both men and women, although women require the service more often than men. The service may be performed by a licensed beautician or esthetician. Basic training in waxing techniques is covered in many beauty school curriculums. Additional on-the-job training may be advisable to build proficiency (see Figure 5-6).

ELECTROLYSIS

Electrolysis is the only method of removing hair permanently. It is fairly expensive to establish but is highly profitable. Most salons that offer electrolysis specialize in the service, but it can be offered with other services. It is a specially good fit with other skin care services and is popular among both men and women. Electrolysis is a highly skilled specialty and, in most states, requires a separate electrologist license. A number of schools offer electrology curriculums leading to the license. Practice is also required to gain proficiency.

SKIN AND BODY CARE SERVICES

Over the past few years, skin and body care services have under-gone tremendous growth. Unlike hair and nail services, relatively few salons offer these services, and competition is not nearly so fierce. They are popular among both men and women and are a profitable source of revenue, although they require considerable capital equipment and supplies as well as special training. As with hair services, many of these services complement each other and may be offered in various combinations. And, like those services, these must also be performed by properly licensed operators.

FACIALS

The facial is the cornerstone of skin care in the salon. It is the most widely offered of the skin care services and has significant profit potential. Facials may be offered to men as well as women. Although women receive most of the facial services, men represent a largely untapped potential customer base (see Figure 5-7).

Facials require a considerable amount of equipment to per-form properly. They may be given by a licensed cosmetologist or esthetician. Most beauty schools cover facials in at least a rudimen-tary fashion in the normal hairdressing curriculum. Many schools also offer specific training in esthetics. In addition, advanced train-

Figure 5-7. Facial services.

ing is available through courses offered by the manufacturers of equipment and supplies.

BODY MASSAGE

Various forms of therapeutic massage are becoming increasingly popular and can be profitable services to offer, either in specialized massage salons or in other types of salons as adjuncts to facials and other skin care services. The services are applicable to both men and women (see Figure 5-8).

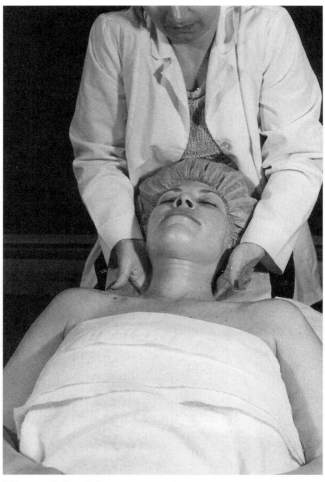

Figure 5-8.   Massage services.

Training and licensing requirements vary from state to state. In most states, licensed estheticians and cosmetologists may give basic facial massages and massages to the hands and feet. Full-body massage, however, often requires a special license as a massage therapist. Check your state laws before offering massage services. The procedures do require considerable training and practice. Basic training in massage of the face, hands, and feet is normally given as part of the curriculum for estheticians and cosmetologists. Training in the various full-body massage techniques is available from special schools.

WRAPS AND PACKS

Body wraps and various packs are used for a variety of cellulite, cleansing, and water retention treatments in spas and salons. These are also gaining in popularity and can be profitable adjuncts to a salon that specializes in skin and body care. These treatments are of interest primarily to women. In essence, these services eliminate or redistribute retained body water or fat cells to achieve a temporary slimming and tightening effect. Some of the services also stimulate and balance certain body systems, such as the lymphatic and circulatory systems, and help cleanse impurities from the body (see Figure 5-9).

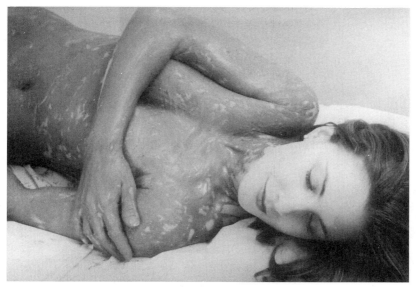

Figure 5-9. Body wraps. (Courtesy of Steve Victor, M.D.)

The services may be given by licensed estheticians and cosmetologists. Training in the application and use of body wraps and packs is included in most curriculums for estheticians. Additional training is offered by manufacturers of equipment and products.

HYDROTHERAPY TREATMENTS

Like wraps and packs, hydrotherapy treatments are highly specialized services for cleansing and balancing internal body systems. Thallassotherapy treatments utilize sea water. Balneotherapy treatments utilize fresh water. They include hydrotherapy tubs, whirlpool baths, hot tubs, and Scotch hose treatment. Scotch hose treatments use high pressure hoses from which jets of sea water at body temperature are played along the main lymphatic channels. These services are profitable for spas and skin care salons, but they require very expensive capital equipment and facilities. These services are of interest mostly to women. State licensing requirements vary, but these treatments may usually be given by licensed estheticians, physical therapists, and massage therapists, although more specialized training in the proper use of these devices is required (see Figure 5-10).

Figure 5-10. Hydrotherapy treatment.

MAKEUP AND COSMETIC APPLICATION SERVICES

Makeup and cosmetic application and consultation services are widely popular. Offered as an adjunct to skin care and hair services, or alone as a specialty, they can be very profitable among women clients. Compared with some other salon services, they are relatively inexpensive to offer and require minimal capital equipment, although supply outlays may be large. The services, which may range from offering advice to women on what makeup to use and how to apply it, to the application of corrective makeup to cover blemishes, to ear piercing services, can be given by a licensed cosmetologist or esthetician. Basic training in makeup use and application techniques is part of many beauty school curriculums. Additional training is available through cosmetics manufacturers and wholesalers (see Figure 5-11).

Figure 5-11. Makeup application. (Photography by Preston Phillips, makeup by James "Romell" Duresseau. Ariah Perez, model.)

RETAIL SERVICES

Retail services involve the sale of products, such as shampoos, skin cleansers, and makeup and beauty care items, to clients for their use at home. Sales of these items can add significantly to your profitability. In addition, they can help reinforce the perception of quality of the other services you offer. They are the finishing touch, so to speak. Sales are made to both men and women (see Figure 5-12).

Retail sales require little capital equipment but require that you stock sufficient inventory to meet your customers' needs. The items can be sold by an unlicensed individual and may offer a way to keep your receptionist or shampoo person busy. Little formal training is required, but the salesperson should be able to discuss the characteristics and use of the products. Training or experience in retail selling is helpful.

Figure 5-12.   Retail services. (Photography by Michael Gallitelli on location at Rielms Hair Salon, Latham, New York.)

SALON RETAIL OPERATIONS

Retailing—that is, selling products and accessories related to your salon services—can add good profit dollars to your bottom line. You must recognize, however, that although there are many similarities in selling services and selling products, there are also differences that you must consider. These include the different products and accessories you stock and sell, the way you display the goods, the competition you face, and a little different thinking in your approach to the business.

To be successful, your retail operation has to be more than just an afterthought. You have to manage that part of the operation with the same zeal and care that you use to manage the salon part. Make the retail operation a profit center for the salon business. Keep the two operations separate. Retail sales represent one mode of business; the services represent another. Don't blur the distinctions between the two.

Keep separate records and inventories for the two sides. As a profit center, the retail operation should earn revenues. Granted, this side of your business is to provide an additional service to the customers. But that's no reason it should lose money. By keeping the sides separate, you can monitor the profitability of both operations. Otherwise, it is very easy to overlook losses from the retail end because of the inability to isolate those dollars from profits in the service end.

Above all, don't lose sight of your primary business—selling services. That is where the majority of your income comes from, not from retail sales. If the opposite is true, you're probably in the wrong business. Don't spend so much time and effort selling products that you shortchange the service part of the business. Give retailing the attention it deserves in your overall operation, but no more than it deserves.

THE MARKET FOR RETAIL SALES

The potential market for retail sales of cosmetics and hair, nail, and skin products by salons is enormous. Industry studies estimate that salon sales of such products are better than $1 billion each year, with tremendous opportunity for further growth. So the opportunities are there. It's up to you to capitalize on them.

You have a captive market for the products you sell. Your retail customers will come from the ranks of your client base. You take care of their beauty needs. You have developed a good relationship with them. They trust your experience and professional expertise. So they are predisposed to buy their retail products from you—as long as you can add value to the product. You have to give the clients a reason to buy products from you rather than from another retail outlet. There's no reason why your client should buy a bottle of shampoo from you for $10.00 when she can buy a bottle of shampoo for $3.00 from the local supermarket, unless you give her more value for her money—that is, better product, better service, and more confidence.

Although your market is captive, it is also limited. Don't expect to get significant walk-in business for retail items in your salon. It won't happen because you haven't built up a relationship with those people, and they have no reason to trust your expertise. To build business for your retail operation, you first have to increase your customer base for the service operation. That should be your priority anyway.

PRODUCTS FOR RETAIL SALES

Your choice of products to sell at retail is important to the success of this end of your business. You want to stock products that will move, not sit on a shelf and get dusty. That means you have to tailor your product mix to the needs and tastes of your clientele. You have to be aware of trends in fashion and in the beauty industry and, in fact, in society as a whole. And you have to be ready to change your product mix as these trends and fashions change.

For example, there is a growing concern with the purchase and use of environmentally sound products. The "green marketing" revolution has concerned consumers looking for products that don't harm the environment. In the salon industry, this includes items such as the newer, lower in volatile organic compound (VOC) hair sprays, which reduce the amount of volatile organic compounds they release into the atmosphere. It also includes an emphasis on using recyclable or biodegradable materials for packaging, and reducing the amount of packaging used for products. And it includes the manufacture, sale, and use of products that do not rely on animal testing. There is also more emphasis on the use of natural materials in products, as opposed to synthetic ingredients.

Choose products that mirror these trends. Your customers will be looking for them.

PRODUCT CHOICES

For the most part, sell the same products you use in your services. These are the products you know and can recommend. They are the products that will complement your services. The fact that you use them in your operations adds credibility to their appearance on your retail shelf. If you don't use the product, you'll be hard put to convince your client that he or she should buy it.

In general, the same strictures apply to your retail products as to your operational products. Limit the number of brands you carry. Stock and sell only quality products. Try to pick products from manufacturers who support the salon business and don't sell their products over the counter to the general public in competition with salons. This can make your choice very difficult, since many manufacturers sell to both sides. A few do not, however.

Sell products that are relevant to your salon business and match the services you offer. For example, you might sell hair care products, nail polishes, makeup, skin and body care products, as well as accessories that enhance these products, such as applicators, brushes, and combs. These all relate to what you do. But you should not sell handbags, ladies' dresses, men's ties, and the like unless you intend to run a general store instead of a beauty salon. Remember your primary business. Don't carry anything in the retail operation that detracts from that business, either by diluting your efforts or by diminishing your professional image.

Know your products well. Know their ingredients and what they do. Be aware of the environmental aspects of their manufacture. Be able to answer your customers' questions. Be able to explain to the customer why that product is best for him or her.

Check with the product manufacturers to see if they offer brochures that you can hand out to your customers. Many manufacturers make promotional materials available, either for free or for a small charge. Take advantage of these when you can get them.

PRIVATE LABELING

You can sell brand name items, or you can sell private label products. Private label products are items you purchase unlabeled from a manufacturer and put your own name on. Unless you have a large operation with an industry-wide reputation, private labeling will probably not work for you. There are a lot of disadvantages to private labeling. You lose the advantages of brand recognition. You can't take advantage of the money and efforts the manufacturer of the brand name products has spent to advertise and promote the products to the general public.

Remember the importance of image. You'll have to spend a considerable amount of money to have a competent graphics artist design a label for you, and then spend more money to have those labels printed or have them silk-screened onto the bottle. In addition, you'll have to buy the labels in a fairly large quantity, which means you'll have to store them so they won't get dirty or damaged until you can use them. Then you have to apply the labels to the bottles or jars. You'll also have to purchase the unlabeled products in larger quantities than you would have to purchase brand name products, increasing the possibility of spoilage or passing an expiration date. And when all is said and done and you've spent the money and done what promotion you could, you still don't have a unique product. You wind up with virtually the same products carried by all the other salons who are private labeling. The only thing different is your label. The ego trip of having your own name brand isn't worth the money or the effort it takes.

Stick with brand name products for your retail sales. Take advantage of the manufacturer's reputation and marketing and promotion efforts. Work with the products best known by your customers and staff.

RETAIL SELLING

You have to market and promote the retail sales aspect of your business, just as you do the services side. Pay as much attention to the details here as you do otherwise.

Decide who in your salon will handle retail sales. You have a number of choices. It might be your receptionist. It could be your shampoo person. You might leave the task up to each operator. Or you might handle the job yourself. Unless retail sales make up a major part of your business, you probably won't need or be able to afford a full-time retail sales clerk.

Whoever you choose to handle sales, however, make sure he or she is fully trained in the products and can answer any questions that arise. Include the duties in the job description for the position so there won't be any disagreements over the responsibilities. Decide on the form of compensation you will give for the job. Will it come in the form of extra pay? Or will you pay a commission on each sale? If you have only one or two people making sales, extra pay might be suitable. However, if you leave the task to each operator, it might be better to offer a commission.

Success in retail sales takes some degree of sales ability. You have to know what motivates people to buy. You have to understand their needs. And you have to be able to show them how the product meets those needs. Know the difference between the features of the products and their benefits. The features are the attributes of the product; the benefits are what it accomplishes for the client. Whether they realize it or not, the clients buy the benefits, not the features. They want to look and feel good. Their concern is whether the product will accomplish that. Your concern is to convince them that it will.

Know both your clients and your product. You've worked on your clients' hair, skin, and nails and should know the condition they're in. You should also know how the products you sell work, especially if you're also using them in the services you sell. Be able to match the correct product with the customer. After all, your marketing edge in the retail end of the business is your professional expertise. You should know what will suit the clients best. They will normally accept your judgment and rely on it.

You might hold an occasional sale, in which you offer selected products at a reduced price, even a price at or below your actual cost. This is especially helpful when you are introducing a new product and want people to try it. Try to avoid loss leaders, however. A loss leader is a product sold at an artificially low price as an inducement to get people to come into the store. It is offered with the idea that, once inside the store, the customers will purchase other items at their normal prices as well. This kind of sales strategy will not usually work with a salon, because you're not drawing customers from outside your client base.

Many of the sales you make will be on impulse as opposed to planned. That is, the customers have not come into the salon with the intention of buying a product. They're there for the service. Rather, they have accepted your recommendation and have understood how the product will benefit them. And they've made the purchasing decision. You have sold them.

You have to sell the products. They won't sell themselves. Customers usually will not buy a product from you unless you have suggested it to them and convinced them that it is right for them. But you won't make the sale unless you ask for the order. Don't be afraid to try to sell a product to a client. But don't overdo it. Hard sells don't work. All you'll do is alienate the customers.

There's an important point about selling: Once you've made the sale, stop selling. The customer has made the decision to buy. He or she doesn't need any more convincing or reinforcement. Many sales are lost because the salesperson kept talking about the product after the customer made the decision to buy it.

Above all, be ethical in your retail sales efforts. This is just as important here as in the other operations of your salon. Don't sell a product just to make the sale. Make sure the product is right for the client. If you truly believe it is, don't be afraid to suggest it. Stand behind the products you sell. Offer a money-back guarantee, whether or not you can return the product to your supplier. Your own personal guarantee is necessary to reinforce the customer's confidence.

SUMMARY

- Product, the first of the classic four P's of marketing, covers more than just physical items sold. It includes the sum total of all of your services as well as the items you sell at retail. In fact, it includes your entire business.
- A product has generic, or tangible, attributes, which represent the core idea of what the product is. It also has intangible attributes, which include what the customer expects to get and what you do to augment the product, or make it even more than the customer expects.
- In a service business such as a salon, image is everything. It's your ultimate product. You must establish the image you want, and then live up to that image. The image you select depends on a number of factors, including your clientele, your decor and salon ambiance, and even the name you choose for the salon. Your image will be a constant from the day you open until the day you close.
- Make the name of your salon appropriate to the image. Once you've chosen the name, protect it by registering it.
- Image includes reliability, so make sure your customers can rely on you.

- Make sure the services you offer are profitable. Your service mix will be built around your core specialties—that is, the services that best reflect your own interests and abilities.
- There are a tremendous number of salon services you can offer, from the simple and basic to the esoteric. These include cutting, styling, permanent waving, scalp treatments, hair straightening, and hair coloring. Nail services, such as manicures and pedicures, are also popular.
- Hair removal services—waxing and electrolysis—are profitable services, as are skin care services, such as facials, body massage, wraps and packs, and hydrotherapy treatments. Makeup and cosmetic services are also important.
- Retail services are good profit centers to supplement and support the sales of your other services. Keep the retail and the service ends of your business separate, and operate each as a profit center.
- The products you can sell are many and varied. But they should be related to the salon business. Tailor the product mix to the needs and tastes of your clientele. Be aware of trends in fashion and in the beauty industry. Sell the same products you use in the salon. You have to market and promote the retail end of the business just as you have to do so with the services. Stand behind the products you sell.

CHAPTER 6

Pricing

Price is the second of the classic four P's of marketing. For a retail or service business, price is of paramount importance. Price directly affects your profits. And profit is the key to your success in business. Profit is not a dirty word. It is, or it should be, the reason you're in business to begin with. You have to sell your services at a high enough margin (that is, cash beyond your costs) to assure that there is enough cash flow to sustain the business and to give you the funds to support your chosen lifestyle. How you price your services will determine how profitable you are and, ultimately, how successful your business is. It is not easy to set prices accurately, and it takes a lot of sound judgment and some courage to do it properly, but the rewards are well worth the effort.

FACTORS IN PRICING DECISIONS

The revenues that come into your salon are a function of the number of customers you service and how much you charge them for the services they receive. The prices you establish go a long way toward determining your success. If they're too low, you will lose money. If they're too high, you will lose customers. Setting prices is more an art than a science. There are a lot of factors involved, not all of them are financial. Figure 6-1 summarizes these factors.

Your costs are, of course, a major factor in your pricing decisions. You have to charge more for the services than it costs you to provide them. In an ideal business world, pricing would be easy. You would figure out your costs, add a suitable amount for your profit, and that would be the price. Unfortunately, it is not that simple. You also have to consider the demand for the services and the competitive situation. How many customers want the service enough to pay the price you want? And how much does the competition charge for the same service?

Then there is the image you've established. That will also affect your pricing structure. Any prices you establish must be con-

- **COST:**   What does each service cost to perform?
                       Direct costs
                           Materials
                           Time
                           Labor
                       Indirect costs
                           Rent
                           Utilities
                           Taxes
                           Expenses

- **DEMAND:**   Who and how many people want your services?
                           Target audience demographics
                           Economic conditions
                           Consumer behavior
                           Promotion

- **COMPETITION:**   How many other salons are offering similar
                       services?
                           Quality
                           Competence
                           Differentiation

- **IMAGE:**   What is the image you project for your salon?
                           Position
                           Consistency

- **GOALS:**   What goals have you set for your salon?
                           Short term
                           Long term
                           Profit Objectives
                           Return on investment
                           Growth

Figure 6-1. Pricing decision factors.

sistent with the image of your salon. Finally, you have to consider the goals you've set for your business. The prices you set have to lead toward accomplishing those goals.

Setting prices properly (and profitably) is a complex juggling act that requires knowledge of your market and the ability to make good, sound business judgments.

THE ESSENCE OF A SALES TRANSACTION

First, you must understand exactly what the sales process entails. Any sale involves an exchange between the buyer and the seller. You give the buyer something, either a service or a product. In return, the buyer gives you something, usually money. When the customer believes that the value of the product or service equals or exceeds the amount of money, the sale will take place. If he or she perceives that the value is less than the amount of money, it won't.

This fact alone determines how much you can reasonably charge for the product or service. It doesn't matter how good the product or service is. It doesn't matter how much it costs you to provide it. Unless it gives a perceived value higher than the amount of money involved, the customer won't buy it. And in all cases, it is the customer who perceives the value, not you.

The problem is in the nature of the difference between the two sides of the equation. Price is "hard." It is finite and quantifiable. Value is "soft." It is ephemeral and changeable, subject to the vagaries of consumer behavior. Your major task in setting prices is to find the balance point where price equals value, as illustrated in Figure 6-2.

Once you understand that perceived value determines price, you can consider the other factors of cost, demand, competition, image, and goals. Even though these factors are discussed separately here, they are all interrelated and all are important. You can't ignore any of them in working out your pricing strategies.

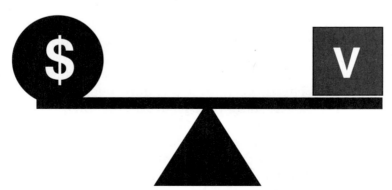

Figure 6-2.   Essence of a sale: an exchange between a buyer and a seller. When value (V) equals or exceeds the amount of money ($) charged, the sale takes place.

COST

Profitability demands that revenues exceed outlays. This means simply that you must get more for your products and services than it costs you to provide them. If this is not the case, you won't last long in business. Therefore, your costs are the first factor in setting your prices.

Determine what each service costs. Calculate both the direct costs and the indirect costs. First, list all of the services you offer. Determine the cost of supplies used to perform each service and the amount of time each takes. The cost of supplies is the direct cost of the service. The amount of time is the limiting factor in how many of the services you can offer. Take for example, a haircut, which includes a shampoo and blow dry. Assume it takes 30 minutes. The only supplies used are shampoo and hair spray, which cost 15 cents. It may seem like nit-picking to consider amounts this small, but they all add up. Even minor expenses are important. In this case, your direct costs are 15 cents. In a service business such as a beauty salon, direct costs are generally low, since they cover only the consumable materials you use.

If the haircut in this case takes 30 minutes to perform, divide that time into the hours of operation, allowing time between clients to clean the station and prepare for the next client. For example, suppose you open the salon at 8:30 A.M. and close at 6:00 P.M. and take half an hour for lunch. That means your actual working time is nine hours. Allowing five minutes between haircuts for preparation, the maximum number of haircuts you could give in that time is 17—that is, if you did nothing else and took no other breaks. More realistically, you probably shouldn't figure on being able to do more than 12 haircuts in that time span. At any rate, you have to consider the number of services you can perform when you set prices.

Your indirect costs are much higher than your direct costs but are no less real. These are harder to figure because you have to consider averages. The indirect costs are a function of your operating and administrative expenses, divided by the number of customers you expect to service in a given time period. This gives you an average cost to service one customer, which you add to the direct cost of the particular service.

For example, suppose you have 400 customers a month. Add up your expenses for the month, including rent, insurance, utilities, telephone, advertising, taxes, debt service, accounting and legal services, etc. Don't add the cost of materials. You've already considered that in the direct cost. Let's say your fixed expenses for the month are $2,500. Now add in the cost of your employees. This includes salaries, your share of social security taxes withheld, and benefits. Don't forget to include your draw if you are taking any money from the salon. Assume your labor costs for the month are $2,500. Your total indirect labor and overhead costs then are $5,000. Divide that by 400 customers. Your total indirect cost per customer is $12.50. Add that to the direct cost to get your total cost of the service. In the case of the haircut, it is $0.15 plus $12.50 for a total of $12.65. So it costs you $12.65 to sell one haircut. Other services will be more or less, depending on the cost of materials used.

This is your break-even price for that service. If you set your price lower, you will lose money. If you set it higher, you will make money. How much higher you will set the price depends on the other pricing factors.

Operate each service you offer as a profit center. That is, make sure all services turn a reasonable profit. Each one should stand on its own and contribute to your overall profit picture. That includes your retail operations every bit as much as your service operations. Don't operate any aspect of your salon at a loss. It's not good marketing. Nor is it good business.

DEMAND

The demand factor considers how much the clientele you've targeted are willing and able to pay. In short, how many potential customers want or need the services you offer? This can be more difficult to determine than cost. Costs are relatively easy to quantify. Through good recordkeeping and proper accounting practices, you can usually know just what everything costs you and how much income you need to operate your business and support your family. But determining the demand for those services is far more complex and depends on the demographics of the area in which you operate, the audience you've targeted as your potential customers, the economic conditions under which you work, your understanding of consumer behavior, and your marketing and promotion efforts.

DEMOGRAPHICS

This is where your knowledge of the demographics of your area really comes into play. Remember the importance of characterizing your audience. It is impossible to overstate the importance of demographics.

ECONOMIC CONDITIONS

The economic conditions prevailing are also important. These go a long way toward determining the willingness of your audience to pay the prices you set. In more prosperous times, price is less of a factor than it is in lean times. When people are uncertain of the economy, they tend to be more price conscious. You may have to charge somewhat less when times are bad than you can in good times. But be careful not to cut prices too low or your customers may perceive a decrease in the value they receive. Value is still an important consideration.

CONSUMER BEHAVIOR

The psychology of the consumer is always an important factor. You have to understand what makes people act the way they do. You have to know the stimuli that make them reach a favorable decision. What are their "hot buttons?"

Consider consumer reaction to prices, for example. If you ask, most consumers will tell you that price is their most important consideration in making a purchase decision. They might even believe that themselves. And, all things being equal, that probably is more or less true. But if you look closely at their actions, you'll find that other factors are just as important.

In many cases, consumers equate price with quality. This is especially true with service businesses like beauty salons, where the product (that is, the service rendered) offers intangible benefits as well as tangible results. Consider a facial, for example. The tangible results include cleaner skin that functions properly. The intangible benefits include a relaxed feeling for the customer. She feels better and looks better. And she believes that she has been pampered and well looked after. In many ways, these intangible benefits will convince her to pay more for the service than just the consideration of the tangible results would allow. They increase the customer's perception of value and make the service worth more.

Identify all the benefits the customer gets from your services and then set your prices accordingly. Use the price as a tool to build confidence in the quality of your services and to support the image of your salon. If you price your products and services too low for your image, you may actually reduce your sales because you will have reduced the perception of quality. You might be able to sell a bottle of skin lotion for 49 cents and still make a profit. It might be the best skin lotion on the market, but customers will wonder what's wrong with it if it's so cheap. But price that same bottle at $5.95, and the customers will think they're getting a bargain.

PROMOTION

One of the functions of marketing is demand creation. To a large extent, you can influence the demand for your products and services through advertising and promotion. These are the tools with which you mold the perceptions of your clients and inform them of the value they will receive. This is how you convince them that your services are worth the money you charge for them and persuade them to reach a favorable buying decision.

COMPETITION

Competition is also a factor. It is somewhat less important than the other factors, but you can't afford to ignore it. You don't work in a vacuum, so what your competition does will affect your operations.

- Study competitors' operations as much as you can and see what they charge for services. Then compare the services they offer with yours.
- Compare the image competitors project to your image.
- Determine the audience competitors are trying to reach. Are they targeting the same clientele that you are?
- You can't let competition dictate your pricing. Don't assume that you will have to charge the same prices for your services that other salons in the area charge for theirs. You may be able to charge more if you are offering a quality of service and competence that competitors are incapable of. The key point is how well you can differentiate your services from theirs. How you justify your prices and how customers will accept those prices is a function of how well you differentiate yourself

from the competition. Customers will pay higher prices for your services than they will for your competition's services if, and only if, they perceive there is a greater value to yours. To compete successfully, you have to be able to demonstrate that greater value. If you can't, then competitive pricing becomes very important.

- Examine your services and compare them with those the competition offers. Learn in what ways yours are better, and then promote those differences.

GOALS

The goals you've set for your shop also affect pricing. When you made your business plan, you set goals for yourself, or you should have. Those goals tell you where you want to be in both the short term and the long term, and they include the profit objectives you have set for your business, the return you expect from your investment, and the growth you've decided you want. Keep your goals in mind, and then set your prices to help you reach them.

CASH AND EXPENSE MANAGEMENT

It is difficult to consider pricing without also considering how you manage cash and expenses. Making a profit is no simple matter. It involves more than setting a price higher than your costs and then counting the revenue that comes into the shop. You must also consider your expenses, your time, and your effort. It is possible to have high revenues but to also have such high overhead that you are actually losing money. That's a trap you can fall into easily.

You can avoid that trap by exercising sound financial management principles and by following proper accounting procedures. These will help you control your expenses, make sure you pay no more taxes than you are obligated to pay, and keep the services you offer profitable. But you must think like a businessperson, not like an operator. It takes time and effort to do the job properly. You have to examine all aspects of the business and keep a close watch over all operations. And you have to do it on a regular basis. Your accountant will help. He or she will set up a bookkeeping system for you, audit your books, calculate your taxes, and make out your returns. The bulk of the effort, though, will depend on you and on your vigilance. One of the major reasons businesses fail is inadequate financial management.

CASH FLOW MANAGEMENT

Cash flow is nothing more than the difference between income and outgo. And it is as much a matter of timing as of dollar amounts. Cash almost always goes out before new cash comes in. You have to spend money—that is, purchase supplies, etc.—often before you generate any revenues. You must have enough cash available to finance your operations and acquire the things you need to make money. There may be a considerable lag between the time you spend the cash and the time you get the payback. You need sufficient funds to overcome that time lag. To put it bluntly, if you run out of cash, you go out of business. This is a hard but incontrovertible fact of business life, especially for a small business with limited resources. It is necessary to balance inflow with outflow so you always have cash available when you need it.

Don't be misled by your profit statement. Profits do not necessarily translate into cash. Profits are a bookkeeping concept, based on total assets, including inventory and accounts receivable. Cash is money in the bank. Profit is theory; cash is reality. You have to pay your bills in cash. You can't pay them with inventory or with money people owe you. Nor can you consider as cash all of the revenue that comes in. A certain portion of that revenue carries obligations, such as income tax payments, wages, and sales tax remissions. This doesn't mean you shouldn't be concerned with profit. Of course you should. Both cash and profit are essential to your business: cash for survival, profit for good long-term business health.

Your cash flow situation is manageable if you plan for it. Proper and timely planning will let you anticipate cash crunches and give you time to raise the funds you need.

EXPENSE MANAGEMENT

The hypothetical cost analysis discussed earlier shows that your 400 customers must generate $5,000 plus the cost of your materials in sales, just so you'll break even for the month. There are only two ways you can change your indirect average cost per customer: Either you increase the number of customers, or you reduce your expenses. It is very important that you keep tight control on your expenses. They can easily get out of hand and wreck your profitability.

Expenses, like the need for cash, are a fact of business life. The efficient management of expenses, like the management of your cash flow, can make or break your operation. Some expenses you can control; others you can't. But you must be aware of all of the expenses you face and be prepared for them.

Your operating expenses are those items that are necessary for the direct conduct of your business. These include the supplies you use for the services you provide, the inventory of products you sell, and the services you purchase, such as towel and uniform rentals. These expenses will vary with your customer flow. The more customers you get, the higher these will go, but not necessarily proportionately. They are also expenses you can control to some extent. For example, you can lower your supply costs by shopping for the best deals and by keeping your inventory levels low.

Your labor costs are also operating expenses, but they depend on the number of employees you have and your compensation levels. Salaries are the major expense, but there are other expenses connected with employees. You also have to consider the costs of benefit packages, such as hospitalization, your share of social security taxes, and worker's compensation and unemployment insurance charges that may be levied by the state in which you do business. You might also factor in costs for sending key employees to training courses. These costs will vary with the number of employees you have.

You can control labor costs by keeping the number of employees low. Have only as many employees as you actually need to do the work. But have enough employees to do the work properly. You can cut your staff too thin. Use some part-time workers instead of all full-time employees. You might also have some employees perform more than one task. For example, your receptionist may double as your bookkeeper. Your shampoo person may handle your retail sales. Of course, you will have to pay them accordingly, although paying one person more usually will still be less than paying two people less.

Administrative, or overhead, expenses are necessary for the indirect conduct of your business. These include fixed expenses such as rent, utilities, telephone, insurance, license fees, trash removal, and water and sewer. These costs generally stay the same month to month and are not affected by the level of business you conduct. There are some variable administrative expenses, too. These include professional fees, advertising, printing, postage, interest payments on loans and notes, and payments on loan principals. And don't forget to pay yourself, too, when you calculate your expenses. Many small business owners fail to do this, but it is an expense item you have to consider.

You can control some of these costs. Advertising costs, for example, will vary with the level of advertising you conduct and with the media you utilize. Except for telephone directory advertising, which you purchase on a yearly basis, you can schedule advertising to fit monthly cash availability. (This may not be the most effective way to advertise, but if you need to reduce expenses, it is a way to do it.) The fees you pay your accountant and lawyer will vary with the amount of work they do in a given month. Interest payments diminish as the principal is reduced. It is also possible to lower monthly payments on interest and principal by renegotiating loan terms.

Then there are the unexpected expenses. Something breaks and needs to be repaired or replaced. Someone gets sick and you need to hire temporary help. One of your suppliers is offering a deal on equipment or supplies that it would be prudent to accept. You can't anticipate everything that will happen at any given moment in your business. But you can anticipate that something unexpected—and expensive—will happen. That something will be just as real an expense as any of the other expenses you face. Your only recourse is to have planned for contingencies and have funds set aside to meet them.

So manage your expenses wisely. And control them whenever you can. Expense management is every bit as important as cash flow management. Make decisions about your expenses as prudently as you make decisions about any other aspect of your business.

PRICING POLICIES

Setting your prices is only part of the job. You must also have firm policies for implementing and enforcing those prices. This is nothing more than formulating rules that govern prices in your salon and then sticking to those rules.

Your prices should be reasonable and fair for the image of your salon and the quality and range of services you offer. If this is so, don't be afraid to implement them. Post your prices clearly in a prominent place in the salon, so there is no question in the minds of your clients about how much any service will cost them.

Don't apologize for your prices. If you've set them correctly, there's no need for apologies. But be prepared to defend your prices by explaining to your customers what their basis is, if you're asked, and without giving more details about the process than necessary. You don't have to tell the customers what your costs or problems are.

Be consistent with your prices. Once you've established them, stick to them. Don't cut your prices to meet a customer's objection. It is better to lose a sale than to make an exception for a particular customer. If you do it for one, you'll have to do it for all of your customers. And don't think you can keep a "special price cut" for one individual a secret. Sooner or later, your other customers will find out about it, and you'll have even more trouble on your hands.

Can you have exceptions to your pricing policies? Yes, of course you can. No policies are ever engraved in stone. Just make sure there's a good reason for making an exception. You can, for example, have special sales, in which you lower the price of a particular service for a short period of time. (Sales will be discussed in depth in Chapter 8.) If you have a sale, make sure you have clear goals and objectives in mind.

It is also possible to charge different prices for different operators. Your more experienced operators command higher prices; your less experienced operators can charge less. This is an especially valid approach for breaking in new operators and building a following for them. Be careful with this approach, however. Don't have too large a disparity between the prices you charge for the various operators. And be very careful not to give lower quality service for the lower price. In theory, the reason for the lower price is that the operator has less experience, not less skill. When the operator gains the experience, however, don't be afraid to raise the price to the existing levels elsewhere in the salon.

RAISING PRICES

At some point, no matter how well you've set your prices, it will be necessary to raise them. Your costs will invariably go up—slower when inflation is low; faster when it is high—but they will go up. As your costs go up, your profits will go down if you keep your prices the same. Unless you're willing to lower your profit goals (and you shouldn't be willing to do this), you have only two ways to offset your rising costs. One is to reduce your costs in other ways. The other is to raise your prices.

Make no mistake, though. Raising prices can be as tricky a proposition as setting your prices was in the first place. You have to be very careful about how you do it. You will probably lose some customers as a result. But if you raise your prices correctly, you should be able to offset that loss and keep your profit levels even.

Communication is a major factor in raising your prices successfully. Let your customers and your employees know what you're doing. Make sure your employees understand why you're raising prices and, more importantly, how the increase will affect them. Give your customers adequate notice of price changes. Don't spring it on them when they come in for the service. Give them time to prepare for paying more money.

Explain your reasons for the price increase. But don't apologize for them. Some clients will complain, but you'll find that most won't. Remember, people are used to prices going up. They pay more for groceries, for food, and for other things they buy. They shouldn't consider your business any different. If they've been happy with the services you've been offering, they will still patronize your salon.

Timing is also important. Some times are better for implementing price increases than others. Busy times are better than slow times. Generally, it is more effective to increase prices in the spring or fall, when holidays such as Memorial Day and back-to-school activities occupy your clients' minds, than in winter or summer, when they are not preoccupied with anything other than how cold or hot it is.

Don't raise all your prices at once. That can be overwhelming and make the price increases seem larger than they are. Raise prices selectively. Increase one service first. Then slowly phase in increases for the others. This way, you give your clients a chance to get acclimated to the changes.

An important question is how much to raise prices. This depends on how much your costs are going up and on how fast they're going up. You obviously have to raise prices enough to cover the increased costs, but you also have to raise them enough to cover what they will rise to in a reasonable time span. You have to anticipate your future cost increases so you can raise your prices enough that you won't have to raise them again soon. Except under unusual circumstances, it is not good to execute a price increase and then have to raise prices again in a short period of time. Generally, you should consider raising your prices by at least 10 percent to give yourself an adequate cushion for your needs. You might be able to justify raising the prices for some services more than for others.

Whenever you raise prices, however, maintain the value of your services. Remember the sales equation. The perceived value of the service must be equal to or higher than the amount of money the client pays. Look for ways to raise the perceived value of the service to help offset the increased price. And, of course, maintain the quality of your services.

RETAIL PRODUCT PRICING

The same factors that determine the prices of the services you offer also affect the prices you charge for the retail products you sell. But there are some other factors you also must consider. How exclusive are the products—that is, who else is selling them at retail? If there is no other source for the products nearby, you can probably sell them at a higher price than if other salons in the area were selling them. Then you would have to be priced more competitively. Your prices will also depend on the image of your salon and the clientele you service. If you operate a low-cost, high-volume salon, your prices would be lower than if you operate a high-cost, exclusive salon. Your product mix would also be different in this case.

Although you should be competitive in pricing with other area salons that sell the same or similar products and cater to a clientele similar to yours, don't try to compete on price with other retail outlets. Simply put, you can't. There's no way you can match their purchasing power and volume. Your edge is in service and expertise, not in price. You should also have an advantage by selling exclusive products.

Whatever your situation, though, don't underprice your products. Charge what they're worth. Allow yourself a fair markup. You have to make a profit from the sales, so you have to charge enough to do so. You know how much the products cost you. Don't forget to add in other costs, such as shipping and handling, commissions, and a fair share of the salon overhead when you figure out the cost of each product. The manufacturers have probably suggested retail prices for the products. These price suggestions are based on their research and on the knowledge of what prices the products will command around the country and include a reasonable markup based on industry averages. Those suggested retail prices are a good starting point. How much you will deviate from those is up to you. You may, if you choose, settle for a somewhat lower price to meet specific situations. You may also charge more, but it will take exceptional circumstances to be able to do this successfully.

RETAIL INVENTORY MANAGEMENT

You have to be just as careful managing your retail inventory as you do your operational supply inventory and other expenses. Like any supplies, those products you stock represent cash. Don't over-buy. You don't want to tie up your capital in items that will sit on a shelf or in your storeroom for any length of time. Remember cash flow management. But make sure you get what you need. You can't sell what you don't have.

This might sound contradictory, but it's part of the balancing act you have to work on. In the beginning, at least, you won't have much information and will have to make educated guesses as to what products will move and what won't. As you gain experience and keep good records, this task will become easier.

Keep your retail stock separate from your services stock. You are operating the retail end as a profit center. If you mix retail with service products, it will be harder to track the results. Even though you should be selling the same items at retail as you use in the salon, many of your retail products will come in smaller, consumer-sized packaging as opposed to the larger, professional packaging. For example, suppose you use a brand name shampoo in the salon and you purchase this in one-gallon bottles. For retail sales, you would purchase that same shampoo in eight-ounce bottles. The unit cost for the smaller bottles is more than for the large containers; thus, it is not economical for you to use the smaller bottles in your salon. It costs you more money and eats into your profitability.

As with other supplies, keep the retail products locked in a storeroom. Limit access to the materials. Limit the number of individual packages of any item you have displayed for sale, and restock the shelves and counters as necessary. For example, you might stock 24 bottles of shampoo, but display only six at a time.

As you would with the operational supplies, set up an inventory control card system so you can keep track of the items. Set minimum, maximum, and reorder point quantities for each item.

Be aware of expiration dates. Many products have a limited shelf life. Know which ones they are. Rotate your stock so you sell the oldest products first. If a product on display passes that date, remove it from the shelf and discard it. Manufacturers put expiration dates on products for a good reason. After a certain time, they may spoil. You might sell an outdated product and it might work fine. But the risk you run, either in customer dissatisfaction or customer health, isn't worth it.

Keep meticulous records on your retail sales. Enter all sales in your log books. Know where and when each item went and for how much it sold. Gather all the data you can and analyze the data regularly. Look for information that tells you which products sell best and how long it takes each product to sell. These data will help you when it comes to deciding which products to keep or which to discontinue and what quantities of each product you should stock. Also keep records on which products you have to discard because they have become outdated. The price data let you figure the profitability of each product.

If a client returns a product, record that information as well. Ask why the product is being returned. Look for patterns. Are particular products coming back with any frequency? Are they coming back for the same reasons? Use this information in your decision making.

SUMMARY

- Price, the second of the classic four P's of marketing, is of paramount importance to your business. Price affects your profits. Profits determine your success.
- Understand the essence of a sales transaction. A sale is an exchange in which you give the buyer the service and the buyer gives you money. The buyer must believe that the service equals or exceeds the amount of money charged for the sale to take place. That fact determines how much you can reasonably charge for the service.
- Costs are an important factor in pricing. You have to charge more for the service than what it costs you to provide it. Know what each service costs, both direct costs and indirect costs.

- Demand is an important factor, too. You have to know how much the clients want the service and how much they are willing and able to pay for it.
- Although most consumers will say that price is the most important factor in their purchasing decisions, in fact most equate price with quality. They will pay more for something with higher perceived quality because their perception of value is enhanced.
- Competition is a factor in pricing, although it is less important than the other factors. Compete on service and quality, not on price.
- You also have to manage your costs and expenses. Profitability depends on both. Exercise sound financial management principles and follow proper accounting procedures. Control your expenses.
- Watch your cash flow. Cash flow is the difference between income and outgo.
- Establish firm policies for implementing and enforcing your prices. Make prices reasonable and fair for the image of your salon and the quality of the services you offer.
- At some point it will be necessary to raise prices. Communication is a major factor in raising your prices successfully.

CHAPTER 7

Place

Place is the third of the four P's of marketing, and it is concerned with the distribution and the availability of your products. It regulates the channels of distribution of products and their physical distribution. At first glance, you might think that this is not so important to you, since in a manner of speaking you are the "manufacturer" of your product (for example, a facial) and you're selling directly to the customer. In actuality, the concept of place is just as important as the other P's in the marketing mix: product, price, and promotion. Quality and service are just as important here.

THE CHANNELS OF DISTRIBUTION

A distribution channel is the route a product takes on its journey from the manufacturer to the end user, with a series of intermediaries in between. An exchange transaction of some type takes place at each step as the product moves from one point in the channel to the next. Usually, the exchange involves money, although that is not necessarily always the case. Each intermediary who handles the product adds some kind of extra value, usually in the form of service.

In some cases, the channel will be short. In others, it will be long. Consider the example of the facial you provide. Here, the main distribution channel is short, consisting of you, the provider and starting point of the channel, and the customer, the receiver and ending point of the channel. Remember, though, that even in this case there are one or more additional distribution channels at work. You use products and tools in providing the facial. Consider the skin cleanser you use. It was made by the manufacturer and found its way into your product inventory, and ultimately onto the client's skin. If you purchased the cleanser directly from the manufacturer, the channel was manufacturer to retailer (you) to the customer—three steps instead of two. If, as is more likely, you purchased the cleanser from a wholesaler, there may be four or more steps in the channel—manufacturer to distributor to wholesaler to retailer to consumer.

Consider the distribution channel as a pipeline that consists of a manufacturer, distributor, wholesaler, retailer, and end user, as illustrated in Figure 7-1. The manufacturer makes the product. Although the manufacturer may sell the product directly to the end user, more often he or she sells it to a distributor, who warehouses the product and sells it, in turn, to a wholesaler. In many cases, the distributor is also a wholesaler. The wholesaler sells it to the retailer, who then sells it to the end user. The retailer may also be the end user. This is the case in the salon. You are both the retailer, for those products you sell to your clients, and the end user, for the products you utilize in providing the services. The local beauty supply store, where you will purchase many of the supplies, is the wholesaler. In some cases, the wholesaler may also act as a retailer by selling the same products directly to consumers. The store may get its stock either from the distributor or directly from the manufacturer.

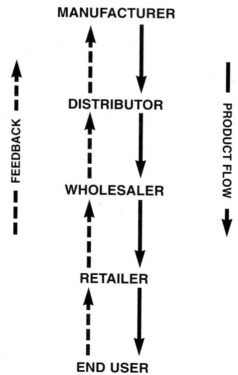

Figure 7-1. Distribution pipeline.

The distributor, wholesaler, and retailer are the conduits through which the manufacturer gets the product into the marketplace and into the hands of the end user. At each step, the number of people handling the product gets larger and the quantities of the product get smaller. Thus, the manufacturer, a single entity, makes the product in a huge quantity. Smaller portions of that quantity go to a limited number of distributors around the nation. Each distributor further breaks down the quantity and sells a smaller number of units to a larger number of wholesalers. Each wholesaler continues the process, selling a smaller number of units to a larger number of retailers. Each retailer sells an even smaller number of units to a larger number of end users. At each stage, the pipe gets smaller but has more branches, as illustrated in Figure 7-2.

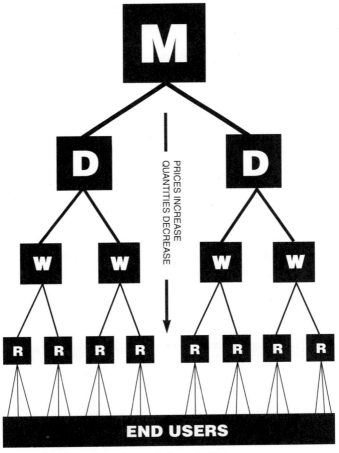

Figure 7-2.   Branches of the pipeline.

The price of the product increases as each handler in the pipeline adds a markup to the cost. The manufacturer sells the product to the distributor at a price determined by the product's cost of research and development, raw materials, manufacturing, packaging, and administration expenses, plus a profit. The distributor adds a markup based on his or her costs plus profit. The wholesaler does the same. And so does the retailer. The consumer pays the highest price. When you use the product in your service, you figure the cost of the product into the price of the service, so you are passing that cost on to the consumer.

At each stage, though, the quantities of the product involved become less as the unit price increases. As an illustration of the cascading price and diminishing quantities, consider this example. Assume each handler adds a markup of 40 percent. Suppose you sell a client one eight-ounce bottle of Brand A shampoo for $10.00. You purchased six bottles from the wholesaler at a cost of $7.14 each. Your 40 percent markup is $2.86. The wholesaler purchased six cases (72 bottles) of the product at $5.10 per bottle. His 40 percent markup is $2.04. The distributor purchased 600 cases (7,200 bottles) at $3.64 each. His 40 percent markup is $1.46. The manufacturer produced 60,000 cases (720,000 bottles) at a cost of $2.60 per bottle. His 40 percent markup is $1.04. Note that these markup figures are not profit. The costs of doing business have to be factored into that figure.

Note also that as prices rise and quantities diminish, the risk diminishes. If the product turns out to be unsaleable, you are only stuck with six bottles and are out $42.84. The manufacturer is stuck with 720,000 bottles and is out $1,872,000.

As a general rule, the higher up the pipeline you can purchase the product, the less you should have to pay for it. If you can buy directly from the manufacturer, you should save a considerable amount, although you won't get a price as low as a distributor would pay, simply because you won't be able to buy the product in the same large volume as a distributor. Some manufacturers will not sell products on a direct basis.

Traffic flows in both directions in the distribution channel pipeline. Product starts with the manufacturer and moves down through the intermediaries to the end user. But the flow of cash starts with the end user and moves up through the pipeline until it reaches the manufacturer. It is not until the product is sold at the retail level that the movement of currency that fuels the entire process begins. Without this currency flow, there would be no profit and, ultimately, no business.

Nor is currency the only thing that flows upstream to the manufacturer. Information also moves through the pipeline. It is the retailer, who is in the best position to know what consumers need and want, who passes that information up the channel. This process gives the manufacturer the information he or she needs to develop new products, improve existing products, and plan more efficient production.

RETAILER UTILITY

An understanding of distribution channels is important to the success of your business. Know where you are in the pipeline. As a retailer—which you are even if you are providing only services—you are a vital link in the network that keeps business moving. Remember the two-way nature of the distribution channel. You operate as a check-valve in the pipeline, regulating the flow of goods from the manufacturer to the end user and the flow of cash and information from the end user to the manufacturer.

As a retailer, you provide a series of utilities that get products into the hands of consumers more effectively. These utilities are of time, place, possession, and form and are important concepts in the distribution function. As a general rule, consumers don't want to travel long distances or spend an inordinate amount of time doing their shopping. You provide time and place utility by operating your business in the general vicinity where most of your customers are located, either at work or in their homes. As a result, you reduce the distance they have to travel and the length of time they have to spend to purchase the product.

You provide possession utility by physically stocking the products so they are readily available for purchase. As a service provider, you give form utility by performing a function that can't be done without you. That is, the consumer can't get a haircut from a catalog.

AVAILABILITY

You are part of the distribution channel, but one of your most important functions is to provide availability of products and services to the customer. This means that it is up to you to have those products and services ready and accessible when the customer wants them. Physical distribution—assuring that the right product is in the right place at the right time—is an important part of your marketing effort.

Keep in mind the time and place utilities you provide. Here is where many of the topics discussed in Chapter 5 come into play, such as location, ambiance, and hours of operation. They all combine to provide convenience and service to the customer. To recap the discussion in Chapter 5, location means that you physically locate your salon where it is most convenient to your clients, making it easy for them to reach you. Ambiance means that your salon is an inviting, friendly place for customers to come to. Hours of operation mean that you are open for your customers' convenience, not yours. It all comes down to customer service. Provide service and you will provide satisfaction.

CONCEPTS IN RETAILING

The concept of physical distribution is valid for retailing services as well as products, and it is evident in both sides of the business. You'll find that you face a number of problems whether you sell services or sell products at retail. You have to be aware of the competition. You have to decide which products to carry. You have to order, inventory, and store those products. And you have to display and promote them. One of the most important things you can do is to find good suppliers and establish good working relationships with them.

RETAILING STRATEGIES

There are a number of strategic concepts in successful retailing. They serve to position you in your marketplace and are a reflection of who you are. They give depth to your product line assortment. Although all are valid and can be used singly, they are best used in combination with each other. It's up to you to work out the set of strategies that works best with your individual image and methods of working.

You can base your strategy on value, efficiency, personal contact, and sensory stimuli. With a value strategy, you stress quality and price. With an efficiency strategy, you make it easier for the customer to purchase your services, through location and hours. A personal contact strategy can also be effective, as you maximize your interpersonal relationships with customers by offering services that pamper them and make them feel good. You implement a sensory strategy through salon ambiance and decor, which you choose to create atmosphere and excitement.

SUPPLIER RELATIONSHIPS

It is important to establish and maintain good relationships with your suppliers. These are the people above you in the distribution pipeline, and they can be manufacturers, distributors, or wholesalers—or a combination of all three. Whatever the type, however, a good supplier does more than just sell products to you. He or she should also be able to provide you with a wide range of services and information. Choose your suppliers with the same care and consideration you use to select anyone with whom you work.

You will undoubtedly purchase your supplies from a number of sources. Different suppliers handle different types of products and different product lines. However, you should limit the number of suppliers you work with. Have more than one supplier for each type of product. It is necessary to have an alternative source for every product. That way, if one supplier can't supply the immediate need, you have somewhere else to turn. But don't have too many suppliers. That weakens any relationships you establish. Two to three suppliers for any given type of product should be sufficient.

Most of the products you purchase will probably come from your local beauty supply wholesaler, although you may also purchase some items directly from the manufacturer. Each source offers advantages and disadvantages. When you buy direct, you shorten the supply pipeline and may get a more advantageous price. In addition, you open a direct channel of communication with the manufacturer and have a better opportunity to ask questions and gather more information about the product and its uses. However, your choices will be limited by the manufacturer's product line offerings. Obviously, you can only buy the products the manufacturer makes. Your orders will be made by mail or telephone and you will have to wait for delivery. It is more difficult to establish a good working relationship with a manufacturer. Your dealings will be more impersonal.

In contrast, your beauty supply wholesaler offers a much wider range of products, produced by a large number of manufacturers. Although you may place orders by mail and telephone, many wholesalers have store locations where you can pick up your supplies. This eliminates the wait and lets you reduce the quantities of the products you have to keep in inventory. You get faster service and can develop a personal relationship with the wholesaler. The disadvantage is that you are farther along the supply pipeline, and prices may be somewhat higher.

Check out all of the suppliers within a reasonable distance from your salon. Visit them and talk to the managers. See what products they handle. Ask questions.

- Do the suppliers stock the products you want to use?
- Is the stock fresh?
- Are the stores clean and tidy?
- Are the salespeople knowledgeable?
- Do you get personal attention?
- What other services do the suppliers offer—training classes, product demonstrations, free delivery?
- Do the wholesalers seem to be reliable?
- What payment terms are offered?
- Do you always have to visit the store location to purchase your supplies, or do the suppliers have salespeople who will call on you?
- Do the suppliers stand behind the products they sell?
- Are their prices competitive?
- Do the suppliers sell only to salons, or do they also compete with the salons by selling the same products to consumers?

Some beauty salon supply outlets sell only to licensed cosmetologists. Others, however, will sell the same salon-grade products to consumers. This practice undercuts your business since it competes, often unfairly, with your salon. Some manufacturers also sell their products directly to consumers. This also gives you unneeded competition. When you can, purchase your products only from suppliers who support the beauty industry and don't try to make a profit at your expense.

Based on your initial survey, choose the suppliers you're comfortable with and begin to establish a working relationship with them. Get to know the people, and let them get to know you. Let them know that you intend to do most of your business with them, but let them know also that they have to earn it. You are their customer and deserve the same treatment your customers expect from you. Discuss your needs and requirements, and make sure your expectations are clear.

Don't choose your suppliers based on price alone. Look for service and quality as well. Reliability is important. You have to be able to trust the suppliers to get you the products you need when you need them. The best price is useless if you can't get the goods on time.

By the same token, the suppliers can expect you to be a good customer. Be fair in your dealings with them. Don't make unreasonable demands. Don't play one supplier against another. Treat the suppliers the way you want your customers to treat you. Remember, the suppliers are entitled to make a reasonable profit, too. Be loyal to your suppliers as long as they provide the products and service you require. If they stop meeting your needs, by all means look for new sources of supply. But don't hop from one supplier to another just in search of the best price.

When you are first starting with a supplier, you will probably purchase your supplies on a cash basis. This will hold true especially if you are just starting your business. Once you've built a relationship, you may be able to purchase on credit terms. If you can, by all means do so. Let your money work for you. But make sure you pay your bills on time. If you get 30 days to pay, make sure you pay the bill within that time. But don't pay earlier unless you get a discount.

Your invoice may contain terms such as 2%10, net 30. This means that you can take a 2 percent discount from the total if you pay within 10 days, but you must pay the total amount if you take the full 30 days. If possible, take the discount and pay within the stated time limit. Given the relatively small invoice amounts and short time periods involved, the discount amount will usually be greater than the amount of interest the money would earn if you left it in the bank for 30 days. The discount adds to your profit.

COMPETITION

Today, the competition for salons is intense. But this competition comes from two sources. The first is, of course, with other salons who are competing with you to sell services. This kind of competition is relatively straightforward. The competitive situation in selling products at retail, however, is not so straightforward. Surprisingly, competition here does not come from other salons. You are competing with other salons for the service business. Clients who patronize your salon for various services are not likely to go to another salon just to purchase products. If they are going to purchase products from a salon at all, they'll buy them in the same place they buy their services.

Your retail sales competition comes from a variety of other sources, which have little or nothing to do with the salon business. These include drugstores, supermarkets, discount stores, department stores, specialty shops, and direct marketing organizations.

Drugstores and supermarkets typically sell mass market products as opposed to the professional upscale products you would handle. They operate on the principle of high volume and low margins, making only a small amount on each sale, but earning their income on the large volume of sales they make. They offer no service or expertise. The consumer just walks down the aisle, drops the product into his or her shopping cart, and pays for it at the checkout counter. There is no value-added benefit. Price alone is the key.

Discount stores, like drugstores and supermarkets, also sell mass market cosmetic products on a high-volume, low-margin basis. They are usually very low overhead, self-service operations. Some discount stores also sell some upscale market products; however, in some cases, these may be gray market or counterfeit products. These stores also sell distressed merchandise—that is, products that they've purchased cheaply from another store that has gone bankrupt or discontinued merchandise from manufacturers or wholesalers. Here, also, price alone is the driving force behind sales.

Department stores usually concentrate on upscale cosmetics, especially makeup and skin care products. They provide service as well as sales, and the products are sold by trained personnel. In many cases, however, the personnel are trained only in one manufacturer's product line and do not have the broad training of licensed cosmetologists. Department stores have reasonably high-volume sales of these products and get good margins. They also enjoy good marketing and promotional support from product manufacturers. The stores' cosmetics department operations are quality oriented, and price is less of a factor.

Specialty shops devote their entire efforts to cosmetics products, usually from one manufacturer, although they may be sold under a private label. Some of these operations can be narrow in their specialization. For example, there are some shops that market only nail products; others that sell only makeup; some that handle only skin and body care products. The specialty shops also enjoy very good marketing and promotional support from the manufacturers, who in some cases, may be their parent company. These shops, like department stores, concentrate on upscale rather than mass market products. Store personnel are usually well trained and knowledgeable about the products and their proper use. Service is normally very good. Quality rather than price is the key to specialty shops' success.

Direct marketing organizations include those who sell cosmetics products door to door, by mail through catalogs, and by infomercials on television. Door-to-door operations utilize a veritable army of salespeople, who either go from house to house or set up demonstration parties in a willing customer's house and solicit orders for the products. These companies normally market upscale products at reasonable prices and usually limit their product lines to their own brand name products. The salespeople are generally better trained in selling techniques and product knowledge than in proper use of the materials. They offer some degree of service, but not at the level of a department store or specialty shop.

Catalog houses send printed catalogs and circulars to mailing lists they either amass or purchase from direct mail list brokers. They accept orders either by mail or by telephone and ship the goods to the buyer. The buyer never sees a salesperson. Catalog houses usually carry a fairly broad line of upscale products, but they sell by price and delivery. Service is nonexistent. Some of the door-to-door operations also sell through catalogs.

Infomercials are one of the newest direct marketing tools. These are paid television broadcasts, usually of 30-minute duration in a format that resembles a talk show or game show. The entire program is devoted to the demonstration and sale of some product. A number of cosmetics products are being marketed this way. Once the province of cable channels and late night television, these programs have begun appearing on network affiliates during prime time. The sales pitches are geared to one specific product or line of products, and sales are made by telephone and by mail. Price is often a factor. Product quality varies with the reputation of the manufacturer. Service is nonexistent. Home shopping networks on cable and satellite television have much the same characteristics

Although there is some degree of competitiveness, you can't really consider yourself in competition with drugstores, supermarkets, and discount stores. You won't be, or at least shouldn't be, selling mass market items. Nor are you targeting the same customers. It would be impossible for you to attract the high volumes of shoppers those store get; nor could you match them in price. (Your major competition in this arena is with discount stores who sell gray market or counterfeit professional, upscale cosmetics products.) Nor are you competing with catalog sellers or those who market through infomercials. These people have targeted a completely different audience from the one you can reach.

You are more in competition with department stores and specialty shops as well as the home sales organizations. Your customers probably shop in the department stores already and have ready access to the specialty shops. And it's very hard to match the convenience of the home sales companies. You cannot compete with any of these retail outlets in price. They have a tremendous advantage in their ability to purchase goods in large quantities at and low prices. With the discount structures they receive, they can sell products at prices lower than your purchase prices. Plus, they get a considerable advantage with the promotional and marketing assistance they receive from the manufacturers.

You do have a tremendous advantage, however: the personal relationships you've built up with your clients. By offering a good mix of products they can't usually get in other locations and selling them on your better service and expertise, you can capture your share of the market, even in this highly competitive atmosphere. Trust and knowledge add value to the products you sell.

INVENTORY MANAGEMENT

In the course of your business, you will need a variety of products, both for use in the salon and for retail sale. To determine your requirements for those products, you need to consider two factors: Which products do you need? What quantities of those products do you need? Note the emphasis on need. Get only the products that enable you to keep your salon operating and enhance your profitability. Don't buy anything that doesn't do just that. Anything else is a waste of your resources. Also, buy only for your immediate needs, not for something you might do or require in the future. When it's time to get those items, you can acquire them.

The types of products you will need will depend on the services you offer. Each service, whether hair, skin, or nails, has its own supply requirements. If you are competent enough to offer the service, you should know what the supply requirements are. Before you buy an item, make sure you know what you will use it for, whether it's for your day-to-day operations or for retail sale.

You have a wide choice of product lines, or brands, from which to choose. In your salon, you may use either brand name or generic products. Which you will purchase will depend partly on the type of salon you operate and the clientele you service. If you operate a high-volume, budget-priced salon, for example, you may want to use only the lower priced generic materials for your services. Conversely, if you service primarily affluent clients and command high prices for your services, you will want to use the more expensive brand name products. In actual practice, you will probably use a mix of both—the less expensive generic products when their use won't adversely affect your image, the costlier name brands when it makes a difference.

If you sell products at retail, you should use those same products in your operations. It is very difficult to convince your client to spend $10.00 on an eight-ounce bottle of brand name shampoo if you've just washed his or her hair with a $3.00-per-gallon generic shampoo.

Whatever products you buy, however, whether generic or brand name, make sure they are of the best quality. Quality products are important to your services. You can't do first-rate work with second-rate materials. Like equipment, good-quality products are a better investment than poor-quality products, even though they may cost more. They will usually do the job better and lead to better customer satisfaction.

Quality varies from one product to another, even among brand names. Even among brands of comparable quality, one may suit your operations and your ways of working better than another. Also, not all of the products in a manufacturer's line are necessarily of the same quality level. You might find, for example, that manufacturer A has the best shampoos, but its colorants are of lesser quality, whereas manufacturer B has outstanding colorants but not so good shampoos. You don't have to limit your selection to one brand, so feel free to mix and match. Choose those products that you're comfortable with and that work best for you, even if they are from different manufacturers. However, don't overdo the mixing and matching. Limit the number of brands you utilize to keep your inventory control manageable.

Test all products thoroughly before you buy them in your normal quantities. Make sure they work for you, through actual experience in your salon under the conditions you face. Read the manufacturer's instructions and any available literature about the products thoroughly. And follow the manufacturer's instructions. They are there for a reason. Know the ingredients of every product you use and know what role each ingredient plays in the product. Get Material Safety Data Sheets (MSDs) for any product that might be classed as hazardous—for example, hydrogen peroxide and acetone. A typical MSDS is shown in Figure 7-3. These are available from the manufacturers on request. If you don't understand any part of the instructions or contents, ask the supplier. Don't use a product unless you understand its composition and use thoroughly.

Keep a file on every product you use or sell in your salon. Include the MSDS forms and complete specifications in the file. Most states now require that businesses have MSDSs on file and readily available for inspection by employees. Keep notes on the performance of each product, especially if you experience a problem with it, and keep these in the permanent record as well. Review the notes periodically to see if there are any changes in the performance of the product. Also review the ingredients periodically to be aware of any changes in the composition of the product. If there are, ask the manufacturer why the change was made. Become so familiar with the products you use that you can answer any question a client may ask about them. Remember, clients view you as the expert in the field. Make sure you don't disappoint them with a lack of product knowledge.

Your job doesn't end once you've made your product selections. You must stay abreast of new developments in the field and be aware of new product introductions. When you see a new product, test and evaluate it. See if it might earn a place in your salon. When you find a better product, don't be afraid to make a change. Just make sure you change for a good reason.

New products are often introduced at regional and national cosmetology trade shows. They are also usually described in the beauty industry trade journals. Attend shows and read the journals. Get all the information you can. Even if you decide a new product is not suitable for your salon, you should still be aware of its existence and its properties. You may not be interested in a new product, but some of your customers may be, so you should have enough information to answer at least basic questions about the product.

MATERIAL SAFETY DATA SHEET
Rohm and Haas Company

---

1. CHEMICAL PRODUCT AND COMPANY IDENTIFICATION

KATHON® CG Preservative

Product Code	:	62369	MSDS Date	:	12/20/94
Key	:	904284-0			

COMPANY IDENTIFICATION
Rohm and Haas Company
100 Independence Mall West
Philadelphia, PA 19106-2399

EMERGENCY TELEPHONE NUMBERS
HEALTH EMERGENCY : 215-592-3000
SPILL EMERGENCY : 215-592-3000
CHEMTREC : 800-424-9300

KATHON® is a trademark of Rohm and Haas Company or one of its subsidiaries or affiliates.

---

2. COMPOSITION/INFORMATION ON INGREDIENTS

No.		CAS REG NO.	WEIGHT(%)
1	5-Chloro-2-methyl-4-isothiazolin-3-one	26172-55-4	1.05 - 1.25
2	2-Methyl-4-isothiazolin-3-one	2682-20-4	0.25 - 0.45
3	Magnesium chloride	7786-30-3	0.5 - 1.0
4	Magnesium nitrate	10377-60-3	21 - 25
5	Water	7732-18-5	74 - 77

See SECTION 8, Exposure Controls / Personal Protection

---

3. HAZARDS IDENTIFICATION

Primary Routes of Exposure

Skin Contact
Eye Contact
Inhalation

Inhalation

Inhalation of vapor or mist can cause the following:
- irritation of nose and throat

Eye Contact

Material can cause the following:
- corrosion to eyes - permanent, irreversible eye injury

Skin Contact

Skin irritation effects can be delayed for hours.
Material can cause the following:
- corrosion to the skin - burns - allergic contact dermatitis

---

PAGE 1 of 8   CONTINUED

FORM 30348 ♻ Recycled and Recyclable!

Figure 7-3. Material Safety Data Sheet (MSDS). (Courtesy of Rohm and Haas Company.)

Many factors go into your product decision. Quality, of course, is mandatory. If the product is of low quality, any price is too expensive, no matter how low it is. Reliability is also important. Does the product perform adequately? Does it do what it is supposed to do, and does it do it consistently? If you can't rely on the product, it is not good for you. Suitability is a concern. Does the product meet your needs? Are you comfortable with it? Does it fit the way you do business? If it isn't suitable, it's not a good buy. Don't discount service, either. Does the manufacturer or the supplier stand behind the product? Can you count on delivery when you need it? And then there's price. Don't base your purchase decision on price alone. Consider price only when everything else is equal. You should be more concerned with value. Value is the sum total of all of the factors.

Once you've decided on the products you will utilize in your salon, you must determine the quantities of each you will purchase and stock. If you are just starting your business, this can be difficult. It is easier when you've been in operation for some time and have developed a business history.

The object is to strike a balance so that you have a large enough quantity of each type of supply to meet your immediate needs, yet not so much of each in inventory that you're tying up your cash needlessly or that the materials pass their expiration dates before you can use them. Don't overbuy. Excess inventory is a waste of valuable resources. The only possible justification for buying more of a particular product than you need for reasonable immediate use is if you get an especially good deal, such as a special sale, or if there is a significant discount in the price for buying in larger quantities. Even then, be careful. Make sure you will use the product within a reasonable amount of time. Analyze the situation on a case-by-case basis. Be certain that the amount of money you will save on the sale outweighs the loss of ready cash you may need for other uses.

The quantity of any given product you should buy depends on two factors: the frequency with which you perform the services in which it is used, and the ease with which you can replace the product. Once you've been in operation for a while, if you have kept adequate records, you will be able to predict how many times you will perform a service in a given time period.

Suppose, for example, that when you analyze your records you see that your salon averages 25 haircuts, seven permanents, nine facials, and 17 manicures each week. Based on these statistics, you know how many of each service you can reasonably expect to perform in any given week. You know how much product it takes to perform each service. Multiply the average number of services by the quantity of product used for each to give you a base quantity requirement for each product. You can consider this number as your minimum quantity requirement.

Statistics, however, give you only an average, not an absolute number. They don't account for variations in your business due to seasonality, holidays, or special promotions you may offer, so you must add a safety factor to your minimum quantity to account for increased business in any given time period. For example, if your base quantity of permanent wave lotion is seven units, you might want to establish a normal stock quantity level at 10 to 12 units, and a maximum stock level at 15 units. This means that for permanent wave lotions, your reorder point will be seven units and you will not keep more than 15 units in stock, unless you have a special promotion on permanent waves that may require more inventory.

Go through this exercise with each product you use. Establish minimum, normal, and maximum stock levels for each. Once you've done this, monitor those levels constantly and adjust them as necessary. You may adjust your maximum stock level according to how easy or difficult it is to replace the product. If you can get the product quickly from a local beauty supply distributor, you can afford to have a lower maximum stock level. If you must order the product from a distant source and wait for delivery, you might want to have a higher maximum.

Note that this discussion is based on a careful analysis of your business. If you are just starting your salon, you will not have these data available, and that will complicate your decisions. In that case, you must make some basic assumptions about the level of business you will enjoy and make your stock level decisions based on those estimates. Make your assumptions realistic and err on the side of caution. You will probably be better off by underbuying until you have a more accurate feel for your business. Adjust your supply purchases as you acquire more information.

Purchase your supplies with the same care and consideration you utilize to buy your equipment. Many of the same principles apply. Investigate your purchases thoroughly. Buy only what you need. Don't overbuy. Consider service as well as price. Choose your suppliers carefully. And don't be in a hurry to buy anything.

INVENTORY CONTROL

It is important to establish strict controls over your inventory. You must manage your inventory just as you must manage all other aspects of your business. Inventory is money. Each item you stock costs real dollars. If these items are lost, stolen, or misused, it means money out of your pocket.

In a busy salon, it is easy to lose track of products. With the hustle and bustle of everyday operations, it is sometimes hard to devote the time and effort to monitoring such a seemingly simple operation as inventory control. You can forget to log in incoming products or neglect to record products you use. Either way, you lose track of them and can't figure out where they went. That represents lost money.

No matter how honest you think your employees and your clients may be, it is a fact of life that some people steal. Products may be stolen from your inventory easily unless you take precautions. Stolen or misappropriated products also mean lost money.

Waste is another profit robber. When products are misused, spilled, ruined, or pass their expiration date, they can't be used to earn income for you. Wasted products are wasted money.

Don't make the mistake of thinking that at most you'll only lose a few small items and that the cost will be insignificant. A trickle can soon become a flood that will drown your profitability and ruin your business. Institute sound inventory handling practices right from the start. Know where every item that comes into your salon goes and how it is used. That means more than buying the right products in the appropriate quantities. It also means storing the goods securely, controlling access to them, and keeping accurate and up-to-date records.

Inventory security starts from the moment you receive the goods into the salon, extends through their storage, and ends when you use the product and discard the empty package. When products are received, don't leave them unattended. If you haven't the time right then to log them in, put them in a secure area until you can log them in. Log them in as soon as you can, but certainly not later than the end of that business day.

Whenever you receive an order, count every item. Match what you received against the invoice. Make sure you get everything you ordered. If the order is short, notify the supplier immediately. Don't pay for goods not received. If items are backordered, ask the supplier when they will be delivered. You don't have to pay for backordered items until you receive them.

Keep your inventory in a locked supply room or in locked cabinets if you haven't a suitable room to use for the purpose. Know where the keys are at all times. Only employees should be allowed in the supply room. You may want to limit access to certain employees. Establish, as part of your salon procedures, who will have the authority to take products from the inventory. Have anyone who takes a product out of the room sign it out, recording his or her name and the date. This is not just for security purposes. It also lets you monitor your business activity.

Organize your supply room so that products are easy to locate. Keep similar products together. Keep the room well lit, clean, and uncluttered. Arrange the stock so that the oldest products are taken first. Be aware of the expiration dates of all products, and use them before that date. Discard any product that has passed its expiration date, and remove it from your inventory. Dispose of the outdated products properly. If you are purchasing the right products in the right quantities, you should not have too many products that go out of date. If you see a pattern developing, adjust your purchases accordingly.

Set up an inventory control card for each product type. The card should contain the name of the product, the minimum and maximum quantities that you have determined for it, and the amount on hand. The minimum quantity is the reorder point for the product. When you reach that point, order more. Whenever a product is removed from the supply room, whoever takes it should sign and date the card. The card should stay in the area in which the product type is stored.

Set up a product log as well. This is your primary record of your supply purchases and use. Record every product that comes into the salon. Record the date received, the quantity and the price, and the supplier. Then note in the log every time you use a product. This is an ideal function for a computer. Keep a running inventory with your supply log. In addition, conduct a physical inventory periodically. You may want to do this quarterly, or even more often if your retail business is sizeable. Note any differences between the physical inventory and your running inventory. This is an indication of product shrinkage and may be due to theft, loss, or waste. Try to account for all discrepancies.

Don't just keep records. Analyze them. They are another business tool that helps you maintain profitability. Accurate records show you patterns of business. They let you utilize your supplies in the most efficient manner and get the most for your money.

THE RETAIL SALES AREA

In Chapter 5, we discussed the importance of salon ambiance and decor. If you have a separate area for making retail sales, the same considerations apply. The area in which you conduct your retail sales is an important feature of your salon and should be designed with the same criteria as any other section. The area should be bright, clean, well lit, and as roomy as possible. If you have a separate room for retail sales, make sure it is visible from the reception area and from the outside. Ideally, patrons should have to pass through the retail area on their way in or out of the salon.

PRODUCT DISPLAY

Your retail area should be inviting, attractive, and should catch the awareness of the clients as they pass through it. Keep it neat and uncluttered, and arrange the products to focus attention on them. Display the products to show them to their best advantage. You can place products in glass display cases, on countertops, in bins, on shelves, or a combination of any of these. In some cases, you might put selected products on a free-standing pedestal to call special attention to them. Keep the more valuable items in locked display cases to help guard against shoplifting. Change your product display frequently to keep a fresh look in the area. If you keep the same display for a long time, your clients can become so used to it that they won't notice it.

Keep glass display cases, countertops, and shelves clean and free of fingerprints and dust. Clean the products frequently, too. Mark the price clearly but unobtrusively on each item. Decide whether you want the customers to serve themselves or whether you will have a designated salesperson wait on them. Self-service items need to be accessible, placed on open shelves or in bins. Items in display cases will not be self-service.

The overall illumination in the retail area should be bright and even, but you can highlight certain products with spotlights. Be careful if the products are exposed to sunlight coming through your windows. Ultraviolet radiation can cause colors to fade and destroy the appearance of the products.

Use appropriate props to show off the products. For example, you might use a bed of autumn leaves to display an assortment of makeup in seasonal colors. Keep a supply of things you can use for props, such as cotton batting, assorted colors of cloth for draping, ribbons, and mirrors. Color coordinate your displays. The displays should be harmonious, not discordant.

Always be alert for display ideas for your products. Visit department and specialty stores and see how they display their goods. Look at various magazines to see how products are shown in advertisements. Start a clipping file of display ideas. And use your imagination.

Take advantage of point-of-purchase displays, posters, and promotional exhibits, all of which you can get from the manufacturers of the products. Ask your supplier what materials are available. Use demonstrations and samples when you can get them. In addition, store fixture distributors sell display accessories. Call them. Ask for a catalog, and visit their showrooms to get display ideas.

SUMMARY

- The third of the classic four P's of marketing, place, refers to the distribution and availability of products. Among other things, place is concerned with the channels of distribution, the route a product takes getting from the manufacturer to the end user, and the functions in the middle of the distribution chain.
- The distribution channel is a pipeline that consists of a manufacturer, distributor, wholesaler, retailer, and end user.
- The distribution pipeline flows in both directions. Products move from the manufacturer down to the end user. At the same time, cash and information move from the end user back up to the manufacturer.
- As a retailer, either of products or services, you offer a number of utilities to the consumer: time, place, possession, and form. These are important to the distribution function.
- There are a number of important strategic concepts in retailing. They include value, with emphasis on quality and price; efficiency, through making it easy for the consumer to buy the product or service; personal contact, by developing good interpersonal relationships with your customers; and sensory stimuli, by the decor and ambiance you choose for your salon.

- Develop and maintain good relationships with your suppliers. Limit the number of suppliers you work with, but have more than one supplier for each type of product you purchase.
- Your competition for retail products may come from drugstores, supermarkets, discount stores, department stores, specialty shops, and direct marketing organizations.
- Inventory management is a vital part of the place function. You can't sell a product or service if you don't have necessary items in stock.
- Choose products that are consistent with your image. Generally, sell the same products at the retail level that you use when providing the services. Be prepared to answer any questions a customer has about any product you use or sell in your salon.
- Keep track of usage patterns for each product. Use that information to establish minimum and maximum stock levels.
- Control your inventory as well. Know where and when every product in the inventory is used.

CHAPTER 8

Promotion

Last, but certainly not least, of the four P's of marketing is promotion. This is the most visible of the elements in the marketing mix, and it encompasses all the means you utilize to present the public face of your salon. Promotion is the factor in the marketing mix that makes the other three factors work. Product concerns what you sell. Price concerns the value of the exchange. Place describes how you get the product into the consumers' hands. Promotion covers how you create the demand for your product in the mind of the customer. Unless the consumer wants the product, it will not be sold, regardless of quality, low price, or availability. It is the task of promotion to make the consumer want the product.

Remember the discussion on customer behavior in Chapter 6, "Pricing." You have to understand the psychology of consumers and why they act the way they do. You have to know the stimuli that make them reach a favorable decision, in this case to patronize your salon. Identify and then push their "hot buttons."

Remember also the essence of the sales transaction. It consists of an exchange between the buyer and the seller, in which you give the buyer a service or a product and, in return, the buyer gives you money. When the customer believes that the value of the product or service equals or exceeds the amount of money charged, the sale will take place. If he or she perceives that the value is less than the amount of money, it won't. The key words here are *believe* and *perceive*. The bulk of the transaction takes place in the consumer's mind. How you see your services is irrelevant to the transaction process. Perception is reality. Regardless of what you think, your salon is what your customers think it is.

Promotion is the part of the marketing mix that convinces consumers of the value of your services. It is how you mold the perceptions of your clients and inform them of the value they will receive. This is how you convince them that your services are worth the money you charge for them and persuade them to reach a favorable buying decision.

A BRIEF THEORY OF COMMUNICATION

In its simplest terms, communication is an exchange of information. All living things communicate in one form or another. In plants, for example, the flower releases pheromones that attract insects. The flower, in effect, tells the insect that it is ready to be pollinated. Bees go through a complicated ritual dance to tell other bees the location and distance of pollen. A dog growls and bares its teeth at a stranger coming up the walk to warn that person away.

All life forms, other than humans, communicate only through the use of signs, which can include smells (pheromones), sounds (growls), expressions (baring the teeth), or gestures (ritual dances). The more complex the life form, the greater its use of signs. Technically speaking, these life forms do not have the ability to utilize language.

Humans also communicate through the use of signs. However, humans also communicate through the use of language, which is the use of symbols that allow the generalization of ideas and actions. Symbols can take the form of words, either spoken or written, or of objects, such as pictures and decorations.

The transmission of information—that is, communication—is a process that utilizes various communications systems. A communications system consists of a source, a transmitter, a channel, a receiver, and a destination, as illustrated in Figure 8-1. The simplest example is speech between two individuals. When you talk to a client, you formulate the idea you want to communicate in your head. Your brain is the source. The idea is converted into symbols—words—in a process known as encoding. Then you articulate the words by modulating air passing through your voicebox with your mouth, which is the transmitter. The sounds of the words travel through the air, which is the communications

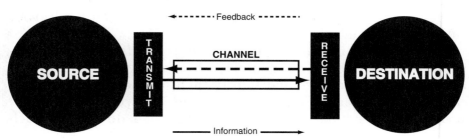

Figure 8-1. Communications systems.

channel, and then to your client's ears, which are the receivers. Here, the symbols are decoded into the idea, which goes to the destination, the client's brain.

The process is the same regardless of the parts. In a telephone call, the transmitter includes the telephone and the channel is the telephone line. In a letter, the transmitter is ink on paper and the channel is the postal service. No matter how complex the communication, the process is constant.

It is also important to distinguish between signals and noise. Signals are the symbols that carry the information, such as the spoken or written words. The stronger the signal, the better the communication. Noise is an unwanted event that interferes with communication. Noise can be physical, such as static on the telephone line that hinders hearing. Or it can be psychological, such as words with double meanings. In either case, effective communication relies on maximizing signal strength and minimizing noise.

The goal of communication is to transmit an idea. You hope the idea the client received is the same as the idea you transmitted. This requires feedback, in which the client communicates his or her reception of the idea to you, in a similar process in which you become the destination and the client becomes the source. In this case, however, the symbols may not be verbal. They could take the form of expressions (the raising of an eyebrow) or gestures (a shrug). Whatever the form, the more feedback you get, the more reliable your communication will be.

You need feedback to make sure the client understood what you said. (You also have to make sure you said what you meant.) Understanding does not necessarily imply agreement. Feedback does not have to be positive. Even negative feedback will give you the information you need to adjust your communications.

You use this communications process to transmit an idea to your prospective client. Simply put, that idea is to purchase your services. Unfortunately, it is not so simple. It is actually necessary to communicate four different messages to get the desired result:

1. You have to let the consumer know the services are available.
2. You have to stimulate a desire for the service in the client's mind.
3. You have to convince the client that he or she should get the service from you and not your competitor.
4. You have to stir the client to come into the salon and buy the service.

Once you've made the sale, you need to transmit a series of different messages aimed at keeping your clients' business. These include reinforcing their belief that they received value for the service, supporting their satisfaction with the service, thanking them for their patronage, and letting them know you want their continued business. This is the essence of marketing.

MARKETING COMMUNICATIONS

Marketing communications are the means you use to transmit that idea to the customer. They represent the toolbox of promotion. Inside that toolbox you have a formidable array of tools (see Figure 8-2). These tools include personal selling, advertising, direct mar-

---

- **PERSONAL SELLING:** Demand Creation and Image Reinforcement
- **ADVERTISING:** Awareness Creation and Interest Creation
  Print media
      Newspapers and magazines
      Telephone directories
      Organization directories and programs
  Broadcast media
      Radio
      Television
      Cable television
- **DIRECT MARKETING:** Interest Creation and Demand Creation
  Direct mail
  Newsletters
  Circulars
  Sales letters
- **SALES PROMOTION:** Action Creation
  Sales
  Rebates
  Coupons
  Contests
  Demonstrations and parties
  Point-of-purchase displays
- **PUBLIC RELATIONS:** Image Building
  Community involvement
  Publicity

Figure 8-2. Marketing communications tools.

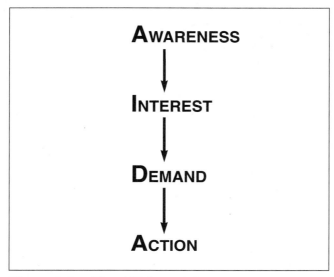

Figure 8-3. The AIDA model.

keting, sales promotion, and public relations. Each of these is important to the marketing communications mix, and each has its own advantages and disadvantages.

Marketing theorists use a mnemonic device known as AIDA as a model to describe the progression of marketing communications (see Figure 8-3). The letters stand for Awareness, Interest, Demand, and Action. From the point of view of the customer, the purchasing process begins with awareness. Awareness fosters interest. Interest encourages demand. Demand leads to action.

The approach you take to the customer in your marketing communications, and which tool you use, depends on where your customer is in the model. If you are trying to create awareness, you would use a different set of marketing communications devices than you would use if you were trying to create demand. Effective marketing communications requires the right tool for the particular job.

PERSONAL SELLING

Nothing replaces the personal touch. You and your staff represent the best voice your salon can put before the buying public. Every time you talk to a prospective client, you are communicating something about your salon.

Personal selling is a good means of creating demand and reinforcing your image. It is effective, and it is inexpensive. There's no expensive media to buy, no advertising agency to pay. Nor are there any materials to consume. You can tailor your presentation to the person you're talking with, and you can get immediate feedback, so you can judge its effect and make adjustments in your approach.

The disadvantage of personal selling is that it is limited in scope. You only have the opportunity to meet and talk to so many people in the course of a day. Hopefully, you'll leave a lasting, favorable impression with each of them. But you can't hope to talk to everyone in your target audience.

ADVERTISING

Advertising is good for creating awareness and interest. There are many forms of advertising. They include those in print media, such as newspapers, magazines, and directories; those in broadcast media, such as radio and television; and those in other media, such as billboards, bulletin boards, and advertising specialties. Advertising is discussed in detail in Chapter 12.

Advertisements tend to be broad reaching, with the ability to get your message to large numbers of people in a short length of time. They are relatively short messages, rarely focusing on more than one idea at a time. They can be expensive, both to create and to run in print or broadcast media. But they are effective when done properly.

Because of the broad reach, however, it is more difficult to target your audience. In most cases, the advertisement will reach far more people than just the potential clients. In that sense, using advertising media is more of a shotgun approach. In addition, there is a lot of clutter in advertising. People are exposed to so much of it in the course of a day that it is necessary to cut through the clutter so they will hear your message.

DIRECT MARKETING

Direct marketing is really a subset of advertising, and it is good for creating interest and demand. It includes direct mail, newsletters, circulars, and sales letters. It is a more personal form of advertising in that you can target the recipients precisely and tailor a message to them. In this regard, it is almost like personal selling. Direct marketing is discussed in detail in Chapter 13.

Costs for direct marketing are generally lower than for comparable levels of media advertising. Creative costs should be similar. The major variables are for printing and postage. Direct marketing pieces can be longer than media advertisements and normally allow space to develop ideas more fully and to include all the information a prospect needs to make a buying decision. It is also easier to include response mechanisms.

The biggest disadvantage for direct marketing for a small business is the "junk mail" syndrome. Like media advertising, most people are inundated with direct mail, so it is necessary to get the recipient's attention and interest quickly so he or she will open and read it rather than toss the envelope in the trash without opening it. This is no easy task, but it can be accomplished if you use some imagination.

SALES PROMOTION

Sales promotion covers all those things you do to sell your services that can't be classified readily as one of the other marketing tools. It is especially good for spurring prospects to take action. Promotion activities include in-store items such as product displays, posters, and point-of-purchase displays; incentive items such as coupons, special sales, rebates, and contests; and items such as demonstrations and parties. Sales promotion is discussed in detail in Chapter 14.

These activities can range in cost from almost nothing to expensive, depending on how you approach them. They can be very effective, although they will most often be used in conjunction with one or more of the other tools. For example, if you held a special sale on permanents (promotion), you would have to advertise the sale in the newspaper (media advertising), distribute circulars (direct marketing), and have signs in the salon (point-of-purchase display).

Advertising, direct marketing, and sales promotion activities are often used together, and the effectiveness of one can be linked to the effectiveness of the others. In a sense, they are tools of each other as well as tools of marketing communications. In many respects, they are similar in that they share goals and objectives.

The difference is in the direction they move. Advertising and direct marketing move the buyer toward the product. Speaking metaphorically, a good ad or direct marketing piece commands the readers' attention, grabbing them by the hand and leading them in the direction of your salon. Sales promotion moves the product toward the buyer. It takes the product and figuratively puts it into the buyer's hand, commanding action.

Sales promotion efforts are an important part of the marketing communications mix if they are handled properly. There is a risk of overdoing activities such as special sales or coupons. It is important with these to know exactly how much they are costing you. You have to make sure that the return is greater than the expense.

PUBLIC RELATIONS

Public relations are those activities that promote your business more than services. They are primarily image builders as opposed to product sellers, although some aspects can be used as sales tools. Public relations activities are good for establishing awareness of your image and for reinforcing the perceptions of your customers regarding the value of doing business with you. Public relations and publicity are also discussed in detail in Chapter 14.

At some point in your business career, you will use all of these marketing communications tools. Whichever you use, however, you'll find that the same rules apply to them as apply to the rest of your marketing efforts. You have to plan them carefully and use them with respect and caution. Otherwise, you run the risk that they will be ineffective or, even worse, counterproductive.

LEGAL AND ETHICAL ISSUES IN PROMOTION

There are a number of legal considerations that regulate promotional activities. You must be aware of these and follow them, just as you do any law. The penalties for breaking laws in this area can be quite severe, whether or not you know the practice is against the law. At a minimum, they will certainly cost you a lot of money. There are also some promotional activities that, although not illegal, border on unethical. You should avoid these as well, not because of potential penalties but for the negative effect they can have on your business.

Any promotional vehicle you use can be held to standards established by various federal, state, and local government agencies. Regulation is not limited to advertising and direct mail materials, either. The same strictures also apply to claims made verbally by you or your staff. Laws governing sales promotion and advertising are complex. It is easy to run afoul of them, so have your attorney review your marketing communications before you commit them to print.

From the point of view of a businessperson, effective marketing communications attract, inform, persuade, and sell. From the consumers' points of view, however, effective marketing communications provide accurate and reliable information that helps them make intelligent buying decisions. Business works best when consumers believe that the information they receive is complete, valid, and true. As long as this is so, they will have confidence in the system and will support businesses. But when consumers believe they are misled or lied to, they lose confidence and businesses will lose their support.

As a result, it is in the best interests of businesspeople to make sure that their marketing communications are complete, factual, and truthful and do not mislead, distort, deceive, or create unrealistic expectations among consumers. Destroy your customers' confidence in your ethical standards, and you will destroy your business. Remember, your major asset for your business is your reputation. If you get a reputation for being dishonest, you can quickly lose your customer base, and your salon as well.

REGULATORY AGENCIES

A number of government agencies have the authority to regulate promotional activities. These regulations have the force of law behind them. In addition, there are a number of private agencies that set industry standards for these activities. Although these standards may not necessarily have the force of law, they are nonetheless powerful and should be followed. Failure to conform to these standards can result in civil lawsuits, which are time-consuming and expensive, even if you win the case. These agencies are listed in Figure 8-4.

FEDERAL AGENCIES

- Federal Trade Commission (FTC)
  Regulates advertising and promotion in the beauty industry
- Interstate Commerce Commission (ITC)
  Regulates common carriers
- Bureau of Alcohol, Tobacco, and Firearms (BATF)
  Regulates advertising and promotion of alcoholic beverages
- Food and Drug Administration (FDA)
  Regulates packaging and labeling of foods, drugs, and cosmetics
- Consumer Product Safety Commission (CPSC)
  Regulates safety of products
- United States Postal Service
  Regulates advertising and promotion through the mail

STATE AND LOCAL AGENCIES

- Offices of States Attorneys General
  Regulate advertising and promotion on the local level
- County District Attorneys
  Regulate advertising and promotion on the local level
- Consumer Protection Agencies
  Regulate safety of products on the local level

PRIVATE AGENCIES

- Council of Better Business Bureaus (CBBB)
  Concerned with self-regulation of business
- Association of National Advertisers (ANA)
  Establishes standards for self-regulation
- American Advertising Federation (AAF)
  Establishes standards for self-regulation
- American Association of Advertising Agencies (AAAA)
  Establishes standards for self-regulation

Figure 8-4. A list of regulatory agencies.

The Federal Trade Commission (FTC) is the major federal agency charged with regulating the conduct of business. If someone complains that your promotion practices are unfair or deceptive, the FTC can order you to stop the practice. The agency can take you to court to impose civil penalties, and it can force you to acknowledge and correct false claims and practices. It can also impose fines and order you to provide documented substantiation of any claims you make.

The FTC has the authority to regulate advertising and promotion in the beauty industry. Other federal agencies regulate advertising and promotion in other industries. For example, the Interstate Commerce Commission (ICC) governs common carriers. The Bureau of Alcohol, Tobacco, and Firearms (BATF) regulates advertising and promotion of alcoholic beverages. The Food and Drug Administration (FDA) has the authority to regulate packaging and labeling of food, drugs, and cosmetics. In the case of defective products, the Consumer Product Safety Commission (CPSC) has jurisdiction and can order the recall of products found to be unsafe or defective. The United States Postal Service is responsible for regulating advertising and promotion that utilizes the mail service.

At the state and local levels, promotional activities can be regulated by the offices of state attorneys general, district attorneys, and local consumer protection agencies. In reality, you're more likely to become involved with the state and local agencies than you are with the federal agencies. However, the laws and regulations will be similar. Most states are authorized to regulate promotional activities by "little FTC acts," which closely follow FTC rules. Most of these rules provide for both criminal and civil action against unfair or deceptive practices.

Private agencies allow for self-regulation of promotional practices in industry. This is a practice that the government agencies encourage. The Council of Better Business Bureaus (CBBB) is the major private agency concerned with self-regulation. The company develops and issues promotion standards and guidelines for businesses. Other agencies involved in establishing standards for self-regulation include the Association of National Advertisers (ANA), the American Advertising Federation (AAF), and the American Association of Advertising Agencies (AAAA).

Self-regulation typically takes two forms. The first is preclearance, in which the advertiser submits its advertising materials to one of the agencies for review before it starts the campaign. The second is industry monitoring, in which the agencies act as watch dogs, monitoring advertising and providing a forum for airing complaints. Although these agencies can't order an advertiser to change his or her practices, they can apply considerable pressure to do so, up to and including civil court action. In addition, many media require the advertiser to submit substantiation for claims before they will run the advertisement.

TRUTH IN ADVERTISING

A promotional message can be true in that every statement made is factual, but it can still be deceptive or misleading. In promotions, the literal truth is often less important than the impression the consumer gets. It is very easy to be misleading, either deliberately or inadvertently. You can be held liable if the courts hold that consumers could be misled by the material, whether that was your intent or not. The courts use a number of standards to determine if a promotional activity is deceptive.

Regulatory agencies look at promotional materials from the point of view of the average person. Could a person of average intellect and knowledge infer the wrong meaning from the message? Is he or she likely to be misled by it? You may think you're developing a message aimed at sophisticated, knowledgeable people. The courts may not agree with you. When you develop your message, make sure it is perfectly clear and understandable to the average reader.

You have to consider the overall impression your promotional package leaves with the reader. Headlines, copy, illustrations, design, etc. all contribute to its effect. The package, in its entirety, can be misleading, even if the individual claims in it are true. For example, a statement in your advertising, "No salon in town gives better haircuts," may be perfectly true. But a court could rule that the average person might take that statement to mean you give the best haircuts in town, especially if the design and illustrations in the advertisement support an idea that you are the best.

Make sure that you give all the pertinent facts that let the consumer make an informed buying decision. You don't have to tell everything in your promotions, but neither can you hide anything that might make the consumer reach a different decision. For example, you can't offer "makeovers at half-price" if the condition for getting the special price is to purchase a facial, unless you explicitly state that in the promotion.

For that matter, don't make any promise in your promotions that you don't intend to honor fully, without reservation. For example, don't use a promise of a low-price service as a lure and then try to sell the customer a higher priced service when he or she comes in. Suppose you run an advertisement that offers "haircut and styling with Cindy, only $10.95," and when the client comes in you tell her, "You really won't like the haircut Cindy gives, she's still getting experience. Why don't you let Catherine cut your hair? Her price is $18.95." This is known as bait-and-switch advertising, and the authorities especially frown on such tactics.

Avoid puffery, or unreasonable exaggeration in any claims you make. You can be enthusiastic about your services without indulging in hyperbole. Some embellishments are acceptable, as long as they don't mislead (remember the average person), or make the statement so outrageous that no one could really take it seriously. You can do this if you're taking an obviously humorous approach in the promotion—for example, "Alley-Oop Would Go Ape Over Our Haircuts."

Any claims you make in your promotional materials must have substantiation. You don't necessarily have to offer the proof in the material, but you better have it on file if someone challenges your claim. If you were to say, "We're the top-rated salon in the area," you must be able to produce the surveys that show that conclusion. And the surveys must be valid and have been run by an independent source. Of course, if you can prove it, you can say it. Be very careful when making claims about public issues such as environmental protection, unless you can back them up.

If you are fortunate enough to know a celebrity or beauty industry expert, you could have them give a testimonial about your services, but only if they use them or are able to make any statements about your salon with reasonable authority. If you use testimonials from your customers, make sure they represent typical experiences.

Also, be careful that any statements you make in your promotions can't be interpreted as giving an implied warranty. For example, a statement that "you're sure to like our permanents" could be taken to mean that you are guaranteeing satisfaction. You can give a guarantee, but make sure you honor it. If you say "your money back if you're not happy with any service," be prepared to make refunds if a customer asks for one. The FTC has specific guidelines for guarantees and warranties. Check with the agency, and then follow its guidelines.

Comparative advertising is legal, but it is risky. If you have a definite advantage over a competitor, and you can prove it, it is acceptable to use that fact in your promotions if the comparison means anything to the consumer. But make sure it is true. Make sure you're comparing similar things. And be prepared for complaints from the competitor and, probably, counterpromotions. Also keep in mind that anytime you mention the competitor, regardless of the context, you're giving free advertising. The consumer may only remember the competitor's name, not that you have an advantage.

As this discussion shows, there are a lot of legal and ethical considerations in developing your promotional materials. Be aware of everything you do in this area. Think it through before you put it before your target audience. If you know it's wrong, don't do it. If you're not sure, check with your attorney or with one of the private monitoring agencies before proceeding. Have a basic understanding of the laws that govern promotions.

TRADEMARKS, PATENTS, AND COPYRIGHTS

Trademarks, patents, and copyrights are legal concepts that protect intellectual property from being used by unauthorized persons or companies. A trademark identifies a product or service and distinguishes it from other similar products or services. It can take the form of words, symbols, or pictures. Typically, a product's trademark is its brand name. Trademark protection keeps others from using the name to market products in the same category, but not from making or selling similar products. So, for example, Xerox® is the registered trademark of the Xerox Corporation for its brands of copying machines. No other manufacturers can call their copying machines Xeroxes, but they can sell competing brands.

A patent, on the other hand, gives the holder the right to keep others from making and selling similar items. A patent protects the rights to an object. The trademark protects the rights to the symbol used to designate the object.

A patent remains in effect for 17 years. After that time, others may manufacture and sell similar items. A trademark becomes effective when it is first used and remains in effect for the life of the product. But the trademark holder has to protect the trademark. If he or she allows others to use it improperly, the trademark can be canceled and become a generic designation that can be used by anyone. Aspirin is an example. At one time, aspirin was a registered trademark. Because the holder didn't protect it, it has become a generic name.

Trademarks and patents are issued by the Patent and Trademark Office, which is part of the U.S. Department of Commerce. A patent is granted after a thorough search has been made to make sure the idea is, in fact, new and innovative, and that no one has invented a similar item before. While the search is going on, the applicant can use the phrase "patent pending."

A trademark should be registered, a process in which the Patent and Trademark Office searches to make sure no similar trademarks are already in use. While the registration process is going on, the applicant can use the notation ™ in conjunction with the name. After the trademark has been registered, the notation ® can be used. A service can use the notation ˢᵐ to indicate it is a service mark.

A copyright provides protection for creative works, such as books, magazine articles, musical compositions, photographs, and art works. It prevents anyone from using part or all of these works unless authorized by the copyright holder. Copyrights are covered by the U.S. Copyright Act of 1976, which ruled that an artistic work is copyrighted as soon as it exists in tangible form. The work does not have to be registered to be legitimate, but registration ensures protection in a court of law. Copyrights are registered through application to the Copyright Office, which is part of the Library of Congress.

A copyright remains in effect for the life of the author plus 50 years. After that time, the work goes into the public domain and can be used by anybody. But be careful with this or you can run into unanticipated problems. For example, suppose you wanted to use excerpts from Mozart's *Eine Kleine Nachtmusik* as background for a radio commercial. The work is in the public domain, so you can use it freely. But the performance of the music that you are using might be copyrighted. So you can't use that rendition without permission from the orchestra that recorded it.

There are some exceptions to copyright law. The doctrine of fair use allows the use of short excerpts of copyrighted works for private or educational use, such as for purposes of review or to use as an example. However, the user must attribute the author, including the title of the work, the publisher, and the publisher's address. Fair use does not allow for commercial use.

Ideas and facts cannot be copyrighted. Anyone can use them freely, without attribution. However, particular expressions of those ideas or facts can be protected by copyright.

Government documents and other materials cannot be copyrighted. So you can freely use any materials found in government publications. Thus, you could not reprint an article from a trade magazine in your newsletter without the publisher's permission, but you could reprint an article from a magazine such as *FDA Consumer.*

Trademarks and copyrights are important concepts for you to remember when you prepare marketing communications. Simply put, you may not use materials that belong to someone else without their permission. Before you use a trademark or copyrighted material, make sure you get written permission from the holder. Follow any requirements the holder specifies as to attribution or the way you use the material. Note the captions used with many of the illustrations contained in this book. Even with permission, however, you cannot alter the work or use it improperly.

Be especially careful with photographs. Copyright laws are very strict in this regard. If you hire a photographer to take a photograph that you will use subsequently in an advertisement, in a newsletter, or in some other marketing communications vehicle, the photographer owns the copyright, even though you paid him or her to take the photo. Unless you have negotiated for the rights and that is specified in the contract, all you have purchased is the right to use that photo in the particular application. You may find that you owe the photographer more money if you want to use it in another application.

MODEL AND PROPERTY RELEASES

You cannot use pictures of people or property in a commercial communications medium without their permission. Before you use a picture, make sure you have a signed model release from every recognizable person in the photo or from the owner of any real or personal property shown. If the person is a minor, the release must be signed by his or her parent or guardian. Keep the signed forms in a permanent file with the project files. Also be aware that even with a signed model release, you can't hold the person up to ridicule in the photograph. If you have any question about the propriety or legality of using a photograph, consult with your attorney.

SUMMARY

- The fourth of the classic four P's of marketing, promotion, is the most visible of all of the elements in the marketing mix. It covers the means you use to present your salon to the marketplace and is the factor that makes the other three P's work.
- Communications is an exchange of information. Although virtually all life forms enjoy some means of communication, humans are the only ones who communicate through the use of language—that is, the use of symbols to allow the generalization of ideas and actions. The transmission of information is a process that utilizes a source, a transmitter, a channel, a receiver, and a destination.
- Signals are the symbols that carry information. Noise is an unwanted event that interferes with communication, and it can be either physical or psychological.
- The goal of communication is to transmit an idea. Feedback lets you know that the receiver has understood the message. Your communications goal in promotion is to transmit the idea that the prospective client should purchase your services. To do this, you have to transmit four messages. You have to let the consumer know that (1) the services are available; (2) he or she should desire them; (3) he or she should get them from you; and (4) he or she should come into your salon. After the sale, you have to keep on communicating to reinforce the client's decisions.
- Marketing communications are the means you use to transmit ideas to your prospective clients. You have a number of tools available to you. These include personal selling, advertising, direct marketing, sales promotion, and public relations.
- You can remember the progression of marketing communications through the use of the mnemonic device, AIDA, which stands for Awareness, Interest, Demand, and Action.
- Personal selling is a good means of creating demand. Advertising is good for creating awareness and interest. Direct marketing, really a subset of advertising, is good for creating interest and demand.
- Sales promotion covers the things you do to sell your services and is good for spurring customers to take action. Public relations are those activities that promote your business more than they promote the services you sell.

- Any promotional vehicle you use has to meet standards set by either the government or by industry agencies. First and foremost, you have to provide your prospects with accurate and reliable information that helps them make an informed buying decision. It is in your best interests to make sure your communications are complete, factual, and truthful and don't mislead, distort, deceive, or create unrealistic expectations.
- The primary regulatory agency that governs promotional activities is the Federal Trade Commission (FTC). Other agencies include the Interstate Commerce Commission (ICC), the Bureau of Alcohol, Tobacco, and Firearms (BATF), and the Food and Drug Administration (FDA). Even the U.S. Postal Service can become involved.
- There are a host of state and local agencies that also play a part in regulating promotions. There are also a number of private agencies, such as the Council of Better Business Bureaus (CBBB), the Association of National Advertisers (ANA), the American Advertising Federation (AAF), and the American Association of Advertising Agencies (AAAA).
- Trademarks, patents, and copyrights are also concerns in marketing communications. These are legal concepts that protect intellectual property from unauthorized use. Trademarks identify products or services and distinguish them from similar products or services.
- Patents protect the holder from unauthorized use of an invention or product. Once registered, a patent is in effect for a period of 17 years. Patents and trademarks are issued by the Patent and Trademark Office of the U.S. Department of Commerce.
- A copyright provides protection for creative works and protects the author from unauthorized use of the work. A copyright lasts for the life of the author plus 50 years. Copyrights are issued by the Copyright Office of the Library of Congress.
- There are three exceptions to copyright law. (1) Fair use allows limited private or educational use of short excerpts from works. (2) Ideas and facts cannot be copyrighted, nor can materials from government publications. (3) You cannot use photographs of people or property in your marketing communications without written permission. This permission comes in the form of signed model and property releases.

CHAPTER 9

Marketing Communications

Your promotions are designed to further your overall marketing objectives. The means you use to promote your salon and your services are marketing communications, as outlined in Chapter 8. Marketing communications, whether they take the form of advertisements, direct marketing pieces, public relations, or sales promotion devices, must be just as carefully thought out and planned as any other aspect of marketing. They cover a vital aspect of your overall marketing plan.

There are a number of essential elements to a good marketing communications plan: objectives, positioning strategies, specific tactics, message, measurement procedures, and budget. These are listed in Figure 9-1. In many ways, this type of plan mirrors the larger marketing plan, of which it is a part. The objectives are a statement of what the communication should accomplish in a specific period of time. These should be quantifiable and measurable. That is, the result must reach a specific amount and there must be some means of measuring the result. For example, a quantifiable, measurable objective might be to increase the awareness of the salon in the neighborhood from zero percent to 20 percent in the first year of operation, as measured by prepromotion and postpromotion surveys.

As with the marketing plan, the strategy describes how you will attain the objective. Here, you determine the theme of your message to the audience and the position of your salon in the marketplace. For example, your strategy might be to use advertisements and publicity items to tell the members of the target audience that your salon uses the latest state-of-the-art technology to provide a complete range of hair, skin, and nail services that are guaranteed to please.

The tactics are the specific actions you take to make the communications strategy work. They should spell out what the actions will be and when they'll take place. For example, your tactics might include the preparation of a series of three advertisements

191

- **Objectives**
  What to accomplish
  Specific period of time
  Quantifiable and measureable
- **Positioning Strategy**
  Theme of message
  Place in prospects' minds
  Image
- **Tactics**
  What specific actions to make strategy work
- **Message**
  What to say
  How to say it
- **Measurement**
  How to measure results
- **Budget**
  How much to spend

Figure 9-1.   Marketing communications plan.

that will run in one local daily newspaper and one local weekly shoppers' guide on a rotating basis each week for the next 13 weeks. Each ad will highlight one specific service—that is, one for hair services, one for skin care services, and one for nail services. In addition, two publicity releases announcing new services will be sent to the local newspapers.

Measurement procedures specify how you will measure the results of the plan. The most typical way is to measure the increase in business, either by the increase in telephone calls to the salon or by walk-in trade. There should be some mechanism to determine why the new people came in. Which ad or publicity notice are they responding to? Make it a point to ask.

The last element, but certainly not the least important, is the budget. Determine how much it will cost to accomplish your objectives and decide how much you want to spend. Calculate your costs carefully and allocate sufficient money to the programs. Marketing communications represent a significant expense to the salon. However, this should be money well spent. The money you spend on these programs will bring in new business and increased revenues, if they are carried out properly. If you don't give them the planning they require, your money is wasted.

- **To Inform**
  Create awareness of services
- **To Interest**
  Create consideration of need and value
- **To Persuade**
  Create conviction in value
- **To Sell**
  Create motivation to purchase

Figure 9-2. Marketing communications objectives.

OBJECTIVES

When you examine marketing communications objectives closely, you'll realize that there are really only four kinds. These are listed in Figure 9-2. Essentially, the objective can be either to inform, to interest, to persuade, or to sell. Remember the AIDA model discussed earlier, which describes the four stages of customer acceptance: Awareness to Interest to Demand to Action. The communications you will utilize will depend on which of these objectives you want to achieve.

The objectives you will choose will depend on what you need to accomplish to achieve your marketing goals and on the location of the members of your target audience in the customer acceptance framework. In all likelihood, you will have multiple objectives, one or more for each segment of your business.

TO INFORM

The first stage in customer acceptance is awareness, and the first objective of marketing communications is to provide that most basic of information. If the need is to create awareness of your salon or your services, you have to inform your target audience about them. Awareness is essential to your business. You can't sell your services if your potential clients don't know they exist or, for that matter, that your salon is in business. In effect, you're saying, "We're here, and this is what we offer."

The primary vehicles for creating awareness are advertising, both print and broadcast, and publicity. These have the ability to reach large numbers of people efficiently. Direct marketing efforts can also be used to build awareness, but they are less effective for this purpose than the other means because of their more narrow reach.

TO INTEREST

Just knowing that your salon and your services exist is not enough, however. In the second stage of customer acceptance, it is necessary to create an interest in the minds of the prospective clients. Here, your objective is to plant the seed in their minds that the services have value and should be considered. Hopefully, that seed will grow into a sale. Interest is the first step in creating demand. The idea is to make prospective clients willing to focus their attention on what you have to offer. This is no simple task. Most people have a lot of things clamoring for their attention in the course of a day.

The primary vehicles for creating interest are advertising and direct marketing programs, ranging from targeted direct mail campaigns to the distribution of flyers. Both can foster appeal and attraction. Sales promotion programs and public relations are less useful for achieving this objective.

TO PERSUADE

By the time you reach this third stage of customer acceptance, you've made your prospective clients aware of your services and have created an interest in them. With this objective, your idea is to convince the prospective clients that the services are valuable, that they need them, and that your salon is the place to get them. The idea is to water and fertilize the seed you planted while creating interest and create the demand for your services. The primary vehicles for persuasion are advertising and direct marketing. Personal selling is also valuable for demand creation.

TO SELL

The fourth stage of customer acceptance is the sale. By now, you have a group of prospective customers who know you exist, are interested in and want the services you have to offer, and believe that your salon will best fill their needs. The objective here is to motivate them to come into the salon and purchase the services.

Customer demand does not bring revenue into your salon. Customer action does. No matter how much your prospective clients want your services, they will not buy them unless you move them to come into your salon and make the purchase. They will not do this on their own. You have to supply the impetus. Newton's First Law of Motion is just as valid in describing inertia in marketing as it is in physics. The law says that an object at rest tends to stay at rest until an external force moves it.

In this regard, customers work the same way as objects. It's not that they're lazy or too busy. In most cases, people are too pre-occupied with their own concerns to pay attention to yours. Unless you spur them to action, they'll always find something else to occupy their attention. The primary vehicles for spurring action are sales promotion activities and personal selling, although action-directed direct marketing and advertising programs can also be effective.

It is one thing to create awareness, interest, demand, and action. Once you've accomplished those, it is still necessary to maintain those states. If you expect repeat business, you have to keep your salon and services in front of your clients, constantly maintaining their interest and motivation. There is an old story in marketing circles about two people sitting next to each other on an airplane. One was a successful businessperson; the other was a young accountant. The accountant turned to the businessperson and commented, "You know, you are very successful. Your products are selling well. Why are you still spending your money on promotion?" The businessperson turned to the accountant and replied, "I don't stop promoting the products for the same reason the pilot doesn't turn off the engines once he's gotten the airplane into the air." Promotion never stops. For as long as you're in business, you will be doing some type of promotion, either to bring in new business or to keep the business you already enjoy.

STRATEGY

The strategy is the basic plan of action you take to achieve your objectives. It describes, in broad brush strokes, what means you will employ to reach the stage of customer acceptance you require and to establish your place in the customers' minds. There are two primary tools of strategy—positioning and message—and both hold the key to your success.

POSITIONING

Positioning is a deceptively simple concept that is difficult to accomplish, because it starts with the mind of your prospective customer rather than with your business. In its most basic terms, positioning is where you reside in the customer's consciousness. Your positioning statement should define just how you want the customer to think of you. Maytag appliances are a good example of positioning. Notice that commercials for the company's appliances all deal with the "loneliness of the Maytag repairman." They never talk about the benefits of the product. The company's positioning statement is summarized in its tagline, "Maytag, the dependability people."

Don't confuse the positioning statement with the messages you use in your marketing communications. Although they may work together, they are two completely different things. Your message conveys the benefits of your service. Your positioning conveys who you are and what you stand for. Unless your prospect has a clear idea of who you are, your message will not get through.

It is not easy to establish your position. You can't force your way into the prospects' minds. You have to work with their preconceptions. People are bombarded with information. Just consider today's mass media—AM radio, FM radio, cable radio, network television, cable television, newspapers, newsletters, magazines for virtually every conceivable interest, billboards, posters, and signs—there is so much that consumers are near sensory overload. The human mind can only work with so much information before it rejects what it can't use. As a result, people are selective in what they retain, keeping what fits their experience and belief and rejecting almost everything else. Therefore, it is almost impossible to put new ideas into their minds.

People's minds are compartmented into categories based on their needs. Your goal is to get into the customer's mental compartment labeled "beauty care." The compartments are small, so there's only room for one salon in the beauty compartment. Think of this as a game of King of the Mountain. The leader is at the peak. The competition is trying to dislodge the leader. Positioning lets you be that leader.

The best way to get to the top of the mountain is to be the first one to get into the customer's mental compartment. That doesn't mean you have to the first salon in the area to open. It does mean you have to be the first to recognize the importance of positioning and go after the share of mind. The first one into the compartment is imprinted on the customer's consciousness. It is virtually impossible to dislodge the king of the mountain, once imprinted.

If you're not first in the customer's mind, the job is much harder. You'll have to analyze the competition and find and exploit their weak points. The idea is to find a particular niche you can claim as your own and then fill it. In essence, if you can't knock the king off the mountain, you have to build a new mountain to occupy. Just don't try to go head to head with an established leader. Find your own unique spot and don't try to be everything to everybody.

Positioning is a long-term concept and can take time and money to establish. You will probably have to do some research to find out where you fit in your prospective customers' minds, and then build your positioning statement from that. Prospective customers view your business much different from the way you see it.

Make sure your position matches your image. Be consistent with both. Be objective when you look for your position. And keep it simple. Concentrate on one concept. Getting one idea into the customers' minds is difficult; getting two or three ideas in is virtually impossible.

MESSAGE

What you say is just as important as where you say it. Although it is vital to pick the right marketing communications vehicle to reach your target audience most effectively, it is equally vital to make sure potential customers get the information you want them to get. The vehicle and the message work together to accomplish your objectives. Your message must lead prospective clients to make the decision to patronize your salon. It must entice the prospects, inform them about your services, and persuade them to spend their money with you.

The message must be oriented to the needs of your prospective customers. It should stress the benefits of your services to them. When people read or listen to a message, their primary thought is, "What's in it for me?" They don't care if your salon is the biggest, the best, the most modern. Nor do they care if you've won every imaginable award for hair styling or if your staff is world famous. Those kinds of claims in your communications are meaningless. You may mention some of them later in your message if, and only if, they will add credibility to your benefit statements. Don't put anything in your message that doesn't work toward the goal you have set. Leave out all superfluous matter.

- **Opening**
    Capture prospect's attention
    Invite prospect into rest of message
    Contain a strong benefit
- **Body**
    Offer proof statements for major benefit
    Provide additional benefits and proof statements
    Provide salon identification
- **Close**
    Ask for the sale
    Make the offer
    Say what prospect should do

Figure 9-3.   Parts of a message.

The principles for developing your message are essentially the same for any type of marketing communication, whether it is advertising visually (print media), aurally (radio), or both (television), direct marketing (flyers, newsletters), sales promotions (demonstrations, special sales), or public relations (news releases). The message has three parts: the opening, the body, and the close (see Figure 9-3). The opening, or headline, has the task of capturing the prospect's attention. It should contain a strong benefit statement—that is, it must tell the reader or listener what he or she will gain. It must also invite the reader into the rest of the message.

Don't begin your message with your salon name. There's no intrinsic benefit in your name. That information comes later. The benefit should be specific. For example, you might open with a statement like, "Get better looking, healthier skin in 30 days." Don't ask any question that can be answered no—for example, don't use a headline like, "Are you unhappy with your skin condition?" If the prospect answers yes, you have a chance. But if she answers no, you've lost her. She won't continue with the message. Don't mention price in the headline. Don't say, for example, "European-style facials, now only $35.00." You haven't yet established whether what you're offering is worth the money. At this stage, there's no perceived benefit.

The body of the message should contain proof statements for the major benefit in your headline. You've told the prospect what she'll gain. Now you have to tell her how she will gain. For example, you might say, "A series of European-style facials given by our professional staff of estheticians will cleanse and condition your skin. Your skin will be healthier and radiant looking. We use the most modern skin care techniques and the finest products, specially formulated for your skin type." You can also put in additional benefit and proof statements, if you have the room. Here is where you put in your salon name, address, and other relevant information.

In the close, you ask for the sale. Make the offer. Tell the prospect what you want her to do. You have to do this. People won't respond unless you lead them to do it. If you are going to discuss price at all, here is where you do it. For example, the close for the skin care communication might be, "Come in for a free consultation and analysis. Call today for an appointment." You might also add a special offer, such as "This week only, get a facial for just $30.00." If you have a coupon, call attention to it. Say, "With the coupon, get a facial for just $30.00."

With printed materials, use illustrations, either photographs or drawings, to add visual interest to the message. The illustration should support your benefit statement, if possible. For example, a photograph of a woman receiving a facial would be suitable. A photograph of the outside of your salon would not be so useful. You might want to utilize an equipment or product manufacturer's logo in your communication vehicle, if the manufacturer is well known. The use of such a logo can add credibility to your salon. Of course, you should be using that equipment or product in your salon. Make sure you get the manufacturer's permission to use the logo. Logos are protected by copyright and trademark laws. As with the copy, don't overdo the use of illustrations. They should support your copy, not interfere with the message.

With radio commercials, background music and sound effects perform many of the same functions as illustrations in the print media. They add aural interest. Here, too, don't overdo them and don't let them interfere with the sense of the message.

Obviously, the amount of information you can put in your message will depend on the size of the vehicle or length of time you buy. The larger the vehicle, the more you can say. However, regardless of the size of the vehicle, don't try to say too much. Limit your message to one major benefit, with its proof statements, plus the offer and your salon name, address, and telephone number. If the ad is fairly large, you may consider a second benefit statement, but don't clutter the advertisement with more than that. Too much information will turn off the prospect and negate your chance for making the sale.

Be absolutely truthful in your communications. Don't exaggerate your claims. Don't promise anything you can't deliver. For example, you should not claim to be able to remove wrinkles permanently unless, of course, you can. Be very careful not to make any statements that could be considered medical in nature. You are operating a salon, not a hospital. You are not licensed to practice medicine. So don't claim to heal or cure anything. Stress the beauty and health aspects of your services. Be as ethical in your communications as you are in the conduct of your business.

TACTICS

Tactics are the methods you use to achieve your objectives. They are the specific steps you take to transmit your positioning and your message to your target audience. The array of tactical devices you have at your disposal is almost limitless, depending on your needs, your imagination, and your budget. They include the various means of advertising in print and broadcast media as well as other kinds of media. These will be covered in detail in Chapter 10.

There is also a wide range of direct marketing devices, such as direct mail pieces, flyers, newsletters, circulars, and cooperative mailings. These will be discussed in Chapter 11. Sales promotion devices include open houses and demonstrations, tie-in promotions, and special sales. Personal selling can also play a big part in your promotional tactics. These are the subject of Chapter 12.

Public relations is an important but often overlooked tactical device that can pay big dividends. Press releases and community service programs are a part of this subject; these will be covered in Chapter 13.

MEASURING COMMUNICATIONS EFFECTIVENESS

It is very important that you know how effective your marketing communications are. You want to make the most effective use of your communications dollars that you can. This means that you have to be able to measure the results. Make sure you have some means of doing that.

There are many ways to measure communications effectiveness. Which you use depend on your objectives and on the tactical devices you utilize. Each device has a measurement system that is most appropriate for it. But for the most part, your most effective measurement will be to count how many new customers or how much increased business you get.

MARKETING COMMUNICATIONS BUDGETS

Marketing communications are an expenditure and are treated as an overhead expense. Just as you do with supplies, equipment, and other expenses, you must budget for your communications efforts. You must allocate money to create the vehicles you need, produce them, and place them in various media, as appropriate. There are three parts to the process: First you have to create the vehicle, then produce it, and then put it before the target audience.

You have to decide how much of your resources you should allocate to your marketing communications. Many businesses do this as a percentage of sales. The rough rule of thumb is to allow 1 to 3 percent. You may need to spend more than that, especially if you are just starting your salon. Or you may need to spend less if you aren't generating the revenues to pay for promotion. The actual amount you spend will be determined in part by your goals and by the vehicles you choose, and in part by how much you can afford. As important as promotion is to your business, you have to temper your efforts with practical considerations of your financial situation. You can't shortchange other aspects of your business just to pay for your communications.

By now, you should know the audience you want to reach and what you want to accomplish with your communications. In the case of advertising, you should gather data about the various media you feel will reach your audience. Talk to the media representatives. Let the media representatives give you all the cost data and demographic data you need to make your decision, and figure out your effective cost per exposure for each medium. Then choose the media that best serve your needs. In most cases, you'll want to use a mix of communications vehicles—for example, a combination of telephone directory advertising and newspaper advertising as a minimum, with perhaps some direct mail and circulars.

You don't have to run all of your communications programs at once. Start with a modest program, perhaps just in one or two media. Evaluate the results, and then expand the program as necessary. Remember frequency, though. The more times you can run an advertisement, the more people it will reach and the more they will remember it. You may be better served, at least in the beginning, by trading size for frequency. Run smaller ads, but run them more often. Also, take advantage of any cooperative advertising allowances you can get from your suppliers.

Evaluate your communications results constantly. Make sure you know what is working and what isn't. Don't be afraid to change either your vehicles or your message if you aren't satisfied with the results. But make sure you give the communications program a fair chance to work before you make the changes.

CREATIVE AGENCIES

There's an old saying that familiarity breeds contempt. That is certainly true in the field of marketing communications. The problem lies in the amount of such communications we receive on a daily basis. We are so used to seeing advertisements, flyers, signs, and posters and listening to commercial messages on radio and television that they take on an undue familiarity. And these messages, especially the better ones, give the impression that they are easy to do. As a result, the profession is one in which almost everyone thinks he or she is an expert. This is not the case.

Marketing communications are complicated. To conduct them effectively requires a thorough knowledge of communications, of media, and of psychology. Although it is possible to do your own communications, it is a task best left to the experts. You don't represent yourself in court; you hire an attorney. You don't deal directly with the IRS; you hire an accountant. You don't erect your own building; you hire a building contractor. You don't take out your own appendix; you go to a surgeon. Just as you utilize the services of these professionals and rely on their aid and advice, so should you utilize the services of marketing communications professionals. Although you will pay for their services, just as you pay for the services of the other people you hire, in the long run you'll save money. Unless you're an expert, don't make the mistake of thinking you can do your own. When it comes to communications, amateurish work is worse than no work at all.

AGENCY FUNCTIONS

A good creative agency performs a variety of functions for you. First and foremost, it helps you make money by bringing in new clients and cementing relationships with your existing clients. It does this by developing and implementing marketing communications vehicles tailored to your needs.

An agency can do many things on both strategic and tactical levels. On the strategic level, the agency can help you enhance your image by designing your salon's look and ambiance. And it can help you develop your positioning and message strategies. On the tactical level, the agency can design and produce print and broadcast advertising and a wide variety of direct marketing vehicles, ranging from simple flyers to complex direct mail pieces to salon newsletters. It can handle publicity, by writing and placing press releases or by coordinating public relations functions. It can also perform basic communications research to gather data to help develop your strategies.

Whatever communications need you have, an agency can handle it for you. If it is a full-service agency, it can perform all of the functions in house. If it is a boutique agency, that is, an agency that specializes in a particular function, it can perform those functions that are within its expertise and either subcontract other functions or suggest other agencies who perform them.

AGENCY COMPENSATION

All agencies, regardless of type, perform these functions for money. It's their business. Like you, they have bills, salaries, and overhead costs. And their aim is to make a profit. How they do that varies, however.

The two major kinds of agency compensation are fee based and commission. In most cases, agencies use a combination. Fee-based systems are essentially charges done for work done. Normally, the fee is set on an hourly basis. You pay for the number of hours worked on your project. Most often, more than one person will work on your project, so time costs are figured on the total person-hours. Some of the people in the agency will have higher hourly charges than others. Also, the larger the agency and, consequently, the larger its staff, the more overhead it will have to cover.

With media advertising, the cost structure can be somewhat different. In this case, the agency purchases the space in a newspaper or magazine, or the time on radio or television on your behalf, and is paid a commission by the publisher. The commission rate varies, but it is currently around 17.5 percent. The commission should offset some or all of the creative and administrative charges for media advertising projects, depending on the overall size of your media budget.

ANATOMY OF AN AGENCY

Like salons, or any kind of business for that matter, creative agencies come in various forms. There are large ones, small ones, good ones, and bad ones. There are generalists, who take on any kind of business. And there are specialists, who limit themselves to certain kinds of business.

There are full-service agencies and boutique agencies. Full-service agencies handle all aspects of the communications spectrum. They conduct marketing research, plan the strategies, design the communications vehicles, produce them, purchase the media, and track the results. They have the capability to manage your entire marketing communications program. A boutique agency, on the other hand, specializes in certain aspects of the communications process. One agency, for example, might conduct research. Another might only do creative work. Yet another might only conduct sales promotions.

AGENCY STRUCTURE

A creative agency staff is made up of a number of different people, who normally work together to get the job done. Larger agencies, of course, will have more people, and those people will often be specialists in one field or another. Smaller agencies, on the other hand, will have fewer people, and each of those people may perform more than one function. In general, though, agency positions are similar in all agencies, even when one person might fill a number of positions (see Figure 9-4).

The account supervisor oversees the work of the account managers and creative teams and is responsible for the overall conduct of the agency's business. He or she may not deal directly with clients, except in the case of a major client, but will review the work done by his or her subordinates.

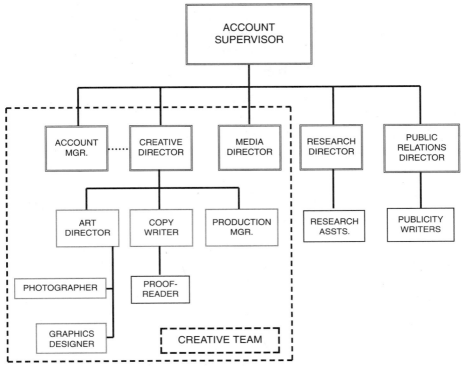

Figure 9-4.   Agency structure.

An account manager is the liaison between the client and the creative team. As the nominal head of the creative team, he or she is the client's primary contact and is responsible for taking care of all aspects of the client's marketing communications needs. The account manager conveys the client's needs to the agency staff and presents the agency's solutions to the client. An account manager normally handles a number of accounts. In many cases, he or she has considerable knowledge and experience in the fields of business of those clients.

The creative director is the chief manager for creative services. He or she supervises the art directors, copy writers, and other creative professionals, either working for the agency or hired as subcontractors. Although the creative director may not perform creative activities for the clients, he or she will review the work done by subordinates and will approve the work before it is shown to the client.

An art director is the person responsible for developing the main illustrative concept for the marketing communication vehicle and for designing the look of the piece. He or she hires and supervises the work of photographers and graphics designers, who actually take the pictures and draw the illustrations. Although some larger agencies may have photographers and graphics artists on staff, in general they prefer to subcontract that work to freelancers who specialize in those disciplines. The art director will also hire other people, such as models and set builders, as the need on any specific project requires.

A copy writer is the person responsible for the words that are used. He or she works closely with the art director on projects. He or she plays a key role in developing the overall theme of the marketing communications vehicle, which will be expressed in headlines and body copy.

The production manager is responsible for turning marketing communications concepts into real physical pieces. He or she prepares materials for printing and works with commercial printers to print the pieces. He or she supervises the work while it is on press and approves proofs. It is the duty of the production manager to ensure that the finished job has been done correctly.

The media director determines which print or broadcast media are best suited for the client's advertising. He or she chooses the publications or radio or television stations in which the advertising will appear and develops a schedule for the advertising. In addition, he or she negotiates prices with the media and purchases the space or time. The director normally has a staff consisting of one or more media managers, who work on specific projects. In addition, an agency may have managers who handle specialized media, such as telephone directories.

The research director is responsible for conducting all marketing communications research for the agency. He or she, with the help of one or more research assistants, designs and conducts surveys of all types, focus groups, and advertising effectiveness studies.

The public relations director is responsible for developing public relations and publicity programs for the clients. He or she supervises one or more publicity writers, who write press releases, feature stories, and other public relations vehicles and who work with magazine and newspaper editors and others to place them in various media.

Like any business, agencies also have a number of administrative managers and support people who are responsible for the many business functions of the agency. These include accounting and billing personnel, purchasing agents, receptionists, clerks, secretaries, and mail room people.

CLIENT/AGENCY RELATIONSHIP

In many ways, the client/agency relationship is as intimate as the relationship between the salon customer and the salon staff. When you hire an agency, treat your relationship with the staff as a partnership. The agency people are experts in their fields. You are the expert in yours.

When you hire an agency, a creative team will be assigned to you. This team will consist of the account manager, an art director, and a copy writer, and other people as the need arises. For example, if you are working on advertising, the media director will be part of the team. If you are working on publicity, a publicity writer will be part of the team. There is one other very important member of the team—you. Your input and direction is as vital a part of the process as the agency's output.

A project starts with a meeting between you and the creative team. Here, you will discuss your needs and give the team members the information they need. They will ask questions and learn what they have to in order to understand your business. As the project progresses, there will be a number of other meetings, sometimes with the whole team, sometimes with just you and the account manager. At these meetings, you will be asked to clarify issues or to look at creative ideas. As always, your input is necessary.

Cooperate with your agency. Be open with the team members. Give them the information they need to develop effective marketing communications campaigns, and listen to their suggestions. That doesn't mean that you have to accept every idea they propose. But give every idea the consideration it deserves. In the creative process, there is give-and-take on both sides. Remember that you are as much a part of the team as the agency personnel working on your account. So feel free to make suggestions and to point out areas you don't like. But don't be overcritical. Give the team the opportunity to explain the reasoning and expected results of every idea, whether you like it or not. Some of the most creative and effective programs may come from ideas you didn't like initially.

On the other hand, do your part. Don't expect the agency people to read your mind. Have a clear idea of what you want to accomplish before starting the creative work. Then give the creative team members all the information they need to develop the programs. Their output can only be as good as the information you give them to work with.

The agency will usually present you with a number of options. Choose the one that meets your requirements and best suits your positioning. Once you and the agency have settled on a creative approach, don't change your mind unless something happens in your business that makes changing the approach necessary. Remember, agency compensation is normally based on time, so the clock is running while the team members are working on your account. When you change your mind, the agency will, in essence, have to start over again. But you'll still have to pay for the work that had been done.

It's the same situation you would face if you got into a taxi and told the driver to take you to the airport, and then halfway there you decide you want to go to the train station. The driver will be glad to take you there, but he or she won't wipe off the charges you've already accumulated on the meter.

There's another very important consideration in maintaining a good relationship with the agency. In fact, it's a major part of keeping a relationship with anyone you hire: Pay your bills on time. Remember that the agency is a business with bills to pay, just like your business. In many cases, the agency will have expended money on your behalf long before you get the invoice. The agency will buy printing services, photography services, print media space, and broadcast media time for you. It has to pay those bills whether you pay the agency or not.

FINDING A CREATIVE AGENCY

Look for a small, local agency that has experience in working with small businesses. Stay away from the large agencies that handle major corporations. If they accept your business at all, which is doubtful, they won't give it much attention. Get recommendations from other small businesses in the area. When you find likely candidates for your business, interview them and review their portfolios. See what kind of work they've done. More importantly, find out the results of the marketing communications campaigns they've run for other businesses.

If there is no suitable agency available to you, you might be able to utilize the services of freelancers. Again, ask other business owners in the area for recommendations. Contact your local colleges and universities. Some of their teachers or students may do freelance work. In some cases, you may be able to work out a barter arrangement with some of these people, in which you trade services for creative work.

In addition, you can often get help from your local media. If you are advertising in the local newspaper, for example, staff members will usually help you write the advertisement and give you assistance in measuring the results.

Wherever you find help, however, use it. Remember the caveat at the beginning of this section: Get professional help for your marketing communications. Your expertise is in salon management and operations, not in communications. If you're not an expert in this area, don't try to do it yourself.

SUMMARY

- A good marketing communications plan has a number of essential elements, including objectives, positioning strategies, specific tactics, message, measurement procedures, and budget. Objectives should be attainable and measurable. Strategies determine how you will reach the objective. Tactics are the specific actions you will take to make the strategy work.
- There are really only four kinds of marketing communications objectives. They are to inform, to interest, to persuade, or to sell.
- The first stage of customer acceptance is to inform your target audience about your salon and services. The primary vehicles for doing this are advertising and publicity.
- The second stage is to create interest in the salon and services. Advertising and direct marketing are the primary tools for this stage.
- The third stage is persuasion. You have to create a demand for the services you provide. As with the second stage, advertising and direct marketing are the primary tools.
- The sale is the fourth stage of customer acceptance. You have to get the prospective client to come into the salon and make the purchase. Sales promotion and personal selling are the

primary tools here, but advertising and direct marketing efforts can also be effective.

- There are two primary tools of strategy: positioning and message. Positioning conveys who you are; message conveys the benefits you have to offer.

- Tactics are the specific steps you take to transmit your positioning and message to your target audience. They include a vast array of advertising, direct marketing, and sales promotion vehicles.

- To make the most effective use of your communications dollars, you have to be able to measure and analyze the results you get. You also have to budget for your marketing communications.

- Marketing communications are complex. You need to understand communications processes, media, and psychology, and you have to be able to write and design effectively. Unless you're an expert in these areas, hire a professional.

- An agency helps you make money by providing you with effective communications that bring in customers. It operates on either a fee-based or commission-based compensation arrangement. Usually, the agency operates on a combination of both.

- Creative agencies have a number of staff functions, ranging from account supervisors and account managers to creative directors and art directors, copy writers, production managers, and media directors. Some may also have research directors and public relations personnel.

- Cooperate with your agency. Be open with the agency's team members and give them the information they need to help you. Listen to their suggestions.

- Look for a small, local agency that has experience working with small businesses. If you can't find a suitable agency, look for freelancers.

CHAPTER 10

Fundamentals of Design

Marketing communications is an art and a craft that requires years of study and practice, as well as innate talent. It is impossible to learn everything you have to know about the subject overnight. In almost all cases, you should be working with professionals to design and produce your promotional vehicles.

At the same time, however, you should understand enough about design and production that you are able to discuss programs intelligently with the people who are developing them for you. This understanding will make communication between you and them easier and more productive.

IMPORTANCE OF DESIGN

Good design is crucial to the success of any marketing communications vehicle. It is more than a matter of good taste or attractiveness. The overall design of the piece leads the eye through the document. It enhances the message and makes it more inviting. Good design also reduces "noise" in the message. It eliminates extraneous matter and makes it easier for the message to get through.

Paradoxically, the design has to be transparent. Even though the first thing the reader notices, at least on a subconscious level, is the overall design of the piece, if the design calls too much attention to itself rather than the message it carries, it is not doing its job. The primary task of the design is to carry the message and present it in the best light. The document exists to transmit the message, not to show off the design. Design is the tool of the message.

PRINCIPLES OF DESIGN

The computer has literally changed the face of marketing communications design. Powerful page layout programs, drawing and painting programs, and photo editing programs, along with easy access to thousands of typefaces, make it quick and easy for almost anybody to put documents together. And that has become a problem.

Making the task easier has not automatically made it better. Good design still requires knowledge, taste, experience, and talent. You still have to understand the principles that underlie good design and follow them. What the computer does is take the drudgery out of the process and allow more concentration on the design process itself. Because of the ease with which the designer can make changes and alterations, it is possible to develop far more options at lower costs than were possible with drawing board and colored marking pens.

The fact is, there is no one right way to approach design. Any project can take a number of different looks and still be effective. By looking at a number of different designs for your various marketing communications, you'll be able to find an approach that meets your needs exactly and projects both the message you want and the image you've set.

Cultivate a sense of design so you'll be able to recognize good design when you see it and so you can intelligently discuss design concepts with the communications professionals you hire.

First, read about design. There are a number of excellent books on graphics design on the market. Many of these can be found in the computer section of your local bookstore or in the book section of your local computer store. The various computer magazines usually have articles about design, also. Pay more attention to the design of various articles that come into your daily life.

Look at the ads you see in magazines. Study the direct mailers that come to your house or salon. Learn to observe what's around you. When you see something you like, analyze it and determine why it appeals to you. By the same token, when you see something you don't like, analyze it to determine why.

Start and maintain a file of marketing communications items that appeal to you. Make notes about them and attach the notes to the pieces. Go through the file periodically to get ideas and inspiration. You'll be surprised how quickly you will gain a basic understanding of good design.

The first step in the design process is planning. Like any other aspect of marketing communications, you have to have a plan before you start. The designer doesn't sit down at the computer and start designing. He or she has to develop a plan first.

Planning starts with a few basic decisions. What are the objectives for the project? You have to know what you want to accomplish. Who is the audience? You have to know who you're trying to reach. What media will you use? You have to know whether you want a newspaper ad, a direct mailer, a brochure, etc. Then you have to develop a design that looks like it belongs in the medium you've chosen. Simply put, if you want a brochure, make it look like a brochure, not like a magazine ad. What is your budget for the project? You have to know how much money you're willing or able to spend. Unless you have a clear idea of how much money you will allocate to the project it is very easy to design something that you can't afford to produce. Let your agency know how much money you've budgeted. That information will save you and the agency a lot of time and effort.

Even though you will most likely work with a creative agency, you should still learn to think like a designer. If you were a designer, here's how your thought process would go. No matter how much high-powered computer equipment and how many sophisticated software programs you have, the first actual design step is to sit down with a notepad and pencil and quickly sketch out a number of ideas. Put down every idea that comes to mind. At this point, don't edit or make judgments. Experiment with different combinations of text blocks and graphics and move them around to different locations on the page. Then sit back and compare the ideas. Now you can start to edit out ideas that don't work. Set aside all the ideas that do work. Then compare those again. Pick out the best two or three (or more) and use those as your basic direction. Now you can get busy on the computer (or at the drawing board) and refine those designs.

DESIGN CONSIDERATIONS

Regardless of the direction the design takes, there are a number of basic considerations to keep in mind. These hold true for any design, and they are summarized in Figure 10-1.

- Don't overdo design. Keep it simple. Make sure every element performs a function, and eliminate all extraneous material. If it doesn't move the message forward, leave it out. This is a very easy rule to violate, especially with computers. You have so many tools for manipulating text and images available that it is very easy to get carried away with them and lose sight of what you're trying to accomplish.

- **Simplicity**
  Don't overdesign
  Make every element count
- **Plenty of White Space**
  Provide eye relief
- **Relevance**
  Every element supports message
  Every element in proportion to its importance
- **Appropriate**
  Every element befits subject and image
- **Consistency**
  Integrate styles
  Have coherent look
- **Direction**
  Move reader through page easily
- **Contrast**
  Provide visual contrast
  Make page readable

Figure 10-1. Design considerations.

- Leave plenty of white space. Just because you have a number of square inches on the page doesn't mean you have to fill up every one of them. White space—that is, areas of the page that have nothing on them—provides eye relief and makes it easier to read the document. If it is easier to read, it will more likely be read.
- Make it relevant. Every element in the design, whether text or graphic, should have something to do with the message or with directing attention to the message. Each element should be used in proportion to its relative importance to the message. In other words, make the more important elements more dominant in the design.
- Make it appropriate. Every element in the design should be appropriate for the subject and for the image you're trying to project. Make sure each element fits into your overall look.
- Be consistent. Maintain a consistency of design among the various elements. Integrate the styles you use so that every element works with every other element.

- Give direction. Make sure the design directs the reader through the page in an orderly and coherent manner. Make it easy for the reader to navigate through the document. A good design provides a natural flow from one element to another.
- Provide contrast. Give visual contrast to the elements to create a more interesting look. If the elements are too similar in tone, size, or shape, the page will look drab and uninviting. Keeping the elements different makes the page more readable and more inviting to the reader.

There are two major elements used in any marketing communications vehicle. These are copy and graphics or, more simply, words and pictures. Every vehicle will have some words. Not every vehicle will have illustrations, but even in these, the words will be treated in such a way, through typographic treatment, that they will provide the functions of graphics. So there are graphic elements present even in those documents that have no pictures.

In addition, there are a number of specific design tools (such as grids, columns, rules, and boxes) that help accentuate and set apart the words and pictures. You also have to consider color, size, and shape. Just about all of these elements will be present in any well-designed marketing communications vehicle. How they will be used depends on the particular requirements of the vehicle. How they are put together is a function of the layout.

LAYOUT

The layout is the arrangement of the words, pictures, and other design elements on the page. It is an essential part of the overall design and determines how each element will interrelate with the others. It is how you organize the page. In multipage documents, layout provides a framework that coordinates a consistent look throughout the document.

Layout consideration starts with the size and shape of the page. Using standard size 8½-inch by 11-inch paper as an example, the layout can be horizontal, with the paper in landscape orientation (wider than it is long), or vertical, with the paper in portrait orientation (longer than it is wide). In the case of a spread, where two pages face each other, the layout covers both pages together rather than each page individually. Figure 10-2 shows various layout orientations.

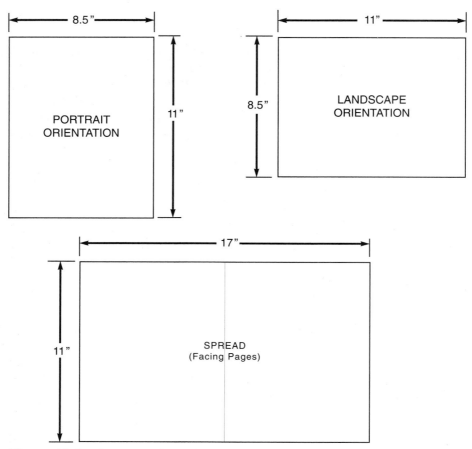

Figure 10-2. Layout orientations.

In addition to page orientation, layouts rely on a variety of other tools. These include grids and columns as well as margins and gutters. All of these affect the color of the page and the readability.

PAGE COLOR

Color in this context doesn't mean the hue. It means the overall density of materials on the page and is a function of column widths, margins, gutters, and the amount of white space available. (see Figure 10-3). The wider the margins and the more space between columns, the "lighter" the page. As margins get smaller and the space between columns decreases, the page gets "dark-

---

Garamond Book, 12 point type, justified, 14 point leading

Color in this context doesn't mean the hue. It means the overall density of materials on the page and is a function of column widths, margins, gutters, and the amount of white space available. The wider the margins and the more space between columns, the "lighter" the page. As margins get smaller and the space between columns decreases, the page gets "darker." Page color affects readability and contrast. Typography also affects page color.

Color in this context doesn't mean the hue. It means the overall density of materials on the page and is a function of column widths, margins, gutters, and the amount of white space available. The wider the margins and the more space between columns, the "lighter" the page. As margins get smaller and the space between columns decreases, the page gets "darker." Page color affects read-ability and contrast. Typography also affects page color.

Color in this context doesn't mean the hue. It means the overall density of materials on the page and is a function of column widths, margins, gutters, and the amount of white space available. The wider the margins and the more space between columns, the "lighter" the page. As margins get smaller and the space between columns decreases, the page

Garamond Book Condensed, 12 point type, justified, 12 point leading

Color in this context doesn't mean the hue. It means the overall density of materials on the page and is a function of column widths, margins, gutters, and the amount of white space available. The wider the margins and the more space between columns, the "lighter" the page. As margins get smaller and the space between columns decreases, the page gets "darker." Page color affects readability and contrast. Typography also affects page color.

Color in this context doesn't mean the hue. It means the overall density of materials on the page and is a function of column widths, margins, gutters, and the

amount of white space available. The wider the margins and the more space between columns, the "lighter" the page. As margins get smaller and the space between columns decreases, the page gets "darker." Page color affects readability and contrast. Typography also affects page color.

Color in this context doesn't mean the hue. It means the overall density of materials on the page and is a function of column widths, margins, gutters, and the amount of white space available. The wider the margins and the more space between columns, the "lighter" the page. As margins get smaller and the space between columns

decreases, the page gets "darker." Page color affects readability and contrast. Typography also affects page color.

Color in this context doesn't mean the hue. It means the overall density of materials on the page and is a function of column widths, margins, gutters, and the amount of white space available. The wider the margins and the more space between columns, the "lighter" the page. As margins get smaller and the space between columns decreases, the page gets "darker." Page color affects readability and contrast. Typography also affects page color.

Garamond Book, 12 point type, ragged right, 16 point leading

Color in this context doesn't mean the hue. It means the overall density of materials on the page and is a function of column widths, margins, gutters, and the amount of white space available. The wider the margins and the more space between columns, the "lighter" the page. As margins get smaller and the space between columns decreases, the page gets "darker." Page color

affects readability and contrast. Typography also affects page color.

Color in this context doesn't mean the hue. It means the overall density of materials on the page and is a function of column widths, margins, gutters, and the amount of white space available. The wider the margins and the more space between columns, the "lighter" the page. As margins get smaller and the

space between columns decreases, the page gets "darker." Page color affects readability and contrast. Typography also affects page color.

Color in this context doesn't mean the hue. It means the overall density of materials on the page and is a function of column widths, margins, gutters, and the amount of white space available. The wider the margins and the more space

---

Figure 10-3. Page color.

er." Page color affects readability and contrast. Typography also affects page color. This will be discussed later in this chapter.

GRIDS AND COLUMNS

Grids are a framework of nonprinting lines that let you define the basic structure of the page. They form horizontal and vertical guides that let you place either text or graphics precisely on the page and help provide consistency from page to page. Vertical grid lines let you set columns—vertical blocks that define the location of copy or graphics.

Most layouts use multiple columns, which can help make text easier to read. You can set almost any number of columns on a page. The more columns, however, the narrower each one is. The space between columns is also an important design consideration, as illustrated in Figure 10-4. Horizontal grid lines help align text from column to column, and help locate graphics.

TWO-COLUMN LAYOUT GRID

THREE-COLUMN LAYOUT GRID

FOUR-COLUMN LAYOUT GRID

Figure 10-4.   Layout grids.

MARGINS AND GUTTERS

Margins are the space left at the edges and at the top and bottom of a page. They allow white space around the borders of a page and provide eye relief. A gutter is the space between columns at the fold separating two facing pages. The size of the gutter depends on how the document will be bound. Some types of binding require more gutter space than others.

COPY

The English language, with some 600,000 words in its vocabulary, is one of the richest, most expressive languages on earth. It is the task of the writer to know which of these words to use and what order to put them in. And that is no simple feat. It takes training and talent to do this right. Almost anyone can put words down on paper. Few have the ability to write.

In any document, copy is indispensable. Words convey the message and express the ideas. Pictures support the words and illustrate the ideas. Design marries the two together to get the maximum effect. Words and pictures are like your eggs and bacon at breakfast. You get the most nourishment from the eggs, but the bacon makes breakfast taste better.

Words are used in a number of different ways in text, depending on the function each particular bit of copy has to perform. These various uses are illustrated in Figure 10-5.

HEADLINES

Headlines are short statements designed to attract readers' attention and entice them into reading the rest of the copy. They should state the major point of the piece so readers get the gist of the idea, whether or not they read the rest of the piece. Set headlines apart from the body copy by using a different typeface or making the type larger and heavier in weight. Limit the length of headlines to three lines, preferably less. Short headlines are more easily read and understood than longer ones.

In many ways, headlines are the most important part of the copy because they are the parts the reader sees and reacts to first. Write them so they have the impact they need.

Headline

- Attract reader's attention
- State major point
- Set apart from body copy

Subhead

- Transition statement
- Guide reader
- Introduce new thought

Kicker

- Introduce headline

Body Copy

- Main text
- Contains message

Pull-Quote

- Short extract from main text
- Add visual interest
- Call attention to a point

Sidebar

- Add further information about a point
- Explain a point

Caption

- Describe or explain contents of photograph or illustration

Figure 10-5.   Copy functions.

SUBHEADS

Subheads are short transition statements that can guide the reader from the headline to the body copy or can be inserted within the body copy to introduce new thoughts. They add visual interest to a page by providing contrast and breaking up large blocks of copy. A subhead should be set in either a different typeface or in a larger size and weight than the body copy, but it should be smaller than the headline type size.

KICKERS

Kickers are short statements that introduce a headline. They should be differentiated from the headline by using a smaller typeface. Use kickers sparingly. They are not often necessary and can confuse the issue as often as they clarify it.

BODY COPY

The body copy is the main text of the document. It contains the message of the communications vehicle. Set body copy in a readable typeface and size. Text set in columns is more readable than text set in one large block.

Cover all the points that have to be made to convey the message. Sell the benefits, not the features. Use proof statements to verify the benefits. Use testimonials if you have them. And don't forget to ask for the order.

Make the copy as long as it has to be, but omit any extraneous copy. Don't use any words that don't have to be there. Just because there are many words in the English language doesn't mean you have to use them all. Write to the audience you're trying to reach. Use language they'll understand. Even if you happen to be writing to Ph.D. physicists, use mostly short words and short paragraphs. Remember, keep it simple and to the point.

PULL-QUOTES

Pull-quotes are short statements extracted from the main text and given prominence by setting them in a different typeface and placing them in the margin or in a box within a column. They can be used to add visual interest to a page and to call attention to a particular point. Pull-quotes should be kept short.

SIDEBARS

Sidebars perform the same function as pull-quotes but are longer blocks of copy. They can be used to explain a particular point or to add further information about the subject. Differentiate the sidebar from the body copy by setting it in a separate box. Use a different typeface or a halftone screen to give it visual contrast.

CAPTIONS

Captions describe and embellish the contents of a photograph or illustration. Behind only headlines in reader importance, captions are the second most widely read of any copy element. Align captions with the artwork they describe. Set them in a different typeface and size to differentiate them from the body copy. But don't ignore captions. They play an important part in increasing the effectiveness of the printed piece.

TYPOGRAPHY

Typography is the treatment of the words on the page. It is concerned with the look of the page, its overall color as it were, as well as its readability and legibility. The way you use type can have a significant effect on the overall look of the document. It can also affect the feel of the piece because the style of type you choose can convey an attitude or a tone as well. Typographic considerations include the type family—that is, the typeface—style and weight, size and case, word and letter spacing, alignment, and column width.

Readability and legibility are two different aspects of typography. Readability means the ease with which long blocks of copy can be seen and understood. Legibility means the ease with which the reader can recognize individual letters. Both are important to comprehension. Serif typefaces, especially oldstyle faces, tend to be more readable, which is why they are generally more suited to long blocks of copy. Sans serif faces, because they are more distinctive, tend to be more legible, which is why they are generally more suited to short copy that needs to attract immediate attention, such as a headline.

FONTS

Before computer typesetting, when type was individually cast in lead as separate letters, the term *font* referred to one size of a particular typeface (for example, 12-point Helvetica Bold Italic). Each size and style constituted a separate font. With the advent of desktop publishing, the term *font* came to include all of the letters, numbers, punctuation marks, and other characters in all sizes of a particular typeface. There are thousands of fonts available, each designed to convey a unique expression of mood and clarity. Typeface choice is extremely important in achieving the effect you want your document to have. The wrong typeface can send the wrong message, even though the words are correct. You wouldn't, for example, use a whimsical typeface when you're trying to set a serious tone.

There are a number of categories of typeface design. The most common are serif and sans serif. Others include decorative, script, and a host of special-purpose typefaces. Some typefaces and styles are illustrated in Figure 10-6.

- **Serif Typefaces**

This is Times Roman in 14-point size.
This is Palatino in 14-point size.
This is New Century Schoolbook in 14-point size.

- **Sans Serif Typefaces**

This is Avant Garde Book in 14-point size.
This is Optima in 14-point size.
This is Helvetica Medium in 14-point size.

- **Script Typefaces**

This is Berthold Script Medium in 18-point size.

- **Display Typefaces**

This is Hobo in 14-point size.

- **Decorative Typefaces**

This is Birch in 24-point size

- **Gothic Typefaces**

This is Linotext in 18-point size.

Figure 10-6.   Sample typefaces.

Serif typefaces have small strokes, called serifs, at the ends of each letter. The serifs come in a variety of weights and sizes and help provide direction to the type by guiding the reader's eye from one letter to the next. Thus, they increase readability and legibility because letter forms are more recognizable. They are especially legible in small type sizes. For this reason, serif typefaces are most often used for body copy.

Serif typefaces can be further categorized as oldstyle, modern, and slab serif. In oldstyle faces, so named because they were designed to resemble Roman inscriptions, the serifs are thin and pointed. Letters tend to be open and round with relatively even stroke weight. Caslon and Garamond type families are examples of oldstyle faces. Modern typefaces, which were first designed two centuries ago, have thin, straight serifs. The letters have highly contrasting stroke weights, varying from thick to thin. The Times Roman family is an example. Slab serif typefaces have thick, square, straight serifs. Letters have even stroke weight. The Clarendon type family is an example.

Sans serif typefaces, not surprisingly, don't have serifs. They are slightly less readable than serif typefaces, especially in long body copy. Sans serif faces are often used for headlines, subheads, captions, pull-quotes, and similar pieces of copy. These typefaces have a simple, elegant look that make them attractive in larger type sizes, but they require more white space and leading (space between lines) for best readability.

Decorative and script typefaces are more ornamental than utilitarian. They are used more for their ability to set a tone than for readability. Because they are harder to read, they should be used sparingly, and rarely for long blocks of copy. Script faces, especially those in which the letters are connected, mimic handwriting and can be used to convey more informal messages. They can be used, for example, for sales letters, to make the letter seem more personal.

Dingbats are special fonts consisting of symbols, such as bullets, stars, asterisks, etc., that can be used to call attention to lists or as design elements on a page. In addition, there are a number of special-purpose fonts for technical and scientific use, or with Greek or Cyrillic characters.

TYPE STYLES

Most typefaces are available in a number of styles as well. A typeface, in all sizes with all of its related styles, makes up a type family. Each style, however, is a separate font within that type family. Thus, Times is a type family. Times Roman is a font within that family. Times Bold Condensed is another font within that family. Style refers to the ways in which the letters vary in stroke and weight. Different styles are used to convey emphasis or contrast to the page. The styles, in ascending order of weight, are ultralight, light, book, medium, demibold, bold, heavy, ultrabold, and ultra-heavy. In terms of letter shape, styles include roman, italic, and oblique. Roman, also called plain, is the normal upright styling of text. Italic is slanted and curved. Oblique is slanted. There is a difference between italic and oblique, although many people use them interchangeably. In addition, type styles can include shadow, underline, and outline. These styles can be used to add emphasis or as decorative elements, but they should be used sparingly. Some type styles are illustrated in Figure 10-7.

Souvenir Family of Type Styles

This is Souvenir Light.
This is Souvenir Medium.
This is Souvenir Demi.
This is Souvenir Bold.

Stone Serif Family of Type Styles.

This is Stone Serif Regular.
This is Stone Serif Regular Italic.
This is Stone Serif Semibold.
This is Stone Serif Semibold Italic.
This is Stone Serif Bold.
This is Stone Serif Bold Italic.

Helvetica Family of Type Styles

This is Helvetica Light
This is Helvetica Regular.
This is Helvetica Oblique.
This is Helvetica Bold.
This is Helvetica Bold Oblique.
This is Helvetica Black.

Figure 10-7.   Type styles.

SIZE AND CASE

Type height is measured in points. One point is 1/72 of an inch. The larger the point size, the larger the type. A 72-point letter would be approximately one inch tall. It would actually be somewhat less than one inch because point size is measured from the baseline and allows for the shoulder of the type block. Figure 10-8 shows a number of point sizes. Another factor in type measurement is the X-height of the font. This is the height of all the lowercase letters that don't have ascenders or descenders. X-heights can vary widely from one typeface family to another, with the result

10 point	18 point	24 point	48 point
Avant Garde	Avant	Avant	Av
Souvenir	Souvenir	Souve	Sou
Helvetica	Helvetica	Helvet	Hel
New Century	New Ce	New Ce	Ne

Note the difference in size of typefaces with the same point size.

Souvenir 12-point size

Type size is an important design consideration.

New Century Schoolbook 12-point size

Type size is an important design consideration.

Figure 10-8. Type measurement.

that the same point size of each family can look larger or smaller on the page. Typefaces with large X-heights are more legible and tend to give a page a darker color. Typefaces with smaller X-heights are more readable and tend to give a page a lighter color.

Type families also have fonts of varying widths, which can be specified as normal, condensed, compressed, or expanded. Normal width is the standard width and is used most often for body copy. Condensed width squeezes letters by changing the width of the letter so more can fit on a line. Compressed width squeezes letters even more. Expanded width stretches letters out so fewer fit on a line. Note that in these widths, it is the width of the letter that is changed, not the space between letters. That is a function of letter spacing.

LETTER AND LINE SPACING

The spacing between letters and lines also affects the look of the page—its color, readability, and legibility. Although the basic spacing is set as part of the design, page layout programs allow a lot of adjustments in these attributes, with tracking, kerning, and leading controls, as shown in Figure 10-9.

Overall spacing between letters in a word is controlled by tracking, a set of spacing specifications set by the designer to achieve the look intended. Tracking changes are global. Increasing or decreasing tracking changes the spacing between all of the letters in the document. Space between two individual letters is controlled by kerning. Letter pairs are kerned to make them fit together better.

The space between lines of type is controlled by leading (pronounced led-ing), which derives its name from the narrow strips of lead that were inserted in type forms to adjust space when using hot melt type. Leading is measured from the baseline of one line to the baseline of the next line. Normally, leading is set as a percentage of the point size, usually 20 percent higher. So, for example, type set in 10-point size would have 12-point leading. However, leading should be adjusted for greater readability and legibility, especially with typefaces with larger X-heights. Leading also affects the color of the page. Increasing leading lightens the page; decreasing leading darkens it.

Letters can also be either uppercase or lowercase. Capital letters are uppercase. The names come from hot melt typography,

TRACKING

Tracking controls the overall spacing between letters.

When tracking is loose, letters are spaced farther apart. (+10)
When tracking is normal, letters are spaced normally. (0)
When tracking is tight, letters are spaced closer together. (–10)

KERNING

Kerning controls the space between pairs of letters and is used to give certain letter pairs a better appearance.

Normal Kerning	Tight Kerning	Loose Kerning
AV	AV	AV
TA	TA	TA

LEADING

Leading refers to the space between lines of type.

10/12

Leading controls the space between lines of type. It derives its name from the narrow strips of lead that were inserted in type forms to adjust space when using hot melt type. It is measured from the baseline of one line to the baseline of the next line.

10/10

Leading controls the space between lines of type. It derives its name from the narrow strips of lead that were inserted in type forms to adjust space when using hot melt type. It is measured from the baseline of one line to the baseline of the next line.

10/14

Leading controls the space between lines of type. It derives its name from the narrow strips of lead that were inserted in type forms to adjust space when using hot melt type. It is measured from the baseline of one line to the base-

Figure 10-9. Tracking, kerning, and leading.

when fonts were kept in compartmented trays called cases. Capitals were kept in the top tray, the upper case, and the other letters were kept in the bottom tray, the lower case.

Long lines of uppercase type are hard to read. For maximum readability, use a combination of upper- and lowercase letters.

ALIGNMENT AND COLUMN WIDTH

The number of columns on a page, their width, the space between the columns, and the alignment of the type all affect the feel of the document, its color, and its readability and legibility.

The more columns you have on a page, the narrower each must be. The narrower the column width, the smaller point size you can use for the type. People tend to read by looking at all the words on a line rather than by concentrating on each individual word. Eight words per line are an optimum number for readability and comprehension. Use a point size that gives you approximately eight words per line.

There are four alignments for type in a column, as shown in Figure 10-10. These are flush left, flush right, centered, and justified. Most body copy is set either flush left or justified, which makes for easier reading. Centered and flush right copy are seldom used except for special effects. They are not as readable because the eye doesn't easily find the beginning of each line.

EFFECTIVE TYPE USE

As the preceding discussion shows, typography can be complicated. Yet few design factors can have such a profound effect on the overall success of your marketing communications vehicle.

Choose typefaces that convey the mood and tone you're trying to achieve. Just because you have a lot of typefaces available doesn't mean you have to use them all. As a general rule, limit the number of typefaces you use in any document to no more than three. More than that gives the piece a jumbled, chaotic appearance. Choose typefaces that work together, and don't overuse decorative typefaces.

Pay attention to the color of the page. Don't make the page too dark or too light. And allow plenty of white space. Keep readability and legibility in mind. Remember, your ad, brochure, letter, or whatever won't do you any good if people can't read it.

Flush Left	Justified
There are four alignments for type in a column. These are flush left, flush right, centered, and justified. Most body copy is set either flush left or justified, which makes for easier reading. Centered and flush right copy are seldom used except for special effects. They are not as readable because the eye doesn't easily find the beginning of each line.	There are four alignments for type in a column. These are flush left, flush right, centered, and justified. Most body copy is set either flush left or justified, which makes for easier reading. Centered and flush right copy are seldom used except for special effects. They are not as readable because the eye doesn't easily find the beginning of each line.
Flush Right	**Centered**
There are four alignments for type in a column. These are flush left, flush right, centered, and justified. Most body copy is set either flush left or justified, which makes for easier reading. Centered and flush right copy are seldom used except for special effects. They are not as readable because the eye doesn't easily find the beginning of each line.	There are four alignments for type in a column. These are flush left, flush right, centered, and justified. Most body copy is set either flush left or justified, which makes for easier reading. Centered and flush right copy are seldom used except for special effects. They are not as readable because the eye doesn't easily find the beginning of each line.

Figure 10-10.   Type alignment.

GRAPHICS

Graphics are the pictures that support the words. They can take the form of photographs, illustrations, charts and graphs, or a host of other graphic devices that add interest and visual contrast to a page. And remember, typography can also be used as a graphic device.

Which type of graphic you use will depend on the situation you face and on your needs. Each type has its particular uses and its advantages and disadvantages. All types can be very effective when used properly. You can see examples of all of these graphics used in the various illustrations in this book.

PHOTOGRAPHS

Photographs provide realistic representations to depict events and ideas conveyed in your message. Because they are perceived as being realistic, they have a credibility that illustrations don't share.

A good photograph can add greatly to the effectiveness of a marketing communications vehicle. A bad photograph, however, can destroy it. A photograph should be well composed and properly exposed. It should be in sharp focus, with good contrast and brightness. And it should tell a story that illustrates the point you are trying to make.

Photographs can be manipulated to fit into your overall page layout by enlarging or reducing to fit. And they can be cropped. Cut out all extraneous matter in the photo, but don't eliminate relevant details. You can also adjust brightness and contrast and retouch imperfections. Computer programs provide the ability to alter photographs substantially. However, there may be ethical or copyright problems if you alter a photograph so much that the subject is distorted.

Photos are available from a variety of sources. You can take them yourself, if you have the expertise. Or you can hire a professional photographer to take them to your specifications. You might also use stock photography.

When you use a stock photograph, you are, in effect, renting that photograph from a company that specializes in providing such images. Stock photography houses have libraries of photographs of all subjects. You tell the firm what subject matter you need. It searches through its data banks and then sends you a number of photographs that fit that subject. You choose the one that fits your needs and return the rejects. When you're finished with the picture you've rented, you return it.

This can be a rather expensive proposition, although it is usually cheaper than hiring a professional photographer. The price of a stock photo depends on how you are going to use it. If you're using it in an advertisement, for example, you'll pay more than if you were using it to illustrate a magazine article. And for the price, you only get to use the photograph one time. If you have other uses, you have to pay more fees. Remember, the photograph and the rights to use it belong to the stock photo house.

The rise of desktop publishing has given birth to another alternative. There are software companies that sell sets of stock photographs on CD-ROM disks. You choose from a catalog of subjects and then purchase the disks for that subject. For the price, you have almost unlimited use of the photos. Although these collections don't have the breadth or sophistication of the offerings in stock photo house libraries, they are often more than adequate for certain uses.

Before you use a photograph, make sure you have a model or property release for subjects shown. And make sure you have the written permission of the photographer. Never use a photograph for which you don't have the rights. It could cost you thousands or even hundreds of thousands of dollars.

ILLUSTRATIONS

Illustrations can be drawings or paintings used to portray realistic or abstract concepts. Like photographs, they can help communicate your message or convey an idea in conjunction with the copy. Illustrations are especially useful for setting a mood, where the realism provided by a photograph isn't appropriate or necessary. Since they are created by an artist, they can stretch the imagination to represent ideas the way you would like them to be rather than the way they are.

Like photographs, good illustrations work well. Bad illustrations are worse than useless. Unless you are a talented illustrator, you will have to have your illustration drawn professionally. It is conceivable that you could take an acceptable photograph. It is not likely you could draw an acceptable illustration.

Although illustrations can be very effective, they are also usually very expensive. It costs a lot of money to hire an artist. And it takes time to conceive and execute a drawing or painting. But there is an inexpensive alternative. That is to use clip art, which is similar to stock photos. Clip art comes in collections grouped by subject matter. It is professionally drawn and available from a wide range of sources. Some clip art collections come packaged on floppy disks; others come on CD-ROMs. They are available in black and white and in color. Clip art can vary in quality. There are inexpensive packages, and there are more costly collections. As with most things, you get what you pay for.

What you are paying for in any collection is a group of professionally drawn images which you have the right to use in a variety of ways. Some collections have more restrictions on use than others, so read the fine print before you use any clip art.

Clip art can be versatile. You can use the images as they appear, or you can manipulate them readily. You can reorient them, flip them from one side to another, change their color, use only parts of the image, or perform any other manipulation that your drawing or painting program lets you do. You can also combine images to create different looks. Figure 10-11 shows some representative clip art.

Figure 10-11. Clip art.

There is a danger, however. Clip art is so easy to use that it is very easy to use badly. So be careful and choose images that work in your vehicle. Then use them with imagination.

CHARTS, DIAGRAMS, AND TABLES

Charts, diagrams, and tables illustrate information. They are best used to show numerical data. They can illustrate trends and comparisons and do a good job of showing relationships. As such, they are a valuable adjunct to copy, often giving life and excitement to cold and drab facts and figures.

Charts are best for showing trends and comparisons. They can take the form of pie charts, bar graphs, or line graphs. You could use a pie chart to show how each service you offer contributes to your overall business, for example. Or use a bar graph to show your business compared with your competitors. You might use a line graph to show the increase in your business over time.

Diagrams are best to show relationships and sequences of events. Thus, you might use a diagram to show the layout of your salon and illustrate where one service center is located relative to another.

Tables offer an efficient method of comparing data. A simple table can often convey numbers more quickly and more understandably than trying to present the same information in words.

OTHER GRAPHIC DEVICES

Other graphic devices include rules, boxes, borders, screens, and drop shadows, all of which can be used to highlight or to set apart a text or graphic element.

Rules are horizontal or vertical lines that can be used to separate one item on a page from another or as a design element. They can have varying line weights, from very thin to very thick, depending on how they are used.

Boxes and borders are frames that hold blocks of copy or graphics. They can be used to delineate boundaries for their contents or to separate the contents from other elements on the page. Boxes totally enclose their contents. Borders sometimes physically enclose their contents, but can often be suggested by the illusion created by the edges of text blocks or graphics. Borders tend to be larger than boxes. Both can have lines of varying widths.

Screens and drop shadows highlight boxes. A screen is a tint of a color, measured in percentage of that color, which serves as a backdrop for copy or art work that is set apart from other copy in a box. Sidebars, for example, are often set apart by boxes and screens. A drop shadow is an outline set behind a box that gives the illusion that the box is floating off the surface of the paper.

EFFECTIVE GRAPHICS USE

Graphics can add considerably to the effectiveness of your marketing communications. You have a wide range of graphics types to choose from, but keep in mind a few guidelines. Don't overdo graphics. Use them sparingly, and don't try to put too many of them in any one document. Make sure the graphics and text work together. Each should support the other, although the text should take precedence. Don't mix different types unless you have to. Be careful of spacing. Leave enough white space to separate graphics from text.

Be judicious in your use of stock photography and clip art. And whatever photographs and illustrations you use, make sure you have the rights to use them.

COLOR

We live in a world of color. Most of the communications we see are in color: color television, color photos in magazines, and even newspapers are using color photos more and more. The reason is simple: Color attracts attention. It also establishes mood and evokes emotions. There are many psychological overtones associated with color.

An object's color depends on the wavelength of the light reflected from it or transmitted through it. Red letters on a page, for example, appear red because they absorb all wavelengths of visible light except for red, which they reflect back to the eye. A piece of yellow stained glass transmits only the yellow wavelengths and absorbs the rest. If the object absorbs all of the visible light, it will be black. If it reflects all of the visible light, it will be white.

Colors are discussed in terms of their hue, value, and intensity. Hue refers to the color itself (for example, green, yellow). Value refers to lightness or darkness (for example, light green, dark yellow). Darker values are sometimes called shades; lighter values are sometimes called tints. Intensity refers to a color's brightness or dullness. Shiny colors appear more intense than matte finish colors.

Colors also have temperature—that is, they can be thought of in terms of warm, neutral, or cool. Colors containing a predominance of red or yellow tend to be warm; those containing a predominance of blue or green tend to be cool. White, gray, and black are neutral.

These aspects of color—hue, value, intensity, and temperature—are important considerations when choosing colors to use in your marketing communications. Although colors can be combined in almost limitless numbers, not all combinations are pleasing. Some combinations are harmonious; others clash.

A color wheel, available from art supply stores, can help you choose appropriate color schemes, whether they are monochromatic, complementary, analogous, or triadic. A monochromatic color scheme consists of one color with varying values. A complementary color scheme consists of two hues directly opposite each other on the color wheel. An analogous color scheme consists of three colors next to each other on a color wheel. Each of these colors will contain some of the primary color. A triadic color scheme consists of three equidistant hues on the color wheel.

There is also a definite psychology of color, both in how colors are perceived and in the moods they evoke. Color is as much a factor of human perception as it is a physical concept. People see colors differently. A shade of red, for example, will look different to a person with blue eyes than it does to a person with brown eyes. In addition, a given color is seen differently depending on the context in which it is viewed. Thus, a bright red dot on a lighter red field would appear more intense than it actually is. However, that same bright red dot on a darker red field would appear less intense than it actually is.

Light or bright colors appear to come forward, or advance. Dark or dull colors appear to move backward, or recede. This perception of color is sometimes used to create the illusion of more or less space. So you can utilize color to give your marketing communications vehicle a different look and feel. Likewise, some colors reflect their hue into adjacent areas, giving those areas overtones of that hue.

The psychological effect of color has long been known. Different colors are associated with different states of emotion. We are "blue" when we feel sad; we are "green" with envy; we refer to a coward as "yellow"; or we "see red" with anger. The color used can have subtle effects on mood and behavior. Green, for example, is soothing and tranquil. Blue promotes a feeling of spaciousness. Yellow is cheerful and stimulating. Red calls for attention and action.

Color should be an important consideration in design and can be used effectively in a number of ways. It can be used as an accent, or to highlight text or graphics. Type can be set in various colors for emphasis. Any of the graphic devices discussed earlier can be used in color. Also remember that color means more than hue. Black and white are also colors.

Color can add considerable cost to a project. It can be used either as spot color or process color. These production aspects will be discussed later in this chapter.

SIZE AND SHAPE

The size and shape of your marketing communications are also factors in their design and effectiveness. Regardless of the vehicle you choose, you have a lot of flexibility with these factors, although you have more leeway with direct marketing vehicles than with print advertisements.

With print advertisements, your choice of size and shape is constrained by the physical limits of the page in the medium you use. Even here, however, you have choices. When you place an ad in a magazine or newspaper, you purchase a block of space, usually a rectangle measured either in column-inches or in fractions of a page.

Be creative with the space. Make your ad stand out from the others that might be on the page. Just because you have a rectangle of space doesn't mean your ad has to be in the shape of a rectangle. If other advertisers have rectangular ads, make your ad a circle. Or a diamond. As long as you stay within the limits of the space you purchased, you can do this. Use the space to give your ad a different look. Or stretch the rectangle. Make it long and thin or short and wide instead of in proportion to the page size. Check with the magazine or newspaper, though, before you commit to a particular shape.

When it comes to direct marketing materials, especially direct mailers and brochures, your options are virtually unlimited. Your imagination and your pocketbook are the major limitations. Nothing says that a printed promotional piece must be in multiples or fractions of an 8½-by-11-inch piece of paper. Odd sizes and shapes can attract attention to the vehicle. And this is good, as long as the message doesn't get overwhelmed by the design.

As with any aspect of design where there are a lot of choices, just because you can make a piece any size or shape you want doesn't mean you have to. There are good reasons why certain sizes and shapes have become standards.

One reason is reader expectations. People are used to certain sizes and expect to see them. Business letters are expected to be a certain size. Books and magazines are expected to be a certain size. We are mentally and physically prepared to handle printed items of a certain size. Look at the filing cabinet in your office. The drawers are sized for 8½-by-11-inch paper. Look at the papers in the various file folders. You'll find that they are mostly this standard letter size. Test yourself. What do you keep? Chances are you keep the standard size documents. What do you throw away? Chances are you discard those documents that don't fit into your filing system.

Another reason is economy. In the United States, paper is sold in standard sizes based on the 8½-by-11-inch letter size. The more you utilize multiples or fractions of that size, the less expensive the piece will be. When you deviate from this standard, you incur costs for cutting and special handling. So, stick with standard sizes and shapes unless you have a good reason for going outside those boundaries. But don't be afraid to stretch these limits when you have to.

SUMMARY

- Good design is important to the success of any marketing communications vehicle. It gives more support to the message. And it reinforces your image for quality.
- It is necessary to understand and use good design principles. There is no one right way to design any project. There are always a number of options you can choose, but any of those options must follow sound design principles to be effective and attractive.
- You have to plan design. The process starts with some basic decisions, such as the objectives for the project, the audience it is intended to reach, the media that will be used, and the budget.

- There are a number of basic design considerations. Keep it simple. Leave plenty of white space. Make it relevant and appropriate. Be consistent. Give direction to the eye. Provide contrast.
- Copy and graphics are the key parts of any marketing communications vehicle. You can't do the job without words and pictures. Also important, are color, size, and shape.
- The layout is the arrangement of words, pictures, and other design elements on the page. Layout factors include page orientation, page color, grids and columns, and margins and gutters.
- Copy is indispensable. Words can be used in a number of ways, including as headlines, subheads, kickers, pull-quotes, sidebars, and captions, in addition to the major use as body copy.
- Typography, or how the words are presented, affects readability and legibility, as well as the overall look of the document.
- There are thousands of fonts available, including serif fonts sans serif fonts, and decorative, script, and dingbat fonts.
- Fonts are available in a number of styles as well. These include normal, bold, and italic styles, as well as a large number of variations on these themes.
- Size of type is measured in points. A point is approximately 1/72 of an inch. The larger the point size, the larger the letter. Widths can vary. A type style can be normal, condensed, compressed, or expanded.
- The spacing between letters is controlled by kerning and tracking. Kerning controls the space between individual pairs of letters. Tracking controls the overall spacing between letters in large blocks of copy. The space between lines of type is measured in terms of leading.
- Type can be aligned flush left, flush right, centered, or justified. Column width is a factor in determining what point size should be used.
- Graphics can take the form of photographs, illustrations, charts and graphs, or other kinds of elements.
- Charts, diagrams, and tables are ideal for presenting numerical information, especially for showing trends, comparing one item with another, or illustrating the flow of various processes.
- Other graphic devices include rules, borders, screens, and drop shadows, all of which can accent a page or highlight text or other graphics.

- Color is also a major design element and can be used to attract attention to a document or to highlight particular elements. Colors also have psychological implications. You can use either spot color or process color.
- In print advertising, you have to live with the parameters set by the publication. With direct marketing vehicles, you have much more flexibility. So use size and shape effectively to attract attention.

CHAPTER 11

Fundamentals of Production

Design is only part of the creative activity required to get your marketing communications vehicles into the hands (and minds) of your prospective clients. Production is the other part. Up to this point you only have an idea, not a tool. It's not the idea that will help you promote your business. It takes the reality of the tool to do that. You get no benefit from the idea until the idea becomes reality.

Production is just as important as design. The finished piece is what the prospects will see. They'll never see the work that went into the design. All of their impressions and attitudes will be formed by the end result, so it has to be good. The best design in the world can be ruined by poor production. You have to spend just as much time and effort on this phase of the communications process as you do with any other. Like the other phases, you must have an understanding of the production process so you can discuss your needs with your agency or printer.

THE PRODUCTION PROCESS

The production process starts at the preproduction stage, with a finished layout, from which a mechanical or other camera-ready art is made. The art is photographed to produce film negatives, which are used to make printing plates. At the production stage, the plates are put on the printing press and the job is printed. Before printing is actually started, however, a series of proofs are generated. These are reviewed and approved by the client before printing continues. The postproduction phase comes after printing, when the job goes to the bindery, where finishing operations such as die cutting, folding, and trimming are completed. The finished job is delivered to the client. Figure 11-1 shows the production process.

Virtually every marketing communications project will go through this general process. Specific steps may or may not be taken, depending on the job requirements. The responsibility for any step may vary. For print advertisements, for example, the

241

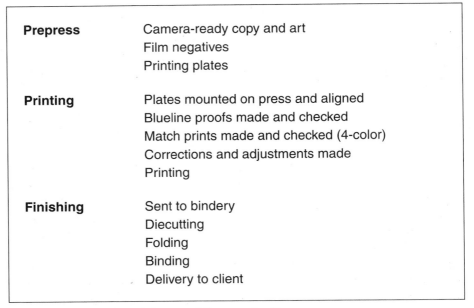

Prepress	Camera-ready copy and art
	Film negatives
	Printing plates
Printing	Plates mounted on press and aligned
	Blueline proofs made and checked
	Match prints made and checked (4-color)
	Corrections and adjustments made
	Printing
Finishing	Sent to bindery
	Diecutting
	Folding
	Binding
	Delivery to client

Figure 11-1. A breakdown of the production process.

agency or client responsibility stops with the production of camera-ready art. The publisher is responsible for printing, finishing, and distribution. For a direct mail brochure, the agency and client may be responsible throughout the entire process.

PREPRODUCTION PHASE

As mentioned earlier in this chapter, the layout shows the design and placement of the copy and graphics on the page. Before the layout can be used, it has to be converted to finished art that can be used to make printing plates. Until computers revolutionized publishing, this was a laborious and time-consuming process in which type was set into columns called galleys and art was sized and photostatted. Then the galleys and art were painstakingly cut apart and pasted into position on a piece of artboard. If more than one color was used, the artist had to make overlays on acetate film and attach those to the mechanical. Each color required a separate overlay. The resulting product was called a mechanical. The mechanical was photographed to produce negatives for making the printing plates.

The computer has made the process faster, more accurate, and less expensive. Now the layout artist can position type and graphics on the page with keyboard strokes and mouse motions. No overlays for various colors are needed. The computer outputs the finished layout to a computer disk, which goes to a machine called an imagesetter. The imagesetter can print the page as a positive copy that can be photographed, or it can print directly as film negatives ready for the plate-making process. New printing technologies that let the process go from computer disk directly to printing plates have been introduced and will probably become widely used once the technology has become established.

The film negatives are attached to photosensitive sheets of aluminum or plastic and exposed to ultraviolet light. When developed, the aluminum or plastic sheets become the printing plates, which make the actual impressions on the paper.

PRODUCTION PHASE

The production phase starts once the plates have been inspected and attached to the press. First, the plates are used on a proofing press with special paper used to make a blueline. A blueline is a proof copy that resembles the final form of the document, except that type and photos have a blue cast to them. (Hence, the name blueline.) The blueline is approved by the client before the job proceeds.

The blueline shows the position of all the elements and can be used for proofreading copy. It does not show color. If color is involved, the printer will make color proofs with color proof presses. These have to be checked for color fidelity.

During the make-ready part of the process, the printer mixes inks, checks the plates for alignment, and gets the paper ready. When the proofs have been approved, the job can be run.

POSTPRODUCTION PHASE

After the job has been run on the press, the printed sheets are sent to the bindery, where all the postproduction steps are taken. These include folding, binding, and trimming to size. It may also include die-cutting operations or other special production factors, depending on what the job requires. Once this phase is complete, the job is inspected and delivered to the client.

PRINTING PROCESSES

Most marketing communications vehicles will be printed in one form or another. There are a number of printing processes in wide use, although three are most important for these applications: letterpress, gravure, and offset lithography. Each has its advantages and disadvantages. Which one will be used on any given job will depend on the requirements of the job.

All three of these printing processes utilize presses, which may be sheet-fed or web. Offset and gravure presses are rotary. Letterpress presses can be rotary, flat-bed, or platen.

Sheet-fed or web presses are characterized by the paper they use. Sheet-fed presses use paper in cut sheet form. The sheets of paper are stacked at the feed end of the press and fed through the press one sheet at a time. Web presses use huge rolls of paper. The paper goes through the press and is not cut into sheets until after it is printed. Web presses are much faster than sheet-fed presses and are most suitable for printing large quantities of material. Web presses are not usually economical unless the quantity exceeds 50,000 copies. Newspapers and magazines are usually printed on web presses. Brochures, on the other hand, are normally printed on sheet-fed presses, as quantities are usually relatively small.

In rotary presses, the plates are attached to cylinders that rotate as the paper passes through. In flat-bed presses, the printing plates are attached to flat surfaces that are lowered onto the paper to make the impression, in much the same manner as you would use a rubber stamp.

LETTERPRESS

Letterpress is the oldest form of printing. It is the process developed by Gutenberg in the mid-1400s, used by Benjamin Franklin in colonial America, and still used today. It has been considerably refined, of course, but it is essentially the same process.

Letterpress is a relief process, in which the ink-bearing surfaces of type and art are raised above the non-ink-bearing surfaces. It is the only printing method that uses cast metal type. Plates must have raised surfaces to carry the ink. In letterpress printing, the ink is applied to the raised surfaces of the plates. The plates are then pressed onto the paper and deposit the ink.

Letterpress is an economical method of printing and is best for printing relatively short runs of documents that are heavy on copy but have few graphics. It is a versatile method in which changes can be made relatively easily and inexpensively, so it is also good for documents that change often, such as printed price lists.

GRAVURE

Gravure, also called intaglio printing, is the opposite of letterpress. Whereas the ink-bearing surfaces of a letterpress plate are raised, the ink-bearing surfaces of a plate for a gravure press are recessed, forming almost microscopic cups that hold the ink. The cylinder that holds the plate rolls through a bath of ink. Excess ink is scraped off the nonprinting surfaces, leaving the little cups full. As the paper passes the plate, the ink is transferred to the paper.

Gravure printing produces work of excellent quality and is especially good for reproducing graphics. Even type is treated like a graphic. Gravure plates are expensive, however, and changes are difficult to make. The process is best suited for high-quality reproduction, especially of color subjects, and is most economical for large runs. Newspaper Sunday comics and magazine sections are commonly printed this way.

OFFSET LITHOGRAPHY

Offset lithography is the most commonly used of the three major printing methods and uses a process different from the other two. It is a transfer process that relies on the principle that oil and water don't mix. The offset plate has no raised or depressed surfaces. Both the printing and nonprinting areas are on the same level.

The ink-bearing surfaces, which will print the image, are treated to resist water and attract oil. The nonprinting surfaces are treated to resist oil and attract water. As the cylinder rotates, the plate first passes a roller soaked in water. The water stays on the nonprinting areas and drains off the other areas. Next, the plate passes a roller that holds the ink. The ink, which is oil based, sticks to the areas that will print and is repelled from the nonprinting areas. The plate then transfers the ink to a rubber blanket. The rubber blanket transfers the ink to the paper.

This method of printing is very good for both type and art. It is a versatile process that can be used for long as well as short runs. It also works well on a variety of paper types and surfaces. Offset lithography is the major printing method used for marketing communications materials such as brochures, direct mailers, and books. It is more economical than the gravure process, but more expensive than letterpress. Making changes can be costly, since it will be necessary to make new plates, although offset plates are less expensive than gravure plates. Depending on the number of copies to be printed, plates can be made of aluminum or plastic.

ALTERNATIVE PRODUCTION PROCESSES

No matter what process you use, printing is expensive. It is a labor-intensive business, from the preparation of plates, to the make-ready operations, to the printing itself. Time is money. Materials aren't cheap, either. Paper is expensive and is getting more so every week.

But much of the cost of printing is at the front end, in the set-up and make-ready. Once the press is rolling, the costs come down. So the major cost lies in producing the first piece. The larger the run, the less expensive the unit cost of each piece becomes. So the more pieces you print, the more economical the process is.

As a hypothetical example, take an eight-page, four-color brochure printed by a commercial printer. To print 1,000 copies might cost $1,500, for a unit cost of $1.50. But to print 5,000 copies might cost $2,000, for a unit cost of $0.40. Quite a difference. If you only wanted 100 copies, the cost might still be $1,500, for a unit cost of $15.00. The extremes can be that different.

But what if you don't want large quantities? Fortunately, there are some alternative methods of production that may work in some cases. There are times, though, when only the quality of fine printing will suffice. Then you'll just have to bite the bullet and pay the costs.

HIGH-SPEED DUPLICATING

Many franchise quick-print shops and office supply chains offer high-speed duplicating services. At these places, you can get copies inexpensively. For many applications, the quality of the duplication is very good, especially for simple circulars and sales letters. Unless you have to reproduce complex art work or photographs, this service may offer an acceptable option.

The copies are made by xerography, utilizing copy machines capable of high resolution and speed, and are economical to use for quantities up to about 1,000. Costs can be as low as 1.5 cents per copy.

COLOR XEROGRAPHY

Many of these quick-print outlets also have copy machines capable of producing copies in color. Although the color reproduction is not as good as that attainable through printing processes, for many applications it could be useful, especially when quantities are low. Costs for color copies can be about $1.00 per copy.

COMPUTER PRINTERS

For very short run jobs, a laser or ink jet printer hooked to your computer may be all you need. High-resolution laser printers are now available that can reproduce copy and art at a quality approaching what you can get by printing. Color laser printers are now coming on the market, although they are still expensive and the quality of the printing can be marginal.

However, there are also a number of color printers utilizing ink jet, thermal wax, or dye-sublimation technology that are capable of color reproduction of very good quality. Although the output may be good, these machines are slow, making them unsuited to the production of large quantities of printed materials. If you need only a few pieces, though, they may offer a very affordable alternative.

If you have a laser printer, there is another possibility. There are a number of firms that offer predesigned and preprinted papers meant to be used in a laser printer. Using templates provided by the company, it is possible to fit your message into the space provided and then turn out finished brochures, newsletters, letters, and other materials that look as though they were printed. The wide array of designs available let you enjoy the advantages of color and graphic design inexpensively.

SILK-SCREEN PRINTING

One other printing process you may encounter is silk-screen printing. In this process, a piece of fine-mesh cloth is stretched tightly in a frame and then coated with a photosensitive emulsion. The negative is placed on the frame and exposed to light. When the emulsion is developed, the emulsion in areas exposed to light washes off and becomes the printing area. The emulsion in the areas not exposed to light hardens and becomes the nonprinting area.

The screen is placed in contact with the object to be printed. Ink is forced across the screen surface with a squeegee and penetrates the exposed areas.

This process is widely used to print on a variety of plain and textured surfaces, as well as on other than flat shapes. T-shirts, for example, are printed by silk-screening, as are bottles. Silk-screen printing is also used for posters. The process is capable of producing work of very high quality, whether in a one-color or four-color process. When you purchase advertising specialty items, they will most likely be printed this way.

REPRODUCING PHOTOGRAPHS AND GRAPHICS

For the most part, printing copy is easy. The ink either goes on the paper or it doesn't. Most type is reproduced in one solid color, generally black on white or on other colored paper. Graphics, especially photographs, are another story.

Except for line art, which is art work drawn in simple black lines with no shades of gray, black-and-white photographs and drawings are continuous tone. They consist of a range of gray tones that extend from pure white to solid black. The printing press can only print in one solid color. It can't reproduce tones. Think of the printing process as a light bulb on a switch. The light is either on (the ink touches the paper) or it is off (the ink does not touch the paper). If you want to vary the amount of light coming out of the bulb (vary the tone of the image), you have to install a dimmer switch.

Fortunately, there is a dimmer switch of sorts that allows the reproduction of continuous tone graphics. It is called a halftone screen and, in essence, is a means of tricking the printing press into thinking that it is printing the graphic in one solid color. Look at a photograph in a newspaper or magazine through a magnifying glass. You'll see that it consists of a bunch of black dots, some closer together than others.

When the continuous tone graphic is photographed onto the film from which the printing plate is made, it is exposed through a clear piece of film on which a gridwork of dots has been printed or etched. Dark areas of the photograph or graphic are reproduced as closely spaced dots. Light areas of the photograph or graphic are reproduced as dots spaced farther apart. When the graphic is printed, ink is deposited only where there are dots. At normal viewing distance, the eye connects the dots and the brain believes it is looking at a continuous tone picture. It's all an illusion, but it works.

Halftone screens are measured in lines per inch (lpi). The finer the screen (that is, the more lines per inch), the better the reproduction. If you compare a newspaper photo with a magazine photo, you'll see that the newspaper photo is made up of larger dots. That's because newspapers use a coarse screen, usually between 60 and 80 lines per inch, to allow for the absorption of the ink in the more porous newsprint. Magazines typically use screens around 133 lines per inch, which reproduce well because they print on coated paper stock that doesn't absorb ink readily.

Before you can print a photograph or other continuous tone graphic, it will have to be converted to a halftone screen. Similarly, if you want to print copy on a lighter-toned background to set it apart from other type, as with a sidebar, you would specify the background as a screen. In this case, the screen is measured as a percentage of black. A 10 percent screen would be very light; an 80 percent screen would be very dark.

For the most part, the printer will take care of preparing halftones. However, some page layout and graphics programs can convert continuous tone materials to halftones and capture the results digitally on disk. In that case, the printer can work directly from the disk.

COLOR

Color reproduction presents its own unique problems and requires careful consideration for the printing process. There are special concerns involved in translating the colors the designer sees on the computer screen to the colors the printer will be able to reproduce on paper. The colors may not be exactly the same, because colors on the screen are generated by an additive color process. Printed colors are generated by a subtractive color process.

In nature, white light is produced by mixing all seven colors of the visible spectrum. However, in the computer, white light is produced by mixing only three primary colors of light—red, green, and blue, or the RGB color model. Mixing these primary colors of light in various ratios produces virtually any other color. The process is somewhat different when mixing inks together.

Unlike the colors of light, the primary colors in pigments are cyan, magenta, and yellow. Complementary colors are made by mixing two primary colors in equal quantities to produce green (yellow + cyan), red (yellow + magenta), and blue (cyan + magenta). In theory, mixing equal parts of cyan, magenta, and yellow would produce black, just the opposite of the RGB color model. In practice, however, since the pigments contain impurities, mixing the three colors together produces only a muddy dark brown. To get a true black, printers add black ink. Four-color process printing, then, utilizes the CMYK model (for cyan, magenta, yellow, black).

Different light sources have different color casts, depending on the color temperature of the source. Incandescent lamps, for example, tend toward the red end of the spectrum; fluorescent lights tend toward the blue end. Even daylight changes color. Depending on the time of day and weather conditions, daylight color can vary from red to blue. So the way color is perceived in a document can change depending on the light the reader sees it under. Printers usually adjust colors to appear most accurate under high-daylight conditions. In the print shop, they use special light sources that simulate the 5,600° K (Kelvin) temperature of daylight.

In marketing communications documents, color is normally used either as spot color or as process color. Spot color is the use of a particular color as a solid block or as a screen. Thus, if you wanted to add a splash of color to a document, a headline in red type, or a logo printed in green, you would use spot color. The printer mixes the ink to the required spot color and applies it to the paper by means of the plate generated for it. There can be as many spot colors in a document that the designer wants, but there has to be a separate printing plate for each one.

If you are reproducing full-color illustrations, however, you utilize process color. The color image is broken down into its four component colors—cyan, magenta, yellow, and black—and a printing plate is made for each. Each of the colors has its own halftone screen. On paper, the dots form patterns to produce the illusion of full color. Look at a color photo in a magazine under a magnifying glass and you'll readily see the dots. In some cases, spot colors are also reproduced by the four-color process.

Printing color requires more sophisticated printing presses. Black and white materials can be printed on single-station presses. There is no concern about registration, since the paper passes by only one cylinder. With color, there has to be a separate printing station for each color. A two-color press would have two stations, each with its own cylinders. Black ink is fed into one, the spot color ink into the other. A four-color press would have four stations, one for each of the process colors. The paper passes through a number of cylinders, making registration critical. Even tiny imperfections in registration can destroy the job.

Four-color printing requires a precision not necessary with black-and-white, or even most two-color printing. That's why it is so much more expensive.

PAPER

No matter what your production method, the medium will most likely be paper. There are a great number of choices. The paper you choose can have a great effect on the quality and appearance of your project. It can also have a major effect on the cost of the project.

Paper manufacture is one of the oldest industries in existence. Modern paper machines are complex and expensive. Capital equipment costs can run into the many millions of dollars. And the machinery is huge. One papermill, for example, has a paper machine that, if it were stood on end, would be as long as the world's tallest building, the Sears Tower Building in Chicago. Manufacturers around the world use the latest state-of-the-art machinery and modern high-tech chemicals. For all that, however, the basic process is still pretty much the same as it was more than 2,000 years ago.

The basic raw material of paper is wood pulp, formed by grinding, boiling, chemically treating, and bleaching wood from trees. The paper-making machine has three sections: the wet end, the press section, and the drying section. The pulp is mixed with water to make a slurry. Additives are added to impart desired characteristics to the finished paper. The slurry is put into the wet end of the machine, where it is distributed evenly on a continuously moving, fine-mesh wire belt. Suction pulls off the excess water, and the pulp fibers start to mingle as the slurry moves through the machine.

When the slurry reaches the press section, it is carried on a felt belt, where it passes through rollers that press the embryonic paper, removing more water and flattening the surface of the sheet.

From this section, the belt carries the paper through the dryers—huge, steam-heated rollers that remove the rest of the water. The paper then goes through calenders, polished steel rollers that press the paper down to its final thickness and smoothness. At the dry end of the machine, the paper is rolled into huge rolls that are stored until they go to the cutters. If the paper will be coated, the coating is applied before the paper is rolled.

PAPER CLASSIFICATIONS

Paper is made in a variety of finishes, weights, grades, and textures, depending on how it is intended to be used. It can be coated or uncoated. Uncoated papers are used as they come out of the machine. They are suitable for applications, such as newspapers, stationery, and copy machines. Coated papers have smoother surfaces that are less absorbent, so they are better for reproducing halftone screens. The surface is treated with a coating made of clays and pigments, with other additives to give other desired characteristics.

Other finishes are antique, eggshell, vellum, machine finish, and English finish, which describe their overall smoothness. Antique is the roughest finish; English finish is the smoothest. Paper can be made even smoother by supercalendering it (pressing the paper between two highly polished steel rollers). Coatings also add smoothness.

Paper is also classified by grade—that is, its intended use—and basis weight—that is, the weight of one ream (500 sheets) of its basic size. The basic size is the trimmed size as the paper is sent to the distributor, and it differs from grade to grade. Figure 11-2 lists the grades and sizes. Paper grades are bond, coated, text, cover, book, offset, index, label, tag, and newsprint.

Bond paper is the type used for stationery and ordinary typing paper. It is sold in 17-inch by 22-inch sheets, which can be cut into four 8½-inch by 11-inch pieces. Coated paper, as mentioned earlier, is used for halftone reproduction and high-quality applications, where gloss and smoothness are required. Coated, text, offset, and book papers are all sold in 25-inch by 38-inch sheets. Book paper is used in books. The more expensive text paper is used in brochures and announcements, especially where coated paper is unnecessary. Offset papers are made specifically for use on offset lithography printing presses. Cover, index, and tag papers are thicker and heavier stocks, designed for the use their names imply. Newsprint is about the least expensive grade of paper and is made specially for use in newspapers and other printed items meant to be read once and thrown away.

Grade	Sheet Size	Principal Uses
Bond	17 × 22	Stationery, typing paper
Coated	25 × 38	Halftone reproduction, high-quality printing
Text	25 × 38	Brochures, announcements
Cover	20 × 26	Booklet covers
Book	25 × 38	Books
Offset	25 × 38	Offset printing
Index	22.5 × 35	Index cards
Tag	24 × 36	Tags
Newsprint	24 × 36	Newspapers

Figure 11-2. Paper grades.

Many of the grades are available in a variety of colors and textures, as well as in other basic sizes. They are also made in a variety of basis weights. The higher the basis weight, the thicker the paper. So, for example, you can have 20-pound bond, 67-pound cover, etc.

PAPER CHARACTERISTICS

The printer is concerned with the printability and the runnability of the paper. Printability refers to the ease with which ink adheres to the paper surface and the print quality of the finished piece. Runnability refers to the ease with which the paper moves through the press. The designer is concerned with the appearance and feel of the paper. It has to look attractive and project a quality feel to the piece. Everyone is concerned with the price.

Characteristics that affect runnability are flatness and moisture content. If the paper is wrinkled or wavy, it will not feed properly. If it is too dry or too wet, the printer can have problems with static electricity or sheets sticking together, both of which can cause press jams. The paper stock also has to be trimmed properly, so it is square, and it has to be free from dirt, either on the surface or embedded in the fibers.

There are a number of characteristics that affect printability. Color is one of these. White can mean anything from brilliant blue-white to dull yellow-white. Colors reproduce best on paper that has a neutral white cast. Brightness and gloss are also important characteristics. Brightness refers to the brilliance or sparkle of the paper. Gloss affects how the ink film will look. Opacity can be critical, especially in thin or low-basis-weight papers. The paper has to be opaque enough that printing on the other side of it doesn't show through. Smoothness is also a factor in quality of printing. The smoother the paper, the better looking the print.

With a publication advertisement, of course, you don't have a choice in paper. The ad will appear on whatever paper stock the publication uses. Knowing what paper the publication uses, however, can help your designer tailor the ad to fit the circumstances. For example, you wouldn't worry about fine-screen halftones if the ad is printed on newsprint.

The paper you choose for your direct marketing project, however, can make or break its effectiveness. It can also break your pocketbook if you're not careful. Generally speaking, you pay more as the smoothness or the thickness increases. You'll also pay extra for color and texture. Coated papers are more expensive than uncoated papers. Use the best paper you can afford, but make sure it's appropriate for the application. You wouldn't use expensive coated stock for a handbill. Nor would you use newsprint for a complex four-color mailer. Let your printer know your budget and let him or her suggest paper stocks. Printers often carry a "house paper" that has very good characteristics. If you specify a paper the printer has to go out and buy, it will be much more expensive.

CHOOSING AND WORKING WITH A PRINTER

There are two general types of printers you or your creative agency will work with: commercial printers and quick-print shops. Both have their uses.

Commercial printers can usually handle larger scale or more sophisticated projects, especially when you need four-color process work. They are also usually more expensive than quick printers. In addition, many of them can handle prepress operations, such as high-quality scanning and typesetting. They also offer proofing services.

Quick printers are geared more to simple, short-run jobs that can be done without extensive prepress work. Their facilities can be somewhat limited. Many can't handle four-color process work, but they can do an adequate job on black-and-white or two-color printing, although some of the large, franchised quick-print outlets are getting surprisingly sophisticated equipment and expertise. These places also often offer high-speed duplicating and color copying services. They cannot normally offer you the range of expertise you get from a commercial printer, however. But they are usually less expensive and may be suitable for printing many of your projects.

You may also deal with a service bureau. A service bureau is a business that acts as an intermediary between the computer designer and the printer. The service bureau takes material on computer disks and converts it to film. Some service bureaus can also do high-quality scanning and halftone screens. Some printers operate their own service bureaus.

Get to know your local printers. They can be valuable assets for you. Involve the printer early in the project. If the printer knows what you have in mind, he or she can often give you money-saving suggestions you can implement before you get to the camera-ready copy stage. Don't wait until you have camera-ready art to approach the printer.

Work just as closely with your printer as you do with your creative agency, even when your agency is handling production. Give the printer all the information he or she needs to do the job. Let the printer know what you expect, your budget, and your deadlines. Then give him or her time to do the job.

Then do your job. Approve proofs promptly. Don't make the printer wait, with his or her press tied up, while you make up your mind. Remember, with printers, time is money. Presses are scheduled weeks in advance. Your job will have an assigned time slot to run. If you're not ready, the press will sit idle and the printer will have to juggle schedules. And that's going to cost you money. Respect the printer's scheduling.

Examine proofs carefully. Make sure everything is correct before you give the proofs back to the printer. Once you've approved the proofs, you have to live with any mistakes.

Make changes judiciously. Make sure the job is ready to go before you take it to the printer. Check it for mistakes before printing starts. The later you make changes, the more expensive it will be. If the printer makes a mistake, he or she will fix it without charge. If you make it, however, expect to pay for it.

SUMMARY

- The production process starts at the preproduction stage, moving from finished layout to camera-ready art work. This is converted to film, from which printing plates are made. Then it moves to the production phase, in which the plates are installed on the press, proofs are made and approved, and the job is printed.
- After printing, the project moves to the postproduction phase, in which the printed sheets go to the bindery for cutting, folding, binding, or other finishing steps.
- The computer has made the production process faster, allowing design and layout to be sent to service bureaus or printers who can convert digital information on a computer disk into camera-ready art or directly to film.
- At the production phase, proofing is a vital step. Before the job can be printed, samples are made in the form of bluelines and, where needed, color proofs. These have to be checked thoroughly and approved before the process can continue.
- Letterpress is the oldest form of printing and is still in use. This process is ideal for documents that contain mostly type.
- Gravure is the opposite of letterpress. Instead of printing from impressions made by raised type, gravure uses recessed printing areas.
- Offset lithography uses flat plates in which the printing area attracts oil and repels water and the nonprinting area attracts water and repels oil. The ink is transferred to a rubber blanket, which transfers the image onto the paper.
- High-speed duplicating is good for many applications, such as circulars and sales letters, which are not heavy in graphics. Small quantities of color documents may be reproduced on color copiers, which offer adequate quality for many applications. Computer laser and inkjet printers may also be used for producing very small quantities of materials. Color printers for computers can also be used. Silk-screen printing is useful for printing on textured or irregular surfaces, such as T-shirts or bottles.
- Although printing copy is easy, printing continuous tone graphics is not. The printing process can only work with solid color ink and has no ability to reproduce shades of gray. The process used to do this is called halftoning, in which the graphic is photographed through a clear film etched with a

series of dots. The dots are close together in dark areas, far apart in light areas. When printed, the result gives the illusion of continuous tone.

- To print in full color requires the use of four different color inks—cyan, magenta, yellow, and black—which combine on the page to create the illusion of full color. Each color is halftone screened and requires its own separate printing plate and press printing station.
- The choice of paper can be crucial to the success of a project. For publication advertising, the publication chooses the paper. But for direct marketing vehicles, the designer has to choose.
- Paper comes in a variety of finishes, grades, and weights, each designed to perform a particular job. There are bond and off-set papers, newsprint and card stock, as well as many others.
- Runnability refers to the ease with which the paper can move through the press. Important characteristics are flatness and moisture content, as well as trimming and dirt. Printability is concerned with the appearance of the piece. Important characteristics are brightness and gloss, color, and opacity.
- There are generally two kinds of printers—commercial printers and quick-print shops. Quick printers are good for small, relatively unsophisticated jobs. Commercial printers are best for large jobs and for printing in four colors.

CHAPTER 12

Advertising

The remaining chapters detail the marketing communications tools available to you. Even though, for the purposes of this book, they will be discussed separately, in the real world, all of these tools work together and many of the techniques presented here overlap. There are elements of technique that are common to all, although they are presented in the section most appropriate to their use, to aid in clarity and comprehension. Thus, for example, many aspects of the message in advertising hold true for direct marketing vehicles and sales promotion, just as do positioning concepts and the necessity of knowing your audience. As you go through each of these chapters, keep in mind that few, if any, of the techniques presented here are limited solely to that tool.

The preceding chapter covered fundamentals of design in general terms. The remaining chapters discuss design concepts in particular and practical terms and show how those concepts apply to specific marketing communications tools.

OVERVIEW OF ADVERTISING

An advertisement is a paid public notice designed to call attention to a product or service with the intent of persuading the people it reaches to form a favorable opinion of the item and to purchase and use it. It can take many forms and accomplish many things. Advertising is the process you employ to develop and use the advertisements.

Advertising is both an art and a science. It can be considered a science, although an inexact one, because it utilizes scientific principles of communication and psychology. It can be considered an art because it requires creativity and imagination to accomplish successfully. Advertising is a means of communication, a marketing tool, and a means of persuasion.

In 1958, McGraw-Hill, one of the major trade magazine publishers in the United States, ran the advertisement shown in

Figure 12-1. Although designed for industrial audiences, the ad nevertheless illustrates the value of advertising effectively and succinctly. It shows just what advertising does.

Advertising vehicles differ from direct marketing and other marketing communications vehicles in their reach. An advertisement takes a shotgun approach to its audience in that it is usually targeted to larger, less specific groups of people rather than to more

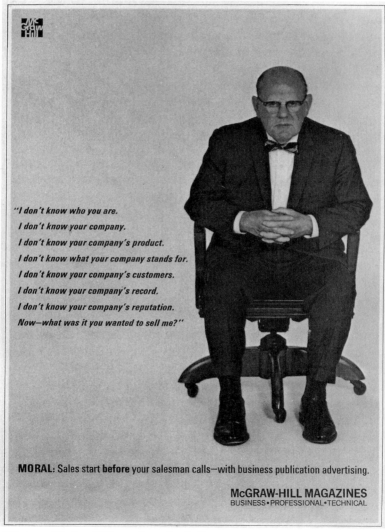

Figure 12-1. Why advertise? (Reprinted with permission from McGraw-Hill, Inc.)

specific groups or individuals. The media in which the advertisements run, whether print or broadcast, send the message out,
reaching large numbers of people in the process. The advertiser has
the ability to reach segments of the population through judicious
choice of media, but it does not necessarily have the ability to tailor
the message to individuals within those segments. As a result, a
portion of the people who see or hear the advertisement fall outside
the audience to which the ad is targeted. The degree to which this
is true depends on how widely or narrowly the medium is targeted.

Think of a fishing boat as an analogy. When you go fishing,
you put your hook (the advertisement) into the water (the medium)
and wait for the fish (prospective customers) to come to you. You
don't know exactly which individual fish will bite. But you can try
to attract certain kinds of fish (your target audience) by changing
the bait (the advertising message) you use and by fishing in waters
(the medium) where you know the fish you want live. The fish
have a lot of hooks to choose from, and they may not necessarily be
looking for food.

ADVERTISING OBJECTIVES

For most small business owners and managers, the ultimate objective for advertising is to increase sales. Advertising can help do
that, thus making an important contribution to profits. But it is only
part of the selling process. Consider a sale as a ladder with seven
rungs, as illustrated in Figure 12-2. On the lowest rung, you make
the initial approach to the prospect, saying in effect, "Here I am."
On the second rung, you create awareness, saying "Here is what I
do." On the third rung, you awaken interest, saying "Here is what
I can do for you and this is how you'll benefit." On the fourth rung,
you instill a preference for your services, saying "Here is why you
should come to me and not my competitors." These four rungs con-
stitute the principal tasks of advertising.

The fifth and sixth rungs are different. On the fifth rung, you
make an offer to the prospect, saying "Here is the deal." On the
sixth, you close the sale, saying "Buy this." These rungs are the job
of personal selling, not of advertising.

Advertising picks up again, however, on the seventh rung. By
the time you've reached this top rung, you've made the sale. Now
the job is to develop customer loyalty. Here you are saying, in
effect, "Thank you for buying. I have satisfied your needs. Please

Figure 12-2.   Sales ladder.

come again." Advertising can be a big help to you here, but it can't do the job by itself. Whether or not the customer keeps coming back is a direct result of his or her satisfaction with your services. Advertising can bring a customer into your salon the first time. After that, it can only reinforce the customer's attitude. If you haven't satisfied the customer's needs, no amount of advertising in the world can bring him or her back.

It is evident, then, that advertising does a number of things for your salon. It creates awareness of your services among your target audience by letting those people know you exist. Awareness is the first step toward purchase. No one will patronize your salon if they don't know you're there. Advertising establishes an image for your salon among your target audience. It tells those prospects that you are a quality salon and are worth their patronage. Advertising creates a demand for your services among your target audience. Once those prospects know you exist, advertising tells them why they should patronize your salon. Advertising changes the attitudes and buying habits of your target audience. It woos the prospects away from their current salon and brings them to you. And advertising reinforces the buying habits of that part of your target audience whose business you've captured. It tells them that they've made the right choice and keeps them coming back to you.

First, you have to catch their interest, so they'll read or listen to your ad. This is difficult. As noted in Chapter 9, people are subjected to oceans of advertising every day. Commercial messages of one kind or another bombard people seemingly constantly. Test it for yourself. Pay close attention next time you listen to the radio or watch television. Count how many commercials you hear or see in one hour of programming. Note how many commercials are bundled together. To a great extent, people tune out advertising. So your ad has to stand out so it cuts through the clutter and impinges on the mind of the recipient. Then you have to tell the audience what you want them to know, in terms that are meaningful to them. Finally, you have to give them good, solid reasons why they should come to you instead of to your competition.

ADVERTISING EFFECTIVENESS

To be effective, advertising must perform three tasks: It must attract, inform, and entice. Advertising can't work if no one sees or hears it.

1. The first task of an advertisement is to capture the prospects' attention and interest. It has to make the prospects stop and pay attention to the message, while competing with all the other things on their minds. This is not an easy job in today's high-volume, media-rich environment, which bombards people with virtually countless messages of all types.
2. The second task is to inform the prospects about the benefits and features of the product or service, and give them the necessary data to make a decision either to purchase the goods or to ask for more information.
3. The third task is to entice the prospects, to persuade them that they need and want the product or service, and invite them to take the next step and purchase the goods.

An advertisement will be effective to the extent it reaches the audience you have targeted, is attractive and memorable, and has objectives that can be measured and if the products referred to in the ad deliver what the ad has promised. Although no one can give an absolute guarantee that an advertisement will be successful, if all of these conditions are met, there is a very high probability that the advertisement will do the job for which it was designed.

KNOWLEDGE OF AUDIENCE

With advertising, as with most aspects of marketing, you must know your audience. You cannot develop your message and target your advertising if you don't know who your audience is. What are their characteristics? What are their beauty needs? What approaches are likely to appeal to them? Go back to your marketing plan. Extract the information from that to determine who you want to reach. Conduct research, if you have to. Don't shortchange this part of the process. Advertising directed to people outside the parameters you've set for your potential clients is money wasted. If you can't identify your audience, how will you decide which media to use to reach them?

KNOWLEDGE OF MEDIA

The media you choose to reach your audience must correspond to their reading and listening preferences and must be accessible to them. If you know the demographics of the people you're trying to reach, you can find media that are designed to appeal to them. There are, for example, countless magazines devoted to specialized subjects. Radio stations broadcast programs designed to reach certain audiences. You wouldn't run a commercial on the local talk radio station, for example, if your demographic and psychographic research showed that your audience listens to golden oldies.

It is also necessary to make sure the audience has access to the media you choose. If your potential clients live or work in a certain area, you need to choose media that service that area. If your salon is located in a large city, for example, you probably would be better off buying space in a neighborhood weekly than a large daily newspaper that covers the entire city and suburban areas. Although your prospects may, in fact, read the daily, it reaches far more people than you want, so you could be wasting money you could put to better use in the smaller paper.

FREQUENCY

You must also run the advertisement enough to make sure that people see or hear it and that it stays in their memories. You can't run an ad once and expect to reap any benefit from it. The frequency of the advertisement—that is, the number of times you run the ad and the time interval between insertions—plays a large part in its effectiveness.

Not every member of the reading or listening public sees every issue of a publication or hears every episode of a radio or television program. So at any given time, there is a lot of missed audience for any medium. If you only run your ad once, your message will not get to those members of the audience who happened to miss that insertion that day. To ensure that you reach the maximum number of potential clients in your audience, you have to run the ad a number of times.

The other aspect of frequency is getting the audience to remember the advertisement. Numerous studies have shown that people forget advertisements very quickly. Much of the experimental data on memory is credited to Dr. Hermann Ebbinghaus, a German psychologist who was a pioneer in the field of memory research. He developed the Ebbinghaus Forgetting Curve, which graphs the rate at which information is forgotten. As the curve in Figure 12-3 shows, forgetfulness occurs rapidly at first and then progresses more slowly. After one day, we retain only 34 percent of what we've learned. After one week, we retain only 24 percent. And after three weeks, we retain only 21 percent. However, the more we are exposed to a bit of information, the more of it we retain. The more often you run the advertisement, therefore, the more it will be remembered. Also, the shorter the amount of time between insertions of the advertisement, the more it will be remembered, simply because the reinforcement of the message in the prospect's mind will be stronger.

Once you've developed an advertisement, let it run long enough to work without changing it. There is a tendency to stop running one ad and use a new one long before it is necessary to do so. The reason for this is familiarity. You have spent so much time and effort to develop the ad, and you've seen it so often, that you quickly become tired of it and want to create something new. Just because you feel that way about the ad, however, remember that your target audience hasn't seen it that often and hasn't had time

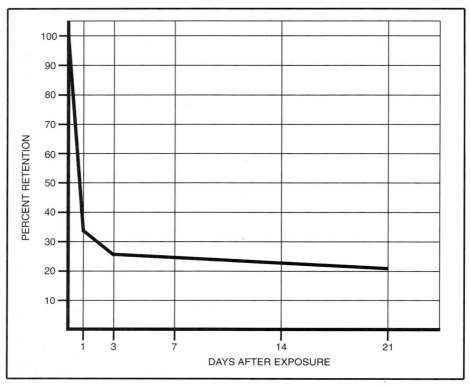

Figure 12-3.   Ebbinghaus curve.

to get tired of it. As long as the advertisement is meeting its objectives, keep running it.

There are only two reasons to change an advertisement that has been running successfully—if the objectives change, or if the ad stops working. If you change your objectives or something happens that makes the ad no longer valid, you will have to change it. By the same token, if the ad stops doing the job it's supposed to do, there is no reason to keep running it. It's time for a new ad. If you are measuring the results of your ad, as you should be, you will know when it no longer works.

Even when you scrap an ad, don't discard it completely. Salvage the basic themes that have worked for you and reuse them. Sometimes it's not necessary to build a new ad when just some refurbishment might do. By the same token, don't make the mistake of falling in love with your ad and becoming so enamored with it that you keep running it long after it has outlived its usefulness.

Be objective when you analyze the results of an advertising campaign. Make advertising decisions with your head, not your heart.

ADVERTISING MEDIA

Advertising takes many forms and utilizes a number of different media. Each medium is designed to reach different objectives, depending on the composition and location of the target audience, the ability to reach certain audiences, and cost. For your salon business, some types are more useful and cost effective than others, although at one time or another you may find use for most of them.

No one medium will accomplish everything you want. You may need to advertise in a number of print or broadcast media to get the most effective reach and results. And you will most likely use advertising along with other marketing communications tools, such as direct marketing, publicity, and aggressive promotion. You need to utilize a good mix of tools. The number of advertising vehicles you can use is limited only by your imagination and your pocketbook.

Keep your message consistent in all the media you use. Make sure the message is user oriented. That is, make sure it appeals to your audience and meets its needs and desires. Sell the benefits, not the features of your services.

WORD OF MOUTH ADVERTISING

In many ways, word of mouth advertising is the most effective form of advertising there is, especially for a service business such as a beauty salon. It has a credibility no other form can match. It is the least expensive form of advertising because it is unpaid. But it must be earned. Word of mouth advertising depends on your reputation, and you can't buy that. You have to offer quality services and good value for the customers' money to get the loyalty that will make your clients want to tell others about you. You also have to make sure they're satisfied, so they tell others how good you are, not how bad you are.

Don't rely on word of mouth advertising to do the whole job. It won't. Remember, statistics show that a satisfied client will only tell five other people. But if the client is dissatisfied, he or she will tell 10 people. And don't count on a dissatisfied customer telling you about his or her complaints. Those same statistics show that only 1 in 25 clients complains to the business owner or manager.

Cultivate word of mouth advertising. Encourage your clients to tell their friends and neighbors about your salon. You may even offer some inducement. For example, give the client a free manicure for every new customer he or she brings into the salon. Just don't try to buy clients' recommendations. It won't work.

PRINT ADVERTISING

There are a number of different print media you can use to advertise your message. Newspapers and magazines are the most obvious, but there are a number of others that can be effective and relatively inexpensive. These include such items as shoppers' guides, church directories, restaurant placemats, shopping center bulletin boards, and even matchbook covers. You can find a wide range of potential advertising opportunities if you keep an open mind and keep your eyes open.

Keep in mind that publications of almost every kind live or die by the amount of advertising space they can sell. It is expensive to publish and distribute a newspaper or magazine. The costs are far higher than publications can recoup solely with revenues from subscriptions or newsstand purchases. It is the revenues from advertising that keep them in business.

As a result, it is to their benefit to run as much advertising in each issue as they can. There is nothing wrong with this. It is just part of the business. But you should be aware of this fact when you talk to the publication's representatives about purchasing advertising space. Although most space sales representatives are honest and ethical and will give you honest information and help, remember that they are working for the publication and not for you. So make your media buying decisions on the basis of factual data about the publication and not based on what the representative tells you. Ask for demographic data. Ask for readership data. If the publication is audited—that is, it undergoes periodic investigation and reporting of its numbers by an independent agency—read the audit statements. Of course, if you're working with a creative agency, they should do all of this for you.

By the same token, because of the pressure to get as much advertising as possible and because of the amount of competition in the business, publications will often give you help in developing your advertisements and will help you measure the results. Obviously, the more space you purchase, the more help you're likely to get.

NEWSPAPERS

Newspapers are publications devoted to disseminating items of news. They also carry opinion pieces, features, and lots of advertising. Newspapers are generally printed on inexpensive newsprint paper stock and are meant to be discarded after reading. There are many kinds of newspapers, ranging from large city daily papers to small rural weeklies. The category also includes shoppers' circulars and limited circulation neighborhood newspapers.

For the salon, advertising in newspapers can be very useful. Newspaper advertising is relatively inexpensive and is cost effective. The medium is flexible and versatile, and advertisements can be changed quickly to meet changing needs, especially in daily newspapers.

The advertising rate depends on the number of readers the newspaper reaches, whether or not it matches your target audience. The larger the newspaper, the more expensive it will be to advertise in it. So a local weekly will usually be less expensive than a metropolitan daily. There will also be less waste, in that the local paper is more likely to reach a larger share of your target audience than the paper with a wider circulation. Know your target audience. Choose the newspapers that they read and that service the area you wish to cover.

Many large daily newspapers also include sections devoted to news and events occurring in individual neighborhoods. These sections are inserted into the papers that are distributed to that neighborhood. The cost for advertising in the neighborhood section is often lower than advertising that appears in the main body of the paper. If you are considering advertising in a major daily, check to see if it offers a neighborhood option. You may save money and reduce the amount of waste audience.

Cost is also based on the space you utilize, usually measured in column-inches—that is, the number of columns wide multiplied by the number of inches high, as shown in Figure 12-4. The larger the ad, the more it will cost. Make sure your ad is large enough to do the job you intend it to do. Remember, it has to attract, inform, and entice. So don't try to save money by squeezing the message into a space too small to present it effectively.

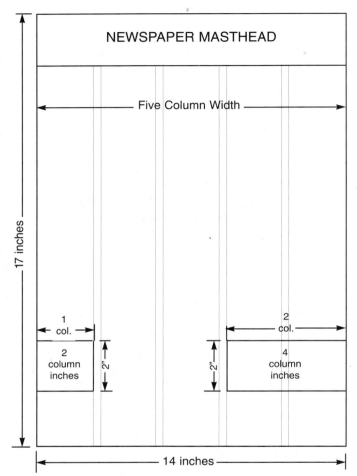

Figure 12-4. Newspaper layout.

The third cost factor is the frequency with which you repeat the advertisement. Advertising effectiveness depends on frequency. Remember, you have to run the ad enough times to make sure that enough people see it and that they see it enough times to remember it. The more times people see an ad, the more likely they are to remember it. When your ad budget is limited and your choice becomes either size or frequency, you will most often be better served by choosing frequency—at least as long as you can get your message across in the smaller ad.

You can place either display ads or classified ads in the newspaper. Display ads are larger, cover a greater amount of space, and often contain some kind of illustration. Figure 12-5 shows typical display ads. This type of ad attracts more attention and conveys more information than classified ads.

Newspaper display ads can range in size from one column-inch to full double-page spreads. Usually, they are sold in fractional page sizes, such as 1/16 page, 1/8 page, 1/4 page, 1/2 page, etc.,

Figure 12-5.   Typical newspaper display ads. (Copyright 1995, Aeone Communications.)

although they may also be sold by the column-inch. Because of the way newspapers are laid out, there is a lot of flexibility in ad size and shape, so don't limit your thinking to standard fractional shapes. You might find that a short, wide ad that runs across the page might be more effective.

Most newspaper ads are black and white, although many newspapers now offer full four-color capability. However, color ads in newspapers tend to be of questionable quality because of the paper stock and inks used. They usually lack the crispness and sharpness found in magazines. For the most part, you should stick to black-and-white ads. They cost less, so you'll be able to increase your frequency. If you must use color, limit it to one standard color used only as an accent.

Your ad may be placed anywhere in the newspaper. When you purchase the space, specify which section you want the ad to appear in. For example, you would probably be better served by having the ad in the Women's Page Section as opposed to the Sports Section. Although you may not be able to insist on a particular page or spot on the page, you should be able to get it into the section you want. But make sure you specify. If you leave the decision up to the newspaper staff, they will put the ad wherever they can fit it in. And you may be unhappy with the results.

Classified ads are smaller, usually single-column width ads placed in special classified advertising sections of the newspaper and are usually devoted to a single purpose. Help Wanted ads, such as the example shown in Figure 12-6, are typical. These are ads soliciting new employees and are contained in the Help Wanted section along with many other ads of the same type. Normally, you would use this type of ad only when looking for new employees.

Classified ads are usually less expensive than display ads but are not as effective for attracting new business. People see your display ad when they are reading the paper and the ad catches their eye. They only see your classified ad if they are looking specifically for the item you're advertising.

MAGAZINES

Magazines are periodicals devoted to a wide range of special or general interests. There are magazines that cover almost any subject, from hobbies, to home improvements, to current events. Most magazines are published on a monthly basis, although there are some weeklies as well as some bimonthlies and quarterlies. They

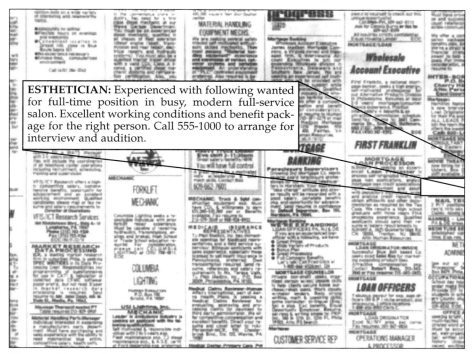

ESTHETICIAN: Experienced with following wanted for full-time position in busy, modern full-service salon. Excellent working conditions and benefit package for the right person. Call 555-1000 to arrange for interview and audition.

Figure 12-6. Typical classified ad.

are printed on better paper stock than newspapers and are meant to have a longer life span, although most are discarded after being read. Unlike newspapers, which aim for a wide audience, magazine audiences are usually more specialized, although they can be quite large. Newspapers tend to be local—that is, their audience resides in a specific city or neighborhood. Magazines, on the other hand, tend to reach national or international audiences, although most major metropolitan areas have magazines devoted to happenings in that city.

Magazine advertising is not usually a good buy for a salon. Advertising in magazines is very expensive and the audience is usually so spread out that there is a considerable amount of waste. As with newspapers, advertising rates in these periodicals are based on circulation. The more people who read the magazine, the more expensive it is. Advertising is typically in the form of display ads, which are sold in page size increments. Thus, you can buy a magazine display ad that is 1/8 page, 1/4 page, 1/2 page, 3/4 page, full page, or multiple pages. In most magazines, you can also have either color ads or black-and-white ads. Color costs more than black and white. Some magazines also offer classified advertising, usually in special sections at the back of the magazine. These are less expensive than display ads and serve much the same purpose as they do in newspapers.

Although magazine advertising is usually not effective for a salon, there may be an exception in local city magazines. These periodicals are devoted to a much more narrow, and usually upscale, audience and feature articles about life in the specific city they service. Although ads in this kind of magazine will be very expensive, they may be worth the cost if you are running the kind of salon whose image would benefit from exposure in the magazine.

TELEPHONE DIRECTORY ADVERTISING

Telephone directories are a form of print media, but the advertising they carry serves a somewhat different purpose. In most forms of advertising, the object is to attract, inform, and entice. The persons who see the ad are not necessarily looking for a particular item or service. So the advertisement has to pique their interest and get them thinking about it. Telephone directory advertising, on the other hand, serves those people who have already decided they want an item or service. The purpose of the advertisement in this vehicle is to tell them where they can get it. Thus, people use the telephone directory when they are ready to make the purchase. They are looking for a source. Remember the fishing boat analogy. In most advertising media, you're trying to attract the fish to the hook. In telephone directory advertising, the fish are already looking for the hook, so the main task is to attract them to your hook instead of your competitor's.

In today's marketplace, telephone directories have gone far beyond the old Yellow Pages concept and have begun to offer special services tailored to meet current advertiser needs. In some areas, there are now ethnic directories available, which list businesses owned and operated by people in those groups. For example, in Texas there is a Muslim Yellow Pages. In Chicago and other cities there are Chinese Yellow Pages. And there are currently more than 50 African American Yellow Page directories throughout the United States. If you are a member of an ethnic minority or if your target audience includes an ethnic minority, check with your local telephone company to find out if there is an ethnic directory in your area. You may find it useful to advertise in that directory, if members of your target audience fit the category.

People use their telephone directories. According to statistics published by the Yellow Pages Publishers Association, directories reach 98 percent of households in the United States and are consulted on an average of twice a week per person. Beauty salons are tenth on the list of most referred to product and service categories, and they draw more than 300 million references annually. Sixty percent of the people who use their telephone directory make an immediate purchase, and almost 90 percent at least call the business. So advertising in this medium can be effective.

Advertising in your local telephone directory is practically a necessity for any business. You receive a free listing in the white pages of the directory as a result of having the telephone service. However, this consists merely of a one-line entry that lists your salon name, address, and telephone number. It provides no information beyond that. To get a listing in the Yellow Pages section, you have to purchase the space. You should consider purchasing more than the minimum listing, however. It can be well worth the cost for its potential to bring in new business.

Advertising in the telephone directory can take a number of forms, depending on how much you want to spend. Like other print media, you pay for the space you use in the directory and pay a monthly fee based on the size for the one-year contract term. The basic rates are determined by the size of the audience the particular directory services. Remember, directory ads run for a one-year period. Once you sign the contract, you are obligated to pay for the full year, even if you change your mind or you go out of business.

In the directory, you can opt for display ads from a full page down to 1/8 page in size. Figure 12-7 shows a typical telephone directory display ad. Some directories also allow the use of additional colors. And you have other options, as well, such as business cards, which are smaller ads in alphabetical order that give some information about the business, or you can purchase extra lines with your regular entry to provide additional information. Or you can have your salon name set in boldface type. The least expensive ad is a plain listing of your salon. You also have a choice of headings under which the ads will appear.

You should advertise under all the headings that cover the services you offer, although the ads you use don't have to be all of the same size or complexity. So if you operate a full-service salon, you might consider using your largest display ad under the major

Figure 12-7. A sample telephone directory ad. (Reprinted with permission from Silva Hairworks, Doylestown, Pennsylvania.)

heading, "Beauty Salons," and smaller display ads or expanded listings under other headings, such as "Makeup and Beauty Consultants," "Manicuring," and "Skin Care."

Check the area the telephone directory services. If you're located in a fringe area—that is, an area on the edge of the directory service area—and your target audience lives or works in areas not covered by that directory, you might also want to advertise in neighboring directories to increase your reach. In your planning, look at the areas covered by all the directories that can reach your customer base. You might need more than one.

Check with the manufacturers of the products you feature in your salon to see if they advertise in your local telephone directories. If they do, they may list salons in that area that use and sell their products. Make sure that your salon is one of those listed.

Regardless of which headings you advertise under, keep in mind that your ad will compete for attention with all of the other ads under that heading. So you must make it stand out from the others. Make the ad as large as you can afford. Keep the layout simple and uncluttered. Make it easy to read. If possible, use some kind of illustration. Use another color of ink, such as red, blue, or green, if that option is available in the particular directory you choose.

Give the readers all the information they need to choose your salon. At a minimum, your ad should contain the name, address, and telephone number of your salon. Include your salon logo, if you have one. If the manufacturers of the products you use have a logo, you might include one or more of those. But get their permission first. Also see if they will help you pay for the ad if you use their logo. Some manufacturers offer advertising assistance programs.

The ad should list the services you offer and list your hours of operation. If you accept credit cards, include that information and say which ones. Finally, add some information that tells the prospective customer why your salon is different from the others.

It is extremely important, especially with telephone directory ads, that you carefully proofread the copy and check the layout. Make absolutely sure there are no mistakes before you approve the insertion of the ad in the book. Once the ad is printed, you have to live with any mistakes for an entire year.

BROADCAST MEDIA

Broadcast media are those that utilize the airwaves to transmit their messages. In this information age, these media—radio and television—have become about the most pervasive source of information and entertainment the world has ever known. Both are extremely effective advertising media.

RADIO

Radio is an almost constant companion for many people. Whether at home, in the car, or at work, there is a radio playing somewhere. Radios are inexpensive and highly portable and are used regularly. Even with the tremendous growth and popularity of television, radio continues to be an amazingly effective means of communication and of advertising. It is also a versatile medium with great flexibility and immediacy. It is very easy to change your advertising quickly on radio, so you have the ability to react to rapidly changing business needs.

There are a wide variety of stations, both AM and FM, which are programmed to reach specific audiences. For example, you can find a station that is programmed for adults from 25 to 54 that plays Solid Gold music. Or you can find a station that services affluent adults and plays only classical music. In addition, there are many radio stations that cater to ethnic audiences.

You can find a radio station that reaches virtually any demographic segment of the population you want. This ability to target a specific audience, plus relatively low cost, make advertising on local radio stations a potentially effective buy for a beauty salon. But you must know your demographics, and you must tailor your message to appeal to your target audience.

Radio advertising rates are based on the reach of the station— that is, how many people listen to it—on the time of day (called day

Segment	Times	Days
A.M. Drive	6 A.M.–10 A.M.	Mon. through Sat.
Daytime	10 A.M.–3 P.M.	Mon. through Fri.
P.M. Drive	3 P.M.–8 P.M.	Mon. through Fri.
Evening	8 P.M.–midnight	Mon. through Sun.
Night	Midnight–6 A.M.	Mon. through Sun.

Figure 12-8. Radio day parts.

part) that the ad runs, and on the length of the ad, usually either 10 seconds, 30 seconds, or one minute. Day parts are important, because people's listening habits vary widely from one time of day to another, as shown in Figure 12-8. This makes some air time more valuable than others. For example, since many people listen to the radio most often when they are driving to or from work, the drive time segments from Monday through Friday are usually the most expensive. These typically run from 6:00 to 10:00 A.M. and from 3:00 to 7:00 P.M. The next most expensive time slots are normally Monday through Friday late morning through early afternoon, from 10:00 A.M. to 3:00 P.M. The 8:00 P.M. through midnight time slot is less expensive yet, and the least expensive time runs from midnight to 6:00 A.M. Sunday time slots are generally less expensive than comparable time during the week.

Even within day-part segments there are premium positions that cost more. Thus, it may cost more to air your commercial on the hour or half-hour than it would at any other time during the period.

The larger the audience the station reaches, the more it charges for running the ads. So you would expect to pay more for an ad on a major metropolitan radio station than you would on a small suburban radio station. Likewise, you'll pay more for a one-minute spot than you would for a 30-second spot, although the difference normally will be somewhat less than twice as much. As with advertising on any medium, frequency is important. You have to air the commercial enough times to ensure that people will hear it and will remember it. Typically, you will purchase radio advertising in units called "flights"—that is, the ad will run for a certain number of times each week during the day parts you chose for a specific number of weeks. Then it may rest for a number of weeks, and then pick up and run again.

Work with radio media representatives the same way you work with print media representatives. Get all the information you need about the station's demographics and reach. Use audited figures. Radio stations are audited just like newspapers and magazines. Let the representatives help you choose a format and schedule. Know your audience, and choose a station and times that match their listening habits.

As with your print ads, design your radio ads carefully to attract the attention of your listening audience and give them all of the information they need to make a purchasing decision. Open the spot with a benefit statement to get their attention. Then follow it with a proof. Make sure you include the name and location of the salon, along with a telephone number customers can call. Put enough information in the commercial to get the job done, but don't overload the time. Have a professional announcer do the talking. Unless you are a trained speaker, don't try to do it yourself. The results may satisfy your ego, but they won't sell your services.

When you listen to the radio, pay attention to the commercials you hear. Note what attracts you and what doesn't. Listen to how other businesses advertise. Get ideas from them, and then utilize those ideas in your radio advertising.

TELEVISION

Television has become the most powerful communications medium in the world. It has tremendous reach and influence, and it has the advantage of combining both sound and sight to transmit messages to watchers. It is also an extremely compelling, wide-reaching, and effective advertising medium, but it can be very expensive.

Broadcast television utilizes the VHF and UHF channels and is transmitted over the airwaves and received free of charge on television sets with the proper antenna systems. There are four major nationwide networks—ABC, NBC, CBS, and FOX-TV—with their local affiliate stations, in addition to local UHF stations and Public Broadcasting Service (PBS) stations. PBS is a noncommercial broadcasting service, with programming and operation costs paid for by a combination of government funding, corporate sponsorship, and private donations, and it does not accept advertising. It does, however, acknowledge its corporate sponsors on the air.

The commercial television stations, however, earn their money through advertising revenues. Like radio, rates are based on the size of the audience they reach and, to a somewhat lesser extent than radio, on the time of day the commercial airs. Top-rated programs command the highest advertising rates, and competition among advertisers for certain time spots can be keen. This is why ratings are so important to the stations. The higher a program is rated—that is, the more people who watch it—the more money the broadcaster can charge for advertising on that program. The costs can reach astronomical proportions—for example, a 30-second spot on the Super Bowl can cost as much as $1 million, not counting the cost of producing the commercial, which can run into the hundreds of thousands of dollars. If there is a celebrity endorsement, the costs are even more.

Advertising rates on local UHF stations are much less, but even here costs are prohibitive for most small businesses. Even the smallest broadcast television stations have far too great a reach to be of much value to a beauty salon. There is far too much waste, and the cost is too high for the results you're likely to get. Under most circumstances, broadcast television cannot be considered a good advertising buy for beauty salons.

Cable television differs from broadcast television in that the signals are transmitted by cable television companies from powerful antenna systems by wire to television receivers hooked up to that company's system. The service is offered through subscription, and viewers pay a basic monthly fee for a package that consists of a wide variety of channels. In addition to the normal channels, most cable companies offer premium channels at extra cost.

The value of cable television for advertisers is the medium's ability to target audiences much more specifically than broadcast television. Thus, cable TV, which some people refer to as "narrowcasting," offers a much wider choice of channels and programming devoted to very specific interests. For example, you can find a channel devoted solely to weather forecasts, one for medical information, one for news, one for sports, and so forth. In addition, most cable television companies offer community service channels, in which small communities can air their own programs, such as local high school football games. Some cable channels serve as video billboards, featuring nothing but a series of short print advertisements with musical accompaniment.

Because of the medium's ability to reach smaller, more highly targeted audiences and the lower costs for advertising, cable television is a better buy for a small business, such as a beauty salon, than broadcast television. This is especially true if the advertising runs on a community program channel or a video billboard channel. However, make the choice carefully. You probably will still be better served by print and radio than by television.

OTHER ADVERTISING MEDIA

In addition to the various advertising media discussed earlier, there are some other forms of advertising that you should be aware of. Some of these are valuable for a small service business; others are not so valuable, but you should have some idea of what they are.

OUTDOOR ADVERTISING

Outdoor advertising includes billboards and posters. Billboards are large advertising displays strategically located along roads and highways to capture the attention of drivers as they pass by. They are a valuable part of the advertising mix for large businesses that cover a wide area. They are not so useful for a small service business, such as a beauty salon. Billboards are expensive and can't target specific audiences as readily as other media. In addition, it is necessary to purchase space on many billboards to make sure enough of the right people see the ad. The only time a billboard should be considered for a beauty salon is if you are promoting a large, multioutlet chain operation. Some salon franchise companies utilize this type of advertising.

Posters are large printed cards that carry an advertising message. They are placed on flat surfaces, such as fences and walls, in the area they are meant to cover. Although they may be fairly inexpensive to print, they may not be very effective for a service business. It is getting harder and harder to find legal places to put up posters. In addition, it is necessary to scatter them over a wide area to get sufficient coverage. Like billboards, they can't do a very good job of targeting specific audiences. Except in rare cases, posters are not a good investment for your advertising dollars.

COMMUNITY BULLETIN BOARDS

Community bulletin boards offer a good opportunity to reach a large audience at little or no cost. These are the bulletin boards you see in supermarkets and other locations, and they are designed to convey information about local businesses and events. Check with your local supermarket to find out about availability, cost, and the requirements for posting a notice about your salon.

DIRECTORIES AND PROGRAMS

Directories, programs, and yearbooks published by local organizations and institutions often offer excellent advertising opportunities. Most churches publish directories and solicit ads. High schools print programs for proms and the like, and they solicit ads from local businesses, as do community cultural organizations. The difference between the types is that directories are published on a regular basis, programs are usually published only in conjunction with a specific event, and yearbooks are usually published annually. Typically, these publications are small and are distributed to members of the organization. Church directories, for example, go to parishioners. A prom program would go to the students attending the prom (and their parents).

Ads in these media are usually sold in fractional page sizes, are relatively inexpensive, and can be a very good advertising buy. Their value to a small business is that their reach is limited to a small area; thus they normally reach a readily identifiable target audience. Look for these advertising opportunities in your area. When you find a directory or program, don't be afraid to ask questions about its reach. Look to see what businesses advertise in the publication, and call a few of them and ask how effective the ads were.

There is a benefit in advertising in directories and programs that you don't get with other media, however. You also get recognition as a member of the community helping support community institutions and activities, so there is a public relations benefit as well. Remember, however, that your decision to purchase ad space in these publications should be governed the same as your decision to purchase ad space in any other medium. It is still a business decision.

Follow the same guidelines for ads in these media as for newspapers and magazines. There is no reason to change the message or the style. If your ad was valid for another print medium, it will be valid for these.

PLACEMATS

An often overlooked but inexpensive and relatively effective advertising medium is on restaurant placemats, as shown in Figure 12-9. Many small family restaurants as well as local franchisees of fast-food chains use paper placemats that contain small advertisements for local businesses. These get wide circulation within the restaurant's operating area and give good exposure for little money.

Typically, the placemat measures 10 inches by 14 inches and has the restaurant's identification in the center. Small ads for local businesses are contained around the perimeter of the placemat. These measure approximately 2 inches by 3 inches, although other sizes and shapes may be available, depending on what other businesses are also advertising. Although the space is somewhat limited, you can still get a surprising amount of information into it. There is plenty of room to include a benefit statement and identification, as well as a logo and an illustration.

When you patronize a restaurant in your operating area, look for placemats. Ask the owner where he or she gets them, and then

Figure 12-9. A sample placemat ad. (Courtesy of Aeone Communications.)

get advertising information from the placemat printer. Don't overlook this simple, inexpensive, yet potentially effective medium.

COOPERATIVE ADVERTISING

Don't overlook the possibilities of cooperative advertising assistance. Many manufacturers offer their customers an advertising allowance if the firm utilizes the manufacturer's logo in their advertising. Although the companies do this most often in conjunction with telephone directory advertising, they also will sometimes offer monetary assistance for advertising in other media. This can help defray your advertising costs while giving you the added advantage of being associated with a large, well-known company. Ask your suppliers about cooperative advertising funds that may be available from the manufacturers whose products you use. Find out how you can qualify. Take advantage of these offers. But you have to ask. The manufacturers won't necessarily volunteer the information.

If you are a franchise operation, your franchiser will probably have a wide variety of advertising and promotional assistance programs available. Make sure you know what they are, and take advantage of them.

ADVERTISING SPECIALTIES

Advertising specialties are the little items you purchase to give away to your clients. They include items such as matchbooks, key chains, pens, and calendars, to name just a few, and they cover a wide price range. The value of the item for the purchaser is that each piece contains the name of the business and other relevant information, such as the telephone number and a brief benefit statement.

These little give-away items can be a valuable source of advertising for the salon, as long as they are chosen with care. Make sure you pick items that the persons who receive them will actually use. The reason for distributing these items is to keep your name in front of the customer. If the item just sits in a drawer, it won't do the job you wanted it for. For example, desk or wall calendars are relatively inexpensive items that lend themselves for Christmas or Chanukah gifts. They are items that the recipient will keep and look at almost constantly for a full year. That makes calendars a very effective advertising specialty.

Almost any item, however, can be effective for you as long as it has some relevance to your salon and will be used reasonably frequently. The space available for your advertising message varies with the size of the item. For example, on a pen you might have room only for the salon name and telephone number. But on a calendar, you might have enough space for a benefit statement.

Advertising specialties are sold by firms that specialize in these items. The better firms offer counseling to help you choose the items that will best serve your needs. Get recommendations from other businesses in the area. Or look in the telephone directory under "Advertising Specialties."

MEASURING ADVERTISING EFFECTIVENESS

There are many different ways of measuring advertising effectiveness. The media salespeople will probably talk to you about your cost per exposure, or how much it costs to reach each member of the audience they service. For example, suppose you advertise in the local neighborhood weekly newspaper. It has a circulation of 10,000 people. Your advertisement cost $300.00. Therefore, your cost per exposure (cpe) is three cents. The cpe figure can be valuable when you're comparing one advertising vehicle with another, so you can make an intelligent buying decision. For example, if newspaper A has a cpe of three cents and newspaper B has a cpe of five cents, A may be the better ad buy, as long as the demographics of the audience it reaches are comparable.

Unfortunately, these figures don't always tell you the whole story. To get the true picture of your cost, you need to know how many of the people that the vehicle reaches are actually in your target audience. For example, even though the newspaper has a circulation of 10,000, how many of those people are potential customers? You have to analyze the newspaper's circulation data to get that information. The newspaper will have this data, or should have it. Ask to see audited figures. Demographic data are audited by independent agencies, who warrant that the data are true and accurate. Be wary of any advertising medium that won't give you audited circulation numbers. Suppose that the newspaper's demographic data show that of the 10,000 people, 1,200 match your audience demographic profile. (Remember, you won't know this unless you know the audience you want to reach.) That makes your effective cpe 25 cents, as opposed to three cents. When you compare one medium against another, you need to use that effective cpe figure, not the overall cpe number. It may change your decision.

The most important measure of advertising effectiveness, however, is how many people responded to each ad, and how many of those people you were able to convert into customers. That is the true test of cost effectiveness. For example, suppose of the 1,200 potential customers reached by the newspaper, 80 people called for more information. That brings the cost per inquiry (cpi) to $3.75. The advertisement has given you 80 new names for your mailing list. That is, you now have 80 more people you can reach with telephone solicitations or direct mail advertising, whether or not you have converted them into customers as a result of the advertisement.

Now suppose 12 of those people actually make an appointment and get a facial. That one advertisement cost you $25.00 for each new customer. Granted, by the time you factor in all the costs of giving one facial—that is, salaries, supplies, and overhead—the money each person pays for that one facial may not give you any profit. In fact, you may even have lost money on that facial. The ad did what it was supposed to do, however. It brought in new business for you. It is up to you to keep those people as customers, so they will keep coming back and earn profits for you. That is up to you. The advertising can help perform that function, but only if you've given the customer satisfaction with the service.

To get the best value for your advertising dollars, you have to know how much business each ad brought in. That means you have to know which advertisement each new customer responded to. If you have a coupon in the ad, put a code on the coupon that tells you where it came from. Have some code in each advertisement that lets you know the source of the business. If someone calls for an appointment or for more information, make sure the receptionist or whoever answers the telephone asks the person which advertisement they are responding to.

Analyze that information. See which advertisements and which media are doing the most effective job for you. Then eliminate the ones that are not effective and concentrate your funds on those that are most effective.

ANATOMY OF A PRINT ADVERTISEMENT

Any print advertisement, regardless of the medium in which it appears, has a definite structure and content. The elements of a print advertisement are:

- headline
- subhead
- body copy
- tag line
- advertiser identification
- response mechanism
- one or more illustrations.

Not every ad will have every element, although every ad must have a headline, advertiser identification, and response mechanism. Without these three elements present, the ad can't work. The size of the ad, the positioning, and the message will determine how many of these elements will be used. Regardless of how many or which elements are used, however, they all have to work together to achieve a unified effect. Figure 12-10 shows a typical advertisement that contains all of these elements.

HEADLINE

The headline performs two functions that make it an extremely important piece of copy, and it is one of the three indispensable elements in an ad. The first function is to alert the intended audience that this advertisement is meant for it. It tells the reader, "this message is for you." The headline brings up a subject that may already be on the reader's mind and persuades him or her to read the rest of the ad. If you were promoting facials for acne treatment, for example, a headline that states "Problems With Pimples?" conveys the idea to acne sufferers that this ad contains information of interest to them.

The second function is to grab readers' attention and pull them into the rest of the ad by giving enough of the message to arouse their interest and get them to read further. Be as specific as you can in the headline. Use verbs and definite articles, like *the* and *this* instead of *a* or *an*. Address the reader directly with words like you.

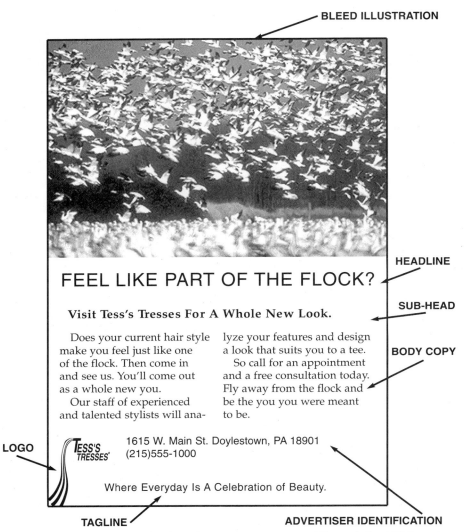

Figure 12-10. A typical advertisement structure. (Copyright 1995, Aeone Communications.)

Don't try to be overly cute. There's a difference between cute and creative. Don't use your salon name in the headline, and don't waste the space by telling everyone how good you are or what awards you may have won. Stick to the major benefit for the reader.

SUBHEAD

The subhead is a smaller headline-type piece of copy that supports the main headline. It is usually set in smaller type than the headline and reinforces the message of the headline. For example, if the headline is "Problems With Pimples?", the subhead might be "Clear up your skin in six weeks." Subheads are also used to break up long body copy, in that they add emphasis whenever the copy brings up a new point.

BODY COPY

The body copy carries the meat of your message and should fit your objectives. It should be clear, concise, and to the point. And it should be appropriate to your positioning and your image. Keep the copy oriented to the benefits of your services. Use the features to support the benefits. And don't forget to tell the people what you want them to do. Don't be afraid to ask for the order. If you don't, they are likely to do nothing. Be wary of comparative advertising. Don't denigrate other salons. Be positive, not negative.

Whether you should mention price in the advertisement depends on the situation. When price is the benefit (for example, if you're holding a special sale), then include it. When price is not a benefit, don't confuse the issue by putting it in the ad. Concentrate on the benefit you're trying to sell. Keep in mind, though, that consumers do look for price information in ads, so the mention of a price may increase memorability.

Copy used in advertisements is relatively short, as compared with that used in other communications vehicles. The amount of information you can put into an ad is a function of the size of the ad. In most cases, your advertisement will be fairly small. You have to make your point quickly and effectively, in as few words as possible, so make every word count. Continuing the example from the previously mentioned headline and subhead, the body copy could describe how you eliminate pimples, discussing the benefits and features. You could also tell the reader what he or she should do next. Remember to ask for the order.

TAG LINE

A tag line is a piece of copy used at the end of the ad. It often summarizes the main idea of the ad and reinforces the major benefit. It can also be used to support your positioning or as the call to action. For example, the tag line for the hypothetical pimple ad could reinforce the headline by saying "Clear skin fast." Or it could state your positioning as skin care experts saying "We're the skin care specialists." Or it could make a call to action like "Call (your telephone number) for an appointment today."

The tag line can be a very important adjunct to your ad. Be judicious in choosing it, however. It is not just a throw-away piece of copy. Make it work for you.

ADVERTISER IDENTIFICATION

Advertiser identification is the second of the three essential elements in an advertisement. Tell readers who and where you are. Don't make them guess. If you don't give them this information, they won't pay any attention to the ad. Even worse, they might develop an interest in the service and go to your competitor simply because you haven't identified your salon to them. This happens more often than you might realize.

The minimum amount of identification in the ad should be your salon name and your telephone number. Don't forget to put at least this much information in. This sounds so basic, you might think it silly to mention, but many advertisers have forgotten to include it in their ads. You're not going to get much business if people don't know who to call. If you have the space, also include your address. If you have developed a logo, by all means, use that also.

Depending on how much room you have, you could also include your salon hours and which, if any, credit cards you accept. Consider getting a toll-free number that people can call for appointments and information. Over the past few years, telephone companies have developed relatively low-cost 800-number services specifically for small businesses. Studies show that 800 numbers in an ad increase memorability and response.

RESPONSE MECHANISM

The third of the three essential elements of an advertisement is the response mechanism. Your advertisement must include a way for the prospect to respond. You want the ad to bring in new business. Make it easy for the prospect to buy. Give him or her a way to act on the interest you've created. If you don't include some type of response mechanism, you risk wasting the effects of the ad.

The response mechanism can be simple, utilizing the call to action by telling the prospect to "Call (this number) today for an appointment." Or it could be a coupon that offers an incentive for coming to your salon. Consider using coupons whenever possible. Studies show that coupons increase memorability. They are also excellent as an inducement to patronize the business that uses them. Whatever mechanism you use, don't forget this essential element.

ILLUSTRATIONS

Illustrations can be drawings, photographs, or charts that explain by example the idea contained in the advertisement. They also add visual interest to the advertisement and help attract attention. Whatever kinds of illustrations you use, however, keep them simple and make sure they support the message of the ad. Don't use an illustration just for the sake of using one. Make it work for you. And don't let it overpower the ad. It is a working element of the advertisement, not a substitute for a coherent message.

For the pimple ad, the illustration might be a before and after photograph of a client you've successfully treated. A picture like this would support the overall theme of the ad and add credibility to your expertise. Don't forget to get the client's permission first.

ANATOMY OF A RADIO COMMERCIAL

Like a print advertisement, a radio commercial has a definite structure. Since radio is an audio medium rather than a visual medium, it relies on sound rather than sight to carry the message. Even so, a radio commercial has a beginning (the headline), a middle (body copy), and an end (call to action and advertiser identification), just like its print counterpart. How much of each part you use depends on the amount of time you have.

There are two types of radio commercial structure: the direct and the slice of life. The direct structure is most like the print ad in that it gets right to the point and asks for the order. Figure 12-11 shows a sample direct radio commercial script. The opening statement performs the function of the print ad headline. Here, you call attention to the members of the target audience and state the

Announcer: SFX: sandpaper on wood	Does your skin feel like sandpaper? Does it feel dry and rough? Are you almost afraid to rub your skin because it might tear?
SFX: paper tearing	Don't fret. Come to Tess's Tresses for a skin-toning, refreshing, moisturizing facial. Relax and enjoy pampering you've never before experienced. Get your skin back to the shape it was in when you were a baby. There's a special on facials this week only, so call 555-1000 today for an appointment and free consultation. That's Tess's Tresses at 555-1000. Where everyday is a celebration of beauty.

Figure 12-11.   Sample direct radio script. (SFX = Sound effects.)

major benefit. In a radio version of the print ad sample used earlier, for example, your announcer might say, "Ladies, now you can get rid of those unsightly pimples in six weeks."

The middle portion of the commercial corresponds to the body copy of the print ad. Here, you provide the listener with the features of your service and the proof statements that support the opening claim. You might also include advertiser identification here, although you might wait until the end to add that.

The ending of the radio commercial combines the call to action, the tag line, and the response mechanism of the print ad. A commercial on the radio is no different than an advertisement in a print medium. You still have to tell the people what you want them to do and make it easy for them to do it. So you might end with a tag line that says something like "Skin care that works from the skin care experts." The call to action might say, "Call (this number) today for a free consultation." Here, the response mechanism will most likely be your telephone number.

The slice-of-life structure is a little skit that gives the advertising message by example rather than by direct statements. A sample slice-of-life commercial is shown in Figure 12-12. There is still

SFX: Street noises.
Two women's
footsteps approaching
each other. They stop.

First Woman	Grace. (surprised) I almost didn't recognize you. You look terrific.
Second Woman	Hello, Ann. Thank you. I feel terrific, too. I just had a facial and it was a wonderful experience. It made me look better and feel better.
First Woman	You know, I've been thinking about doing that, too. I've heard that facials are great for helping your skin. Where did you get yours?
Second Woman	They are great. Especially at Tess's Tresses. You know, that new salon on Main St. Why don't you give them a call? Their number is 555-1000. You even get a free consultation, first.
First Woman	555-1000. That's an easy number to remember. I think I'll call them as soon as I get home.

Figure 12-12. Slice-of-life radio script.

a beginning, a middle, and an end, but they are not so clear cut as in the direct structure. The beginning sets the scene and states the benefit by implication. So, for example, the opening might be a meeting between two women on the street. One says, "Gee, Grace. Your skin looks terrific." The other woman replies, "And I feel terrific, too. I just finished a skin care program at XYZ Salon and they cleared up my pimple problems. The esthetician there did a great job."

The middle can take either of two directions. The skit can continue as the two women discuss the features and proofs of the services, or it can proceed as a "doughnut." In radio advertising jargon, a doughnut commercial is a structure in which a direct message is inserted in between two parts of the slice-of-life skit. In this case, an announcer would deliver the main part of the message and the call to action.

In the normal structure, the end would have Grace deliver the call to action and the response mechanism as part of the conversation. She would say something like "You should try XYZ Salon. They can do wonders for your skin. Call them at (your telephone number)." In the douyhnut structure, the end would reinforce the call to action given by the announcer. The dialogue could still be the same.

Since radio is an audio medium, you can't use illustrations in your commercial. Instead, you can use music and sound effects to add aural interest. As with illustrations in print ads, however, be judicious in your choice of sounds. Make sure the sound effects or the music support the message. Don't add them just to have them. They have to work with the rest of the commercial.

SUMMARY

- An advertisement is a paid public notice that calls attention to a product or service and tries to persuade the reader (or listener) to purchase that product or service. Advertising is a means of communication, a marketing tool, and a means of persuasion.
- Advertising vehicles differ from direct marketing vehicles in their reach. Advertisements are generally targeted to larger, less specific groups of people and are placed in media that carry many advertisements.
- The ultimate objective for advertising is to increase sales. But it is only part of the sales process. If you consider a sale as having seven steps, advertising plays a part in all but two of the steps, making the offer and closing the sale.
- Advertising creates awareness of your services, helps establish your image, creates a demand for your services, persuades the prospect to patronize your salon, and reinforces the buying habits of your customers.
- To be effective, advertising must perform three tasks. It must attract, inform, and entice.
- You must know your audience before you can create effective advertising. You also have to know the media.
- Frequency of advertising is important. You have to keep running an advertisement long enough and often enough to let it do the job for which it was designed.
- There are a large number of advertising media, each of which is designed to reach different audiences and accomplish dif-

ferent objectives. No one medium will accomplish everything you want.

- Word of mouth advertising is the most credible form of advertising, especially for a service business. But you have to earn it. Customers will only "spread the good word" about your salon if they've been satisfied.
- There are many different kinds of newspapers, ranging from large metropolitan dailies to small-town weeklies. Shoppers' circulars and neighborhood newspapers also fall into this category.
- The rate charged by the newspaper depends on its circulation, the size of the space you buy, and the number of times you run the ad. Choose the newspaper based on how well it reaches the audience you've targeted, not on its total circulation. Your ad can take the form of a display ad or a classified ad.
- Magazines are less attractive as advertising media for salons because their scope is usually too large. They are more expensive than newspapers and reach too many people outside your target audience.
- You will almost always have to have an ad in your local Yellow Pages Directory. Buy the largest ad you can afford. Use a second color, if possible.
- Broadcast media use the airwaves to transmit messages. Radio and television are very pervasive media and have extraordinary power to persuade.
- Radio advertising rates are based on the time of day, the size of the audience, the length of time of the commercial, and how often it runs.
- Television is probably the most powerful communications tool in existence today, but its use as a medium for salon advertising is limited. Broadcast television is expensive and has a reach that is far too large for most small businesses, even on local UHF stations.
- Outdoor advertising—billboards—is a good medium for large businesses that cover a wide area, but it is not so useful for small businesses. Posters can be placed more conveniently than billboards, but it is getting harder to find places that allow them.
- Community bulletin boards and directories can reach a large, usually local audience very inexpensively. Community bulletin boards can be found in local supermarkets. Directories are published by many churches and local organizations.

Don't overlook programs published by various organizations in conjunction with special events.

- Check with your local restaurants to see if they use advertising placemats. Also look for cooperative advertising assistance from your suppliers and manufacturers of the products you purchase.
- Don't overlook advertising specialties, items you give away to your clients. Imprinted with your salon name, address, and telephone number, they serve as reminders to your customers.
- You can measure advertising effectiveness in a number of ways. In media advertising, one method is to measure the cost per exposure. What you really want to know, however, is how much new business the ad generated. To learn this, you have to ask your customers how they learned about your salon.
- Any print advertisement has a definite structure and content. The elements include a headline, subhead, body copy, tag line, advertiser identification, response mechanism, and illustrations.
- Don't forget advertiser identification. The best ad in the world is useless if it doesn't tell the prospect who and where you are. Similarly, you must have a response mechanism. You have to tell readers or listeners exactly what you want them to do and make it easy for them to do it.

CHAPTER 13

Direct Marketing

Direct marketing is a means of reaching out to your target audience and delivering a message designed to bring the members of that audience into your salon, utilizing vehicles that go straight to the audience without first passing through a middleman. Like advertising, direct marketing is a tool for promoting your business. Both tools are like two people setting out on a trip. Both have the same destination—the customer. Both have the same starting point—the business. But each takes a different route to get there.

DIRECT MARKETING AND ADVERTISING COMPARISON

Direct marketing and advertising share a lot in common, but they also have some major differences. Each tool has its own advantages and disadvantages. To get the maximum effectiveness, it is necessary that you understand when each should be used.

For either tool, however, it is imperative that you know your audience. Neither will do you any good if you don't know who you want to reach. You must know the demographic and psychographic makeup of your target audience before you can utilize any means of marketing communications.

REACH

One difference is reach. Advertising is ideal when you know the general characteristics of your audience but you can't identify them by name and address, or when the audience is so large that you can't economically use direct marketing. Advertising utilizes a shotgun approach to reaching audiences in that the target is more diffuse. It is aimed to spread out and reach a particular demographic segment, without being very specific about individuals. Remember the fishing boat analogy from the previous chapter.

With advertising, you're dangling the baited hook in the water and hoping to get a prospect to bite.

Direct marketing is ideal when you can identify specific groups or individuals and when their numbers are relatively small. It provides a rifle approach to reaching audiences in that the target is more focused and tightly defined. It lets you tailor your message and approach to appeal to different audience segments and lets you set limits on the size and scope of the advertising effort. Consider the analogy, not of a fishing boat, but of a hunter. The hunter (you) sets out in search of particular prey (the customer), stalking the quarry through the fields and forests (the target area), armed with the right weapon and ammunition (the direct marketing vehicle) for that particular prey. You don't hunt for pigeons with an elephant gun, or vice versa.

CONTROL

Control over message content and delivery is another factor. You exercise control over the message with either advertising or direct marketing. You decide what you want to say and how you want to say it. The major limitation is space. In an advertisement, you have limited space, so you must keep the message fairly short. With direct marketing, you have more space, so you can develop the message more thoroughly and include more supporting material.

This does not mean, however, that you can ramble on in a direct marketing vehicle. Copy for a direct marketing campaign must be just as well written as it is for an advertisement. It is important that you make every word count here, too. With direct marketing vehicles, however, you have the flexibility and space to expand on the message.

Positioning is important in either case. You have to develop a positioning concept that carries through your marketing communications, no matter what form they take. How you state that positioning will vary, of course. No matter what marketing communications tool you use, you have to stay true to your positioning.

When it comes to delivery, you get more control with direct marketing vehicles. When you place an advertisement, you are at the mercy of the publication in which it appears. Certainly, you specify in which issue or on which day you want your ad to appear. And you can ask for certain general positions in the publication. But your ad will appear where the publication puts it, depending on how the editors make use of the space in the publication. Also, you will be sharing that publication with all of the other advertisers in that issue. So not only does your ad have to attract the attention of the reader, it also has to compete with all of the other ads for the reader's attention.

With a direct marketing vehicle, on the other hand, you have the stage all to yourself. Your competition for the prospect's attention comes only from other mail or things that are delivered to the home or office, and not from a myriad of other advertisements. Also, you control the timing. You decide when the best time to deliver the piece is, so you can match delivery with the greatest opportunity to get the maximum impact. You're not controlled by a publication's schedule.

You have more control over who sees your direct marketing vehicle as well. You can deliver the piece to as many or as few people as you want, without paying for excess circulation, much of which may be wasted with an advertisement in a publication.

Direct marketing vehicles also give you more control over the quality of the finished piece. When you place an advertisement in a publication, you (or your agency) prepare it to the camera-ready stage. That is, you supply film, which the publication uses to make printing plates. The publication then prints the ad in the newspaper or magazine, along with editorial, features, and other ads. Although most publications do a very good job of printing, you're nevertheless faced with a take-what-you-get situation. You are also limited to the paper stock and the inks that the publication uses. Newspapers, for example, print on newsprint, which is a relatively low-cost, uncoated paper stock with high absorbency in which ink tends to spread, limiting sharpness and definition. Most magazines, especially the large mass circulation ones, use higher-quality coated paper stocks, but even here printing quality can be variable.

With a direct marketing vehicle, you control the entire production. You have the ability to work closely with your printer to make the piece the best it can be. You can choose from a wide range of paper stocks and from a wide range of inks and varnishes to assure the best sharpness and snap. Your direct marketing piece can be as good as the time and effort you take to make it so.

FREQUENCY

Frequency is as important with direct marketing as it is with advertising. The Ebbinghaus Forgetting Curve, as well as the discussion on frequency in the previous chapter, is as valid for this tool as it is for the other.

The more often you can put your message in front of the prospect, the more chance you have for increasing awareness and creating a demand for your services. As with any other marketing communications tool, get there often. Keep at it. Success comes with repetition.

With direct marketing vehicles, you have the opportunity to establish frequency on your terms. You're not locked into the schedule of the publications in which you advertise. It is up to you, however, to utilize that frequency to your best advantage by establishing a regular schedule for getting your direct marketing pieces into the hands of your prospects.

COST

In many ways, direct marketing is a more cost-effective means of promoting your business than print or broadcast advertising. Direct marketing vehicles are usually less expensive than media advertising, and you have more control over the costs. With a print advertisement, you incur costs for producing the ad and for the space in which it runs. With a direct marketing vehicle, you pay only for producing the piece and for the means of delivering it to your audience. Since the direct marketing piece is targeted more closely and waste is limited, your overall costs are often less than for a comparable advertising campaign.

The cost of producing a direct marketing piece varies with its complexity. Some vehicles cost more than others because more is involved with their production. With direct marketing, however, you can tailor a vehicle to meet your budget with far more effectiveness than you can with print or broadcast advertising.

DIRECT MARKETING LISTS

The greatest direct marketing program in the world is useless if it doesn't get into the hands of the people who can act on its hopes and suggestions. Unlike print and broadcast advertising, in which distribution is in the hands of others, with direct marketing, it is up to you to deliver your message. You have full control over that aspect.

That's why you build a customer list. In your business you will have few assets more valuable than your own customer list, which you compile and keep. The names and addresses on that list are like money in the bank. Make sure you keep meticulous records of your customers. Know who they are and where they can be reached. Add new customers' names to the list immediately, and keep all information up to date. Your current customers are your best source of future income and will remain in your target audience until they move away or die. Even if you lose a customer, don't discard the name. Put it into an inactive category, perhaps, but continue promoting to him or her. Always remember that it is easier and cheaper to keep an existing customer than it is to get a new one.

However, your customer list is just your base. If you want to increase your business, you'll have to reach out to more people than you have already. So you will have to get names from other sources. One good source of names and addresses of prospective customers is recommendations from your clients. Other businesses can also be an excellent source of new names. In some cases, you might be able to trade lists with other noncompeting businesses for names and addresses in the neighborhood you service. Once you've developed your list, keep it up to date.

An excellent source of names for your list, especially of people new to your area, is the real estate transactions section of your local newspaper. This section lists the names and addresses of people who have recently settled on houses. These people should make excellent prospects. Make sure to send them your promotional materials. You might even want to make up a special "Welcome to the Neighborhood" package just for them.

You may also be able to purchase mailing lists from a number of sources. Your local newspaper, for example, may sell you a list of subscribers in a particular area. If it won't sell the list to you, it may do the mailing for you. Or you might be able to find a list from a list broker. There are a number of agencies that do nothing but sell mailing lists. Many of these businesses offer catalogs of mailing lists that break down names and addresses by almost any category you can imagine.

For instance, suppose you wanted to mail a brochure to other beauty salons. One list broker can sell you the names and addresses of 226,986 salons in the United States, delineated by state. Just want to mail to salons in New Jersey? The list contains 5,648 names. To California? 30,768 names.

It is not likely that you would need to purchase a list from a broker. In most cases, there would be too much waste if you're only looking for new customers to patronize your salon. However, if you were selling a beauty care product you had developed and were manufacturing, such a broker could be very helpful. Just be aware that these services are available to direct marketers.

DIRECT MARKETING VEHICLES

Direct marketing is a very versatile tool. The number of vehicles you can develop is limited only by your imagination. You have few limitations with this means of promotion. The design possibilities are virtually endless, and you can work within almost any budget. The traditional vehicles include:

- direct mailers
- sales letters
- brochures
- circulars
- newsletters
- cooperative mailings
- annual reports.

But the computer age has opened up new direct marketing possibilities that offer exciting promotional possibilities. These include telemarketing, e-mail, and telefaxing. Video technology also offers a range of possibilities. Any or all of these vehicles, traditional or new, can provide you with effective marketing communications.

As with almost any other communications device discussed in this book, direct marketing vehicles are interrelated. Even though they may be discussed separately, they often work together. Thus, a sales letter can stand alone or it can be part of a direct mailer. The same holds true with brochures. These can be self-mailers, handouts, or an element in a direct mail package. By the same token, there is a lot of similarity among types. For example, the differences between brochures, circulars, and catalogs is more of scope than of type.

The ability to mix and match devices is one of the advantages of direct marketing or of any other form of marketing communications. Once you understand the principles involved with each type, you can use your imagination to make them work for you.

DIRECT MAILERS

Direct mail has an unfortunate reputation as "junk mail." Too often, that reputation is well earned. Households are seemingly flooded with direct mail offers of all kinds, and many people find the flood annoying. As a result, many people don't even bother to open mail they consider useless. Most of the time, they're right. Too many lazy marketers confuse quantity with quality and bombard prospects with rafts of poorly thought-out pieces that offer no real benefit to the recipient.

It doesn't have to be this way, however. A well-designed, creatively conceived, and expertly prepared direct mailer can be an effective means of communication with your prospective clients, as long as you remember to provide them with something they perceive as valuable to them. In other words, sell the benefits, not the features. It's no different here than with any other marketing communications effort.

Direct mail involves nothing more than developing a promotional package describing your services and the benefits and then mailing it to a preselected audience, by name and address. It can be as simple as a postcard or as complex as a multipart package that utilizes every classic direct mail element possible.

Direct mail is an effective and relatively inexpensive way to keep awareness high among your existing customers and to reach out with a personal message to new prospects. The cost depends on the complexity of the piece. You pay for preparing and printing the mail piece and for postage. Because it is a targeted communication, your return should be reasonable.

The direct mail piece you send must be attractive and command attention. It has to compete with all of the other direct mail the audience receives on a given day, so you want to make sure it will intrigue them enough so they'll open and read it. (As with advertising, you should hire qualified professionals to design and produce your mailers.) Here too, frequency is important. Make frequent mailings. Once a month is not too much. You can also do a direct mail campaign whenever you have something new to offer.

Whatever form the mailer takes, the message is paramount. Limit the message to one basic idea and offer. Stress the benefits. Describe the features. Include all the information needed to make a purchasing decision. You might want to add a coupon for a special sale or other inducement. Don't forget to include your name, address, hours of operation, and telephone number. Make sure the overall design and concept fits the image of your salon and of the market you're trying to penetrate.

Study direct mail packages that come into your home or business. Look closely at the elements they contain. Note how the various pieces fit together, each one reinforcing the others. What appeals work with you? What don't? Use the direct mail you receive as a learning experience, and put what you learn from it to use in your direct mail efforts.

POSTAGE

A key factor in direct mail decisions is postage. How much will it cost you to mail the package, and what mechanism will you use? You have several choices. Consult with your local postmaster for the latest guidelines. Keep up to date. Postal regulations change frequently.

The first decision is whether to mail first class or third class. Third class, or bulk rate, is less expensive but takes longer for delivery, and you generally have to sort and bundle the mail by zip code before taking it to the post office. From the point of view of the recipient, whether the package comes by first class or third class mail is of no consequence. All things being equal, you might as well opt for the less expensive alternative.

The only time the mode of delivery may matter to the recipient is if you use a service such as Federal Express or UPS to deliver the package. You would do this to add emphasis to the mailing (in effect telling the recipient that this offer is really hot) or if you were including some rather expensive premium in the mailing and wanted to make sure of prompt delivery. You will probably never find it necessary to go to this extreme, or this expense, for mailings to promote your salon.

The choice you make will depend on how time-sensitive the offer you're making is. In most cases, your timing will not be critical, so bulk rate will be adequate. It will also depend on the size of the mailing. If you're mailing only a few packages, say 100 or fewer, then you might as well use first-class mail. The cost difference won't make up for the extra work you'll have to do.

Another decision is whether to use stamps or metered mail. Some direct mail experts feel that stamps increase the perception of value for the mailer in the mind of the recipient. Others disagree and feel that using metered mail is just as efficient. So the choice is really up to you. Use whichever is more convenient.

If you are looking for a response to your direct mail package by mail, you will include a reply card or envelope. The question is

Figure 13-1.   Business reply card. (Courtesy of Aeone Communications.)

whether you should have the recipient put a stamp on the response card, whether you should put a stamp on it, or whether you should use a business reply format, as illustrated in Figure 13-1. Generally, you will get far better results if you pay for the return postage than if you make the recipient pay for it.

For large mailings, business reply is less expensive because you only pay postage for the cards that are actually returned. If you put stamps on the reply cards, you've paid for a lot of postage that will never be used. So unless you are making very large mailings, you'll probably find that using stamps is more convenient than using a business reply format, even though it may cost you somewhat more. Whichever you use, though, replies will be charged at first-class rates.

To get a business reply permit, you have to:

1. register with the post office
2. get a permit number, which will be printed on the reply mechanism
3. print precise bar code information on the mechanism
4. make sure you get the details from your postmaster

5. have the postmaster approve the proof copy of the form before you print it.

ELEMENTS OF A DIRECT MAILER

There are a number of basic elements that can be used in a direct mail package:

- an envelope
- a letter
- a promotional brochure
- a lift letter
- an involvement device
- a premium
- an order form.

Not every direct mail package will utilize all of these elements, however. You can pick and choose from the elements to develop a package that best fits your needs. Whichever elements you choose, however, all the elements in your package must work together to get the attention of the reader and to influence a purchasing decision.

ENVELOPE

The envelope is a crucial part of the direct mail package. It does far more than merely hold the contents during delivery. Often, it determines whether the recipient will even open the package to read the message.

The envelope is the first thing the recipient sees. Your package will fight for attention with all of the other mail the recipient receives that day, so your envelope must grab the reader's attention and invite him or her to open it. Use strong, benefit-oriented copy on the envelope. Choose a size other than standard No. 10 business envelope to make it stand out from the rest. Oddly shaped and oversize envelopes can work well, but before you commit to production, check with the post office to make sure you meet its requirements for delivery. Spend extra effort on the envelope. The benefits of strong envelope design and copy should more than make up for any increased costs of production or postage. Figure 13-2 shows a typical direct mail envelope.

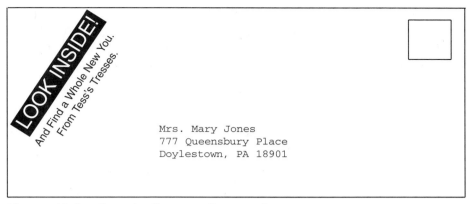

Mrs. Mary Jones
777 Queensbury Place
Doylestown, PA 18901

Figure 13-2.   Sample direct mailer envelope.

SALES LETTER

The direct mail letter is the primary communication vehicle in the direct mail package. It should contain the benefits and the proof statements, and it should introduce the offer and other items that are included in the package. It should be well designed, but simple and in letter-like format. Sales letters are covered in detail later in this chapter.

PROMOTIONAL BROCHURE

The promotional brochure supplements and reinforces the message of the sales letter. It can take a wide variety of sizes, shapes, colors, and complexity, and it can expand on the information you impart to the reader. The brochure is the medium to use when you need illustrations or graphics to convey the message. Typically, the brochure will make far more use of color than the letter. Brochures are covered in more detail later in this chapter.

LIFT LETTER

A lift letter is a supplementary letter, usually on smaller paper folded in half, normally with a message on the outside that says something like, "If you've decided not to accept this offer, please read this." The inside of the letter reinforces the offer made in the rest of the package or adds further inducements to purchasing. The lift letter is designed to give a second chance for the recipient to reach a buying decision. Figure 13-3 shows a typical lift letter.

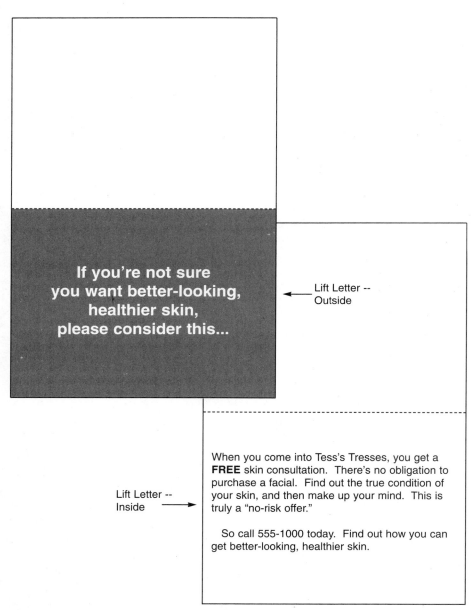

Figure 13-3. Sample direct mailer lift letter.

PREMIUM

A premium is an artifact of some type that serves as an inducement to accept the offer in the direct mail package. Like an advertising specialty, it can take a variety of forms, but it should have some relevance to the message contained in the package. For example, if your message was "Give us a call today," you might include a quarter in the package.

It is not always necessary to include a premium in a direct mail package, although a well-chosen premium can greatly increase your response. However, depending on what the premium is, it can greatly increase your cost. In many cases, the premium item can cost more than the mailer itself. Also, depending on the size, shape, and weight of the premium, it can greatly increase your mailing costs.

INVOLVEMENT DEVICE

An involvement device is an artifact designed to increase the reader's involvement with the package and, therefore, his or her attention to its contents. Unlike a premium, this type of device may not have any intrinsic value as an item. Rather, it is more of a curiosity device, meant to pique the recipient's interest and get him or her to do something. Typical involvement devices used frequently in direct mail packages are tokens, scratch-off cards, quizzes, and puzzles. Sweepstakes and contests are also often used devices.

OFFER

If there is, in fact, one single, most important part of a direct mail package, it would have to be the offer. This is where you repeat the proposition and ask for the order. Without this step, you probably won't get a response. You have to tell the recipient what you want him or her to do. Figure 13-4 shows a typical offer mechanism.

You can present the offer in many ways. It can take the form of a coupon or an order blank, or even just a telephone number with an admonition to "call today." Having an 800 number can help in this regard. The object is to make it easy for the recipient to respond by giving him or her an easy way to take the next step.

If you are selling a product through the mail, then you would have to include a reply card or reply envelope, along with an order

Figure 13-4. Direct mailer offer mechanism.

blank, to elicit a response. For the most part, however, your objective in direct mail promotions will be to build traffic coming into your salon. Therefore, including these will generally not be necessary. A coupon offering a special deal would be a better choice.

The design of the offer piece is just as important as any other part of the package. Often the offer piece is the first part of the package the recipient actually reads. This is the part that will generate the most action. So make it stand out. Repeat your offer and the major benefit. If you mention price in the direct mail package at all, this is the place for it. Include a guarantee, if you can.

SALES LETTERS

Never underestimate the power of a well-written letter. Letters project a feeling of credibility that other vehicles sometimes lack. They are viewed as more personal than other vehicles, and they lend themselves to a wide variety of uses. Whether you use a letter as a stand-alone mailing or as part of a more comprehensive direct mail package, it can be a very effective promotional device for your salon. It can also be one of the more inexpensive forms of promotion, since printing and mailing costs can be relatively low.

Computers give you the option of personalizing letters. Some word processing and database programs let you add in the recipient's name and other information as the letter is being printed, so that it looks like it was written specifically for that person. If you have this capability, use it. However, you can still produce an effective letter without the customization. Even plain form letters are an effective and valuable means of promoting your salon.

An effective sales letter starts with a well-designed letter-head. You can use your salon stationery for the letter, or you can have a letterhead designed specially for a particular campaign. Design and copy are both important. The letter should be attractive and inviting to draw the reader's interest. Use a second color as an accent to focus attention on specific points. Use attention-getting typographic devices such as indentations, bullets, capitalization, bold and italic typefaces, and underlining to lead the reader's eye through the document. But be judicious in the use of these devices. They are more effective when used sparingly. And allow plenty of white space for visual relief.

Spend a lot of time developing the copy. The design attracts and holds the reader's attention. The copy does the persuasion. Consider your objectives and your audience. You have to know the characteristics of the people you are writing to. Have a definite offer in mind, and name all of the benefits of the offer. Remember, sell the benefits, not the features. Don't worry about length. Longer letters generally perform better than short ones, so use more than one page. Say everything that has to be said, but don't ramble. Keep copy direct and to the point. The same standards for ethics and credibility discussed in the previous chapter also apply to direct mail.

The most important part of the copy is the lead. This is the first part the reader sees and should get him or her right into the letter. Very often, the lead will determine if the recipient will read the rest of the letter. A good lead can take a number of forms. You can use a provocative question as a lead, such as "If I could guarantee you perfect skin, would you make a five-minute phone call to find out how?" A news lead is often effective, if you can tie your offer into a newsworthy event, such as "Scientists find that aminophylline creams actually reduce fat deposits in thighs. Let us prove it to you."

One of the first things journalism students learn is to begin news stories by answering who, what, when, where, why, and how. These are the questions any reader has, and addressing them up front allays the initial curiosity and leads the reader further into the story. You can use the same approach as a lead to a sales letter. For example, "How 45 women in Doylestown managed to look five years younger." Numbers also work well in leads, as in "Six simple steps you can take for perfect skin."

Start the main part of the copy with your most important benefit. Put it right up front. Then expand on that benefit immediately with supporting information. Add other benefits. Describe the features of your offer, along with proof statements. If you have testimonials, by all means use them. Testimonials from actual satisfied customers carry a lot of credibility.

Close the letter by making the offer. Restate the main benefits, and give a call to action. Be specific. Tell the reader exactly what the offer is and how to take advantage of it. Then tell him or her what to do—for example, "Call today for an appointment."

Always add a postscript to the letter. Use the postscript (P.S.) to summarize the key benefit and to restate the offer. A good P.S. is a surprisingly effective part of a sales letter, ranking only behind the lead as a persuasive device. Many people read a sales letter by looking at the lead, then scanning quickly through the letter, perhaps stopping at a point that attracts the eye, and then moving quickly to the P.S. Often, the P.S. piques their interest enough to go back and read the letter thoroughly.

BROCHURES AND CATALOGS

A brochure is a printed piece that describes and promotes your services or your business. It can show the capabilities of your salon, highlighting the services you offer and your qualifications for providing those services. Or it can be limited to one specific service. Properly designed and written, this piece of literature can be the primary promotional piece for your salon, used as a self-mailer, part of a more comprehensive direct mail package, or as a handout to people who visit your salon. Figure 13-5 shows a sample self-mailer brochure format.

The format of a brochure is limited only by your imagination. It can be as small as a folded sheet containing copy and graphics, or it can be a multipage booklet. It can be simple black and white, or it can be multicolor, using either spot color or four-color process with varnish overlays. And it can be any size, shape, or configuration.

Catalogs are usually larger booklets that list services or products, along with descriptions, prices, and order forms. These vehicles are usually designed to produce orders directly. Although

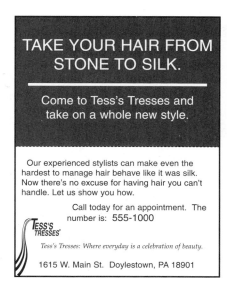
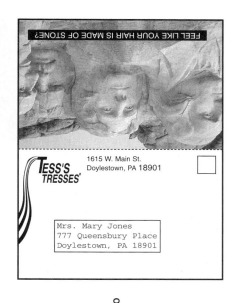

INSIDE

OUTSIDE

Figure 13-5. Self-mailer.

catalogs may be good for selling products, they may have little value for selling your salon services. You would be better off with a well-designed and well-written capabilities brochure.

Brochures can be among the most expensive of direct marketing vehicles, although the cost will depend on complexity. They tend to be of higher quality than letters and are usually printed on better paper stock. They may or may not contain illustrations. In some cases, you can lower the cost of preparing a brochure by using preprinted paper stocks that have been designed specially for brochures capable of being printed on laser printers. These papers are available from a number of suppliers. They offer the advantage of good design at low cost. And, since you do the printing yourself with your computer, you can print as many or as few as you need at any one time. A brochure of this type is shown in Figure 13-6.

As with any marketing communication, a brochure should be designed with objectives and audience in mind. Copy should be direct and to the point and should stress benefits, supported by features and proof statements. The writing style tends to be more

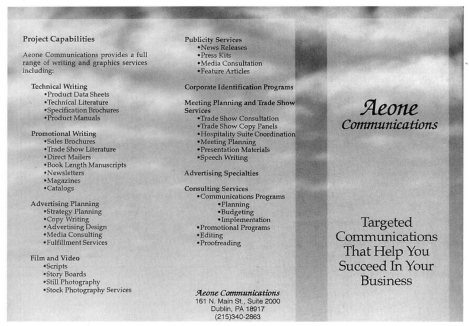

Project Capabilities

Aeone Communications provides a full range of writing and graphics services including:

Technical Writing
- Product Data Sheets
- Technical Literature
- Specification Brochures
- Product Manuals

Promotional Writing
- Sales Brochures
- Trade Show Literature
- Direct Mailers
- Book Length Manuscripts
- Newsletters
- Magazines
- Catalogs

Advertising Planning
- Strategy Planning
- Copy Writing
- Advertising Design
- Media Consulting
- Fulfillment Services

Film and Video
- Scripts
- Story Boards
- Still Photography
- Stock Photography Services

Publicity Services
- News Releases
- Press Kits
- Media Consultation
- Feature Articles

Corporate Identification Programs

Meeting Planning and Trade Show Services
- Trade Show Consultation
- Trade Show Copy Panels
- Hospitality Suite Coordination
- Meeting Planning
- Presentation Materials
- Speech Writing

Advertising Specialties

Consulting Services
- Communications Programs
  - Planning
  - Budgeting
  - Implementation
- Promotional Programs
- Editing
- Proofreading

Aeone
Communications

Targeted
Communications
That Help You
Succeed In Your
Business

Aeone Communications
161 N. Main St., Suite 2000
Dublin, PA 18917
(215)340-2863

Figure 13-6. Tri-fold brochure. (Courtesy of Aeone Communications.)

formal in a brochure than in a sales letter, but don't be too formal. Keep the writing simple.

CIRCULARS

Circulars are simple printed sheets describing your services, and they are another effective form of direct marketing (see Figure 13-7). All that is necessary is to create and print the circular and then hire someone to go from door to door and stuff them into mail slots or hang them on doorknobs in the neighborhood you've targeted. Check with the postal authorities before you put things into mailboxes. It may be illegal.

Circular distribution is one of the most inexpensive methods of marketing communication. It also has the advantage of letting you reach an area without necessarily knowing the names of the people, since you can deliver to households rather than to individuals. Thus, it can extend your reach beyond that of your mailing list.

BRIDAL SPECIAL

All this month at Tess's Tresses -- Our Bridal Special
Look your best for that special day. Great values for the
entire bridal party. Call for an appointment -- **555-1000**

1615 W. Main St., Doylestown, PA 18901

Figure 13-7. Sample circular. (Courtesy of Aeone Communications. Clip art copyright Metro
ImageBase, Inc.)

The message is important. Like any means of communication,
you have to capture the readers' attention first and then give them
the benefits of your services. Limit the size of the circular to one side
of a standard-size paper. Include an offer. Consider using a coupon or
other inducement to come into the salon. Use colored stock to attract
attention, but make sure the piece is readable. Again, don't forget
your name, address, hours of operation, and telephone number.

COOPERATIVE MAILINGS

Cooperative mailings consist of stacks of small circulars from a number of companies, bundled together and mailed to occupants in various neighborhoods. These present a good opportunity to reach a large number of people in an area with your message and offer. The cost varies with the size of the mailing and the complexity of your particular circular. The advantage is that you are sharing costs with every other advertiser in the mailing. These mailings can be an effective advertising tool for your salon.

There are a number of firms that specialize in making these mailings. To find the one servicing your area, ask your advertising agency, check your local telephone directory, or ask other business owners in the area if they're using such a service. Also, pay attention to the direct mail pieces that come into your home. The odds are that you are receiving one or more of these cooperative mailings yourself. Open them up and look through them. They usually contain information on contacting the mail service. While you're looking, note how the other ads are made. See what message they give and what style they take. Use this experience to get some ideas for your own promotions.

The firms that do the cooperative mailings will also print the pieces and take care of the mailing list. Since they print a number of these pieces on one sheet of paper, you can often use four-color process printing at a lower cost than printing it yourself. Again, this is because you are sharing the cost with other advertisers.

In many cases, the firms will also help you develop your message. As with other media, keep your message oriented to the user. Stress the benefits and give the necessary information, including your salon name, address, hours of operation, and telephone number. You may also have a special offer as part of the mailing as an inducement to come into the salon for the first visit.

NEWSLETTERS

Newsletters are excellent promotional vehicles for a salon. Develop your own newsletter, your own salon newspaper that you mail periodically to your customers and others on your mailing list. The advent of relatively low-cost desktop publishing programs for personal computers makes this a very feasible task. Although it can take some time to put a newsletter together, the cost is fairly low and it is an effective means of keeping your salon name and services in front of your clientele. The costs involved are for printing and for mailing the newsletter (as well as paying someone for its preparation, if you don't have the writing or graphics skills to do it yourself). Figure 13-8 shows a salon newsletter.

Newsletters work well because they address items of interest to your clients and promote the image of your salon as progressive and modern. But, like any advertising medium, they must be done properly. The newsletter should have a well-designed nameplate—an identification panel that contains the name of the newsletter, the date and issue, and identification for your salon. Include in your newsletter items about your salon. For example, you can feature a particular service in each issue. In one newsletter, you could describe a facial, discuss the benefits, and talk about your esthetician. In the next issue, you could describe the benefits and features of your hair coloring services. You might also want to profile one of your employees in each issue, describing his or her skills, background, and what benefits he or she brings to your salon. You probably should not discuss anything about your clients in the newsletter, however.

Use the newsletter to announce new services and new products you will offer and include notices of demonstrations or sales you will hold. Also include beauty industry items you think might be of interest to your clients, such as new products coming on the market, fashion trends, etc. You can get this information from the trade magazines. However, don't just copy the items. Take the information and write the article yourself. If you want to reproduce any item you see in a magazine, call the editor and ask for permission. Then give credit to the source of that item in your copy. Ask your suppliers for information you can use in your newsletter.

You might also add black-and-white illustrations and photos in the newsletter to give it more eye appeal and explain the subject matter better. Your suppliers may be able to supply some of these as well. If you show people or property in the photos, don't forget to get model and property releases first.

It may be possible to defray the costs of producing and mailing the newsletter by offering to include news items from other businesses in your area at a small fee. The businesses you approach, however, should be somewhat related to the beauty and fashion industry and should not be in competition with you. For example, the local bridal salon or flower shop would be good candidates, but the neighborhood saloon might not be suitable. This is an opportu-

Headlines

salon norman-dee

1619 Grant Avenue ○ Philadelphia Pa.,19115 ○ 215/676-0554

'94 Beauty and Fashion Forecast

Styling: Rina
Make-up: Trish
Photo: Alan Harris Studios

Our beauty forecasters report that making a resolution to exercise "freedom of choice" is the key to looking your best in 1994. This choice will result in numerous opportunities for you to express your individuality and to bring exciting variety into your life.

Skirts and dresses: long or short; pants: wide legs or tapered. A tailored, conservative look or a sexy, daring one: the choice is yours! Watch the fashion runways and you'll see lots of sheer, see-through fabric, and check out your favorite clothing outlet or boutique and you'll discover that the layered, eclectic look is "in" too.

Hair: short, mid-length or long. Curly or straight. Classic tailored cuts or elegant, natural cuts. Upswept 'dos or low maintenance styles. Color: choices are bountiful! Currently, warm tones are in vogue. Redheads from strawberry and fire to auburn and black cherry. Sultry brunettes with cognac and burgundy highlights. Golden blondes. But if the runways at Intercoiffeur's fall Atelier and at the spring fashion shows are any indication, the "cool" blonde is making a comeback in '94. Can we expect double-processed blondes too? Make your choice by consulting with your Salon Norman-Dee hair specialist to find a versatile style and an appealing color just right for you.

Nails: the long and short of it is --the choice is yours! You can move easily from the short, natural looking nails that are becoming increasingly popular with the busy career woman of the '90's to longer, more glamorous ones for special occasions. For the best of both worlds, talk to one of our nail specialists about the new sculptured acrylic that results in a long lasting French manicure look -- without the polish and without the time.

Make-up: the easiest way to experiment and exercise your freedom of choice. If the results are not exactly what you had pictured, just wash your face and start anew. Color and definition are back, and with high quality products and expert application, they need not be synonymous with a face that is unnatural or overdone. Schedule an appointment with **Pam** or **Helena**, and you'll walk away with the tools and know how to put your best face forward.

The staff at Salon Norman-Dee welcomes the challenge of being your choice for all of your beauty needs in the coming year.

Figure 13-8.   Sample newsletter. (Courtesy of Salon Norman-Dee.)

nity for these businesses to increase their customer base, so they ought to be interested in letting your clients know about new things happening in their businesses. They might also give you the names and addresses of some of their customers to supplement your mailing list. Just be careful not to overdo items from other businesses. You don't want to dilute the focus of your newsletter or let it get too far afield from your primary beauty business.

The newsletter doesn't have to be long. It can be anything from one page to many pages. Make it as long as it has to be to say what you want to say. Publish it as often as you have material to fill it. If you can publish your newsletter monthly, that's fine. But if you only publish it every other month or quarterly, that will work, too. And get feedback from your clients. Ask them how they like the newsletter, whether it's interesting and valuable to them. And ask them for suggestions about what they would like to see printed in it.

ANNUAL REPORTS

Corporations are required by the Securities and Exchange Commission (SEC) to send an annual report to their stockholders. This report details the company's finances for the year and informs the stockholders of profits and losses. Corporations take advantage of this SEC requirement to use the annual report to promote the company and to describe its accomplishments during the year. It becomes a major tool in persuading new investors to buy the company's stock.

Send out your own annual report to your customers and other prospects you can identify. In your case, you wouldn't produce a true annual report. You probably wouldn't want to disclose your finances. Unless you are registered as a corporation, there's no legal requirement to do so, except to your stockholders. How much, if any, profit your salon made and what your expenses and incomes were is really none of your customers' business. But the fact you were successful is of concern to them. And that's what the annual report would show. People are more comfortable dealing with successful people. Success inspires confidence in quality and in longevity. After all, a successful business is more likely to stay in business than an unsuccessful one. Nor is a successful business likely to cut corners on quality to reduce costs in order to stay open.

Your annual report doesn't have to be long or complicated. In fact, the simpler you keep it, the better. Identify it as an annual report, and then design it so it radiates success. Keep it bright and cheerful. If you can afford it, use some color, at least on the cover. And don't skimp on quality. Make it as good a piece as you can. Figure 13-9 shows an example of an annual report for a salon.

Although you won't discuss financial matters in your annual report, you should let the readers know you've had a successful year. Highlight your salon's accomplishments during the year, including any awards you or your operators may have won. Showcase your operators. Include their pictures along with a brief description of their skills. Describe the services you offer, highlighting any new services you instituted during the year. Talk about any new equipment you purchased to perform these services, keeping in mind the benefit to the customer. Also, talk about any special training you or your staff received.

Print enough copies to send to your customer and prospect lists and for distribution to your staff. Remember, your annual report is also an excellent vehicle for internal communications. Make sure you have enough copies to keep in the salon to use with new clients. The annual report is a tool that will keep working for you for the whole year.

VIDEO MAILINGS

We live in a television age. In most households, people have grown up with television. They are influenced by it and, correctly or incorrectly, rely on it for information. Many households have VCRs and often purchase or rent videotapes, or videotape shows for later viewing. Television watching is a deeply ingrained habit. It's a habit that can give you excellent marketing communications opportunities.

Not only have VCRs proliferated, but video cameras have become more inexpensive and easier to operate, as the technology has improved greatly. You might be able to use this technology to your advantage by making your own videotapes (a mini-infomercial) to send to your prospects. This lets you combine sight, movement, and sound to give your message more impact.

TELEMARKETING

Not all direct marketing involves printed materials. You can get excellent results simply by using a tool found in every salon: the telephone. Use it to call prospects and clients and solicit new or

1615 W. Main St., Doylestown, PA 18901
Telephone: (215)555-1000

ANNUAL REPORT 1994

A Progress Report To Our Clients, Friends, and Associates

Tess's Tresses has finished its first full year in operation and we are very happy to report that 1994 exceeded all of our expectations.

This is our first Annual Report, and it's meant to share our success with you and to thank you for making it possible.

We reached a number of milestones this past year.

•Staff: Our family grew with the addition of three new stylists -- Cindy, Bob, and Alice. All three of these hightly trained and talented people brought considerable experience to our shop.

•Services: We instituted our skin care department, which has been very successful and is growing in popularity faster than we imagined. We finished construction of our electrolysis center, which will open as soon as Catherine finishes her training.

•Hours: Due to the demand, we expanded our hours last October. The new hours are

Figure 13-9. Annual report sample.

increased business. It is a relatively inexpensive method of direct marketing in that your major cost is for the telephone calls—that is, if you do the calling yourself or utilize your staff. If you hire a professional telemarketing agency, the cost will be higher.

The advantage to telemarketing is that it gives you one-on-one contact and is an extension of personal selling. You can talk directly to the prospect. The disadvantage is that it can be intrusive. You run the risk of interrupting an activity or annoying the person you call.

Telemarketing requires just as much planning as any other form of marketing communications. You have to have a clear objective, and you have to know the audience. Prepare a script and work from that. Know what you want to say and have a definite offer in mind. Keep the calls short. Call when people are most likely to be available, but don't call at mealtimes or late at night. Never call prospects at work.

Start the call by identifying yourself and your purpose. Ask if the person has the time to talk now or if you should call back later. If the person says this isn't a good time, don't force the issue. Ask when you should call back, thank the person, and end the call. Use the call to update your information to add to your database. At the end of the call, thank the person for his or her time and attention. Ask for the order. Remember, nothing happens until you do that.

Your telemarketing list will come from your customer database. You might be able to get other names and telephone numbers from the telephone directory or from other businesses in the area. Keep accurate records of your calls and the results you get.

FOR THE FUTURE

Technology is pointing the way to the future of direct marketing. Computers and fax machines have become more sophisticated and powerful. And they have become more affordable. No longer are these machines limited to businesses. They are becoming almost essential items in homes across the country.

The implications for direct marketing are enormous as technology opens new doors for marketing communications. One new door is telefaxing, either through fax/modems in computers or through stand-alone fax machines. In the future, you may be sending promotional faxes to your clients. This combines the best of direct mail and telemarketing. The cost would be relatively low, mostly for telephone time. Printing costs would be almost nonexistent, since you prepare only one piece of paper rather than printing hundreds or thousands of copies.

E-mail may be another door of opportunity for marketing communications. As electronic mail systems proliferate and people get accustomed to receiving mail through their computers, this service could provide the next major avenue for direct mail, without the cost of printing.

Although neither of these technologies has been adopted by the masses required to make them viable direct marketing tools, they are growing quickly. Start planning now for using these exciting new tools.

MEASURING DIRECT MARKETING EFFECTIVENESS

Unlike print or broadcast advertising, you can't measure the effectiveness of direct marketing vehicles by factors such as cost per exposure or similar numbers. Your best measure for these vehicles, however, is to count the increase in traffic coming into your salon. This is relatively easy to do if you take the time to do it. When you get a new client, ask how he or she found out about you. Note which direct marketing vehicle the client responded to. If you have enclosed a coupon or reply card in a printed piece, code it so you'll know which vehicle it came from. It is important to know which vehicles are working and how well they are doing for you. Keep accurate records so you can repeat successes and discard failures.

SUMMARY

- Direct marketing and advertising have a lot in common. For both, you have to have clear goals and objectives, and you have to know your audience. They also have a number of differences. One of these is reach. Advertising works best when you have a large, not readily identified audience. Direct marketing works best when you have smaller audiences or audiences that you can identify.
- Direct marketing vehicles usually give you more space to develop your message. You also get better control over delivery, since you deliver the message straight to the prospect, following your own time schedule.

- There is more control over quality with direct marketing since you can be more closely involved with the actual production of the printed piece.

- The more often you get your message in front of the audience, the more likely it is that it will be remembered. With direct marketing, you can set the frequency to suit your needs without relying on publication schedules.

- Direct marketing can also be more cost effective than advertising. You have more control over costs and can tailor the complexity of the vehicle to meet your budget.

- The customer list is one of your most valuable assets. Your current customers are your best source of income. But you also need to add to the list, so you'll have to get names from other sources. There are a number of sources you can use, including other businesses, client referrals, newspapers, and list brokers.

- Direct marketing vehicles include direct mailers, sales letters, brochures, circulars, newsletters, cooperative mailings, and annual reports.

- Telemarketing is also a good way to promote your business. Exciting new possibilities for the near future include video, faxing, and e-mail.

- Basically, direct mail is a package of promotional materials that is sent to your preselected audience. It can be as simple or as complex as you want.

- Whatever form the direct mailer takes, the message is paramount. Stress the benefits. Make the offer. Include all the information the prospect needs to make a decision. And don't forget to ask for the order.

- Postage will be a big part of the cost of direct mailing. You can mail either first-class or third-class bulk, depending on the size of the mailing and its sensitivity to time. Bulk rate is usually most cost effective unless the size of the mailing is very small.

- The classic elements of a direct mail package are an envelope, a letter, a promotional brochure, a lift letter, an involvement device, a premium, and an order form.

- Don't underestimate the power of a well-written letter in increasing sales. Letters have a lot of credibility and are a more personal means of communication.

- Pay special attention to the letter's lead. This is the first part recipients see, and it has to get their attention and persuade them to read the rest of the letter. State the major benefit up front. Then follow it with proof statements. Close the letter with the offer. Restate the benefits and ask for the order. Use a postscript with the letter.

- Brochures, catalogs, and circulars are printed pieces that describe and promote your business and services. A brochure can be anything from a single folded sheet to a multipage booklet. A catalog is generally a multipage booklet that shows and describes products for sale. A circular is usually a simple single sheet document designed for door-to-door delivery rather than being mailed.
- Cooperative mailings are stacks of small circulars from a number of companies bundled together and mailed to occupants in various neighborhoods.
- Desktop publishing makes production of a newsletter practical for small businesses. It gives you an opportunity to discuss a wide range of topics with your customers and keep your name in front of them.
- Consider making your own videotape message and sending it to your mailing list. Produce your own mini-infomercial.
- Don't forget the telephone. Telemarketing—that is, calling your prospects and talking to them one-on-one—is also an effective means of communication.
- As with print and broadcast advertising, it is important to measure effectiveness. Take just as much care to do this with direct marketing vehicles as you do with your other advertising vehicles. Repeat the successes. Discard the failures.

CHAPTER 14

Sales Promotion and Public Relations

In a sense, all marketing and marketing communications involve the promotion of your business. However, there are many things you can do to promote your business and increase sales in addition to your communications programs. With some imagination and effort, you can keep your salon name in front of people in the community, bring them into the salon, and convert them into customers. And you can use many of these same methods to help keep your current customers loyal to your salon.

Sales promotion and public relations cannot exist in a vacuum. Neither can advertising and direct marketing, the other two marketing communications activities. You need all of these tools, working together, to get the most from your marketing efforts. Even though these tools are discussed separately, it is important that you remember to support one type with the others. The various sales promotion and public relations activities discussed here, for example, will be more effective if they are backed up with targeted advertising and direct marketing assistance.

Sales promotion and public relations are closely tied together. They do essentially the same thing, except that sales promotion activities are oriented toward promoting your services, whereas public relations activities are oriented toward promoting your salon. Both are aimed at increasing your business. For many activities, the distinction between the two is blurred. Do you characterize an activity as a sales promotion effort? Or as a public relations effort? Actually, it doesn't really matter what you call it. What is far more important is that you do it—and do it right, with adequate thought, planning, and budget.

Involve your staff in sales promotion activities. You don't have to do everything yourself. Train staff members in various sales promotion techniques. Solicit their suggestions. Hold promotion idea contests among your staff members. And share the successes with them. Offer your staff various incentives, such as bonuses or increased commissions, when they've helped increase your business. Be lavish with praise. Sometimes praise can be a tremendous incentive. Give your employees a stake in increasing business for you, and they'll respond in ways that will amaze you.

When it comes to public relations, look constantly for things you can do to call attention to your salon. Here, too, your staff can be a big help if you involve them in the process.

PERSONAL SELLING

Personal selling is the first of your promotion tools. As long as you're in business, you have to sell your services and you have to sell yourself. That means you have to be outgoing and friendly. You also have to be in a position to meet and talk to people. Other sales promotion methods give you the opportunity to do that.

This tool provides the personal touch that is so crucial to success in a beauty salon, which, more than most businesses, relies on intimacy. And you are in the best position to provide that intimacy. Only you have the passion for your business and the fire to succeed. If you don't have a passion and fire for what you're doing, you probably shouldn't be in business.

You represent the best image and impression you show to your clients. Use every conversation to promote your salon. That doesn't mean you have to do it alone. Involve your staff. Train them in personal selling techniques. Pass along to them the fire and enthusiasm you feel. Make selling a team effort, and get everybody you hire on the team.

Encourage your clients to promote your salon. Remember that word of mouth advertising is the most effective message you can send out. Make each client a salesperson. Ask them to tell their friends and associates about you. You'll be surprised how often they'll readily do this, even without incentives. But they'll only do it if they are completely satisfied with your services and believe you can offer the same benefits to their friends.

Personal selling is possibly the least expensive, yet one of the most effective, promotional tools you can use to help create demand and reinforce your image. It is flexible. You don't work from a script. You can use the best argument for the person you're selling to. As you get feedback, either verbal, through questions and comments, or visual through expressions or body language, you can alter your presentation. You're limited only by the number of people you can reach personally or through your staff.

THE SALON

Your salon itself can be its own best sales promotion tool. Make your salon distinctive. Think of your salon as a giant display case, highlighting your wares—that is, your services and retail products—to the best advantage. Promote your image. Call attention to your salon. Make every element of decor work for you. Remember that the salon is your most important product. Review the discussion on decor and ambiance in Chapter 5.

Choose your decor carefully. Keep it appropriate to your image, and be consistent. Use the best-quality equipment and supplies you can. Utilize in-store displays. Decor starts with your sign outside and continues throughout the entire working area of the salon—that includes more than just the public areas of the salon. Make other areas just as attractive and friendly. You and your staff deserve the same considerations your customers expect.

Decor extends to more than just appearance. Ambiance is a sensual experience. Sight is only one of the senses. Don't overlook the smells or sounds, or even the tactile experiences you subject your clients to. Make sure the salon is always bright, cheerful, clean, and inviting.

Attitude is a key part of the salon experience for your clients. It starts in the reception area and continues in the working areas of the salon. It extends through the time the client pays the bill. This is where you can utilize what, perhaps, is the single most important promotional device for keeping customers satisfied. It is a simple two-word phrase—"Thank you." Let the client know you appreciate his or her business.

DISPLAYS

Help promote services and products with in-store displays. There is a large variety to choose from, ranging from window streamers to floor displays, window and door stickers, wall posters and hangers, counter cards, and counter displays.

Window streamers and window and door stickers are designed to attract attention from the outside of the salon. Their function is to

Figure 14-1. Window streamers and door stickers.

invite passersby inside. So they should be bright and inviting and offer a major benefit. Figure 14-1 shows examples.

The other types of displays are used inside the salon. Their function is to increase sales from your customers, to get them to buy services or products other than the ones they initially came in for. Like the outer-directed displays, these should also be inviting and offer a benefit, but they can be more product oriented. Figure 14-2 shows typical counter displays.

Make wall posters and hangers do more than decorate. Whether they illustrate current fashions or colors or just set a mood, these items on the walls help carry your image. Make sure they sell as well. Whatever you put on the walls should have a theme and an objective and should promote a service or product, even if the promotion is subtle. Figure 14-3 suggests a use.

You can have these display items made for you. Utilize your creative agency for ideas. At the very least, hire a graphics artist to do the design and production. Treat these vehicles the same way you would treat an ad or a direct marketing vehicle. Consider your goals and objectives.

Change your displays frequently to keep a fresh look in the area. If you keep the same display for a long time, your clients can become so used to it, they won't notice it.

Figure 14-2. Examples of counter displays. (Courtesy of OPI Products Inc.)

Figure 14-3. Sample poster. (Clip art copyright Metro ImageBase, Inc.)

Manufacturers and suppliers also offer a wide variety of display materials, often in conjunction with a special promotion they are running. These displays are professionally done and are well designed and produced, even though they may be oriented to a specific product. Talk to your suppliers. Find out what display materials they offer. Then make use of them. Also, store fixture distributors sell display accessories. Call them. Ask for a catalog, and visit their showrooms to get display ideas.

Use display techniques in your retail area, too. Make the area inviting, attractive, and able to catch the awareness of the clients as they pass through it. Keep it neat and uncluttered, and arrange the products to focus attention on them. Display the products to show them to their best advantage. You can place products in glass display cases, on countertops, in bins, on shelves, or in a combination of any of these. In some cases, you might put selected products on a free-standing pedestal to call special attention to them. Keep the more valuable items in locked display cases to help guard against shoplifting.

Keep glass display cases, countertops, and shelves clean and free of fingerprints and dust. Clean the products frequently, too. Mark the price clearly but unobtrusively on each item. Decide whether you want the customers to serve themselves or whether you will have a designated salesperson wait on them. Self-service items need to be accessible, placed on open shelves or in bins. Items in display cases will not be self-service.

The overall illumination in the retail area should be bright and even, but you can highlight certain products with spotlights. Be careful if the products are exposed to sunlight coming through your windows. Ultraviolet radiation can cause colors to fade and destroy the appearance of the products.

Use appropriate props to show off the products. For example, you might use a bed of autumn leaves to display an assortment of makeup in seasonal colors. Keep a supply of things you can use for props, such as cotton batting, assorted colors of cloth for drapings, ribbons, mirrors, etc. Color coordinate your displays. The displays should be harmonious, not discordant.

Always be alert for display ideas for your products. Visit department and specialty stores and see how they display their goods. Look at various magazines to see how products are shown in advertisements. Start a clipping file of display ideas. And use your imagination.

SALES

Sales have long been used as promotional devices to build store traffic. You can offer special sales to promote your services. When you introduce a new service, you might give a special price to first-time buyers of that service, either as a stand-alone offer or piggy-backed onto another service. For example, suppose you are introducing electrolysis services into your salon. You could make an introductory offer of a lower price for the first treatment, or have a "buy one, get one free" promotion, regardless of whether the patron buys another service.

You could also offer another service free or at a lower price when a client buys a standard service (for example, free makeover with a facial). In some cases, you might offer products free or at a reduced price with a service, such as, free makeup kit with makeover. This is especially effective when you can get the products at a lower cost as part of a manufacturer's promotion.

Don't overdo sales. If you've priced your services properly, they should be acceptable and fair to your clientele. If you run sales too often, clients may start to wonder about the fairness of your price schedule. Or they might not come back until your next sale. Don't reduce the price too drastically. Try to at least cover your cost. Remember, when you have a sale, you're trading current revenue for future revenue.

Have specific goals in mind for the sale. Have a clear idea of what you want to accomplish. Think it through before you make the offer. Limit the time for the sale. Don't let it run too long. Advertise the sale so people will know about it. Use a coupon or some item that the client has to redeem to take advantage of the sale. This will help you keep track of how well both the advertising and the sale worked. After the promotion is over, analyze the results. Did it meet your goals? If not, try to find out why. Use what you've learned to guide you in making further promotions.

SPECIAL EVENTS

Take advantage of special events, such as holidays, birthdays, and anniversaries, to promote sales. These events have natural ties to promotions that many businesses run. Just look at how you're inundated with commercials and ads for special sales for holidays such as President's Day. Get on the bandwagon with these. People expect special promotions to coincide with major special events. Don't disappoint them.

Develop a theme built around the event, and use display materials that carry that theme. Then supplement the promotion with advertising and direct marketing. Put an ad in the newspaper. Have someone distribute circulars in the neighborhood. Promote the event to help promote your business (see Figure 14-4).

Special events don't have to be limited to national holidays. They can also be keyed to local affairs or graduation time; even the change of seasons can be an event. Keep track of your own special events, too. Your salon's anniversary is an ideal time for a special sales event. Figure 14-5 shows one way of handling this. Have a sale on your birthday. Celebrate the birthdays of members of your staff by offering specials on services they perform. Offer clients a free or reduced-price service in conjunction with other services on their birthdays. Remember, when it comes to promotion, a special event is defined only by your imagination.

Figure 14-4.   Examples of holiday promotion displays. (Courtesy of OPI Products Inc.)

TESS'S TRESSES IS ONE YEAR OLD!

BIRTHDAY CELEBRATION

Help us celebrate our first anniversary. Join us in a day of fun, prizes, food, and great values.
JANUARY 30, 1995
Reserve your place. Call 555-1000

Figure 14-5. Sample anniversary promotion. (Courtesy of Aeone Communications. Clip art copyright Metro ImageBase, Inc.)

OPEN HOUSES AND DEMONSTRATIONS

An informed consumer is more apt to purchase your services. Hold an occasional open house in your skin care salon so people can come in and see what you have to offer. Hold demonstrations to explain the benefits and features of your services. Show the people what you're selling. You might even have a guest speaker to talk about beauty and health, current fashion, or any relevant subject. Make it a party atmosphere. Have light, nonalcoholic refreshments, door prizes, and make sure each person gets a small gift—an advertising specialty item that has your salon name and telephone number on it. Have members of your staff on hand to answer questions.

Schedule the open house for a day or evening that you are not normally open. Open the affair to invited guests only. If you know your audience, choose your guest list accordingly. Send invitations by mail. Ask for a response so you can get an idea of how many people will come. Let the size of your facility determine how many people you can accommodate. Don't overcrowd the facility. You want the people to be able to mill around without being uncomfortable.

Get your suppliers involved, either to provide a speaker or to help with decorations. Many suppliers will be happy to give you some promotional help. Talk to them when you start making your plans. They should be able to give you some good ideas.

TIE-IN PROMOTIONS

Make promotional deals with other businesses in your area. For example, you might work with your local bridal shop. Let them promote your services for you in exchange for a piece of the profits generated by their customers. For example, the bridal salon might send brides in for a facial and makeover the day before or the morning of the wedding. Similarly, you might promote the bridal shop to your clients who are getting married. Figure 14-6 shows an example.

If you feature skin care services, visit dermatologists in the area. Explain your skin care services and show how you can help the doctor's clients with deep pore cleansing. Try to establish a relationship with the dermatologist, in which he or she will refer patients to your salon and you will refer clients to his or her practice. Don't be afraid to try this. Dermatologists know the value of clean, healthy skin, and many will be receptive to some kind of tie-in.

1615 W. Main St., Doylestown

JUNE IS BRIDAL MONTH. AND WE'RE OFFERING A BRIDAL PARTY SPECIAL.

Bring the bridal party in for hair styling, manicure, and facials, and get 10% off your bridal accessories from Billie's Bridal Bower.

Call 555-1000 to make arrangements for your big day.

Outfit your bridal party at Billie's in the month of June and get a special treat.

Receive 10% off all hair, skin and nail services at Tess's Tresses. Call 555-9999 for an appointment for a consultation.

2180 N. State St., Doylestown

Figure 14-6. Tie-in promotion. (Courtesy of Aeone Communications. Clip art copyright Metro ImageBase, Inc.)

Limit your tie-in deals to businesses that are relevant to your salon. There should be some reason their clients might utilize your services. The tie-in has to be a good deal for both sides, so don't attempt to take any unfair advantages.

OTHER PROMOTION STRATEGIES

Sales, open houses, etc., as discussed earlier, are the most common promotional strategies. They are widely used because they have proved effective time after time. But you don't have to limit your promotional efforts to these. There are many other simple, yet effective, strategies you can employ.

PHOTO GALLERY

Take photographs of your clients and display them. Use photos that show especially good styles or makeup. Highlight your customers. They'll enjoy it. And they'll be perfect illustrations of your successes for other clients to see. In some cases, you might even use before and after shots. Just make sure that the pictures are well exposed, in focus, and well lighted. Both color photos and black-and-white photos will work. Get the customers' approval before displaying the photo, however.

These photos are good sales promotion devices. You might also be able to use them in other ways, once you have them. Use them in your salon newsletter, for example. Or use them in ads and direct mailers. You might even make your own salon calendar, using your clients' pictures as illustrations. For these uses, it is imperative that you get signed model releases from the people whose pictures you show.

VIDEOTAPE

Still photography is one thing. But videotape is another alternative. Make your own salon videotape. Highlight a service with an on-screen demonstration. Show the latest in styles or fashions. Or use the videotape as a "catalog" of your salon's services. Play the tape in your reception area. Let the tape create a selling atmosphere with your clients as they wait for their appointments.

Keep the tapes short. Make sure they tell a story and are not just a jumbled series of shots. Shoot footage carefully, paying attention to focus and lighting. Have the tapes edited professionally. Have the tape put onto a continuous loop, so it will repeat over and over. Keep the volume low.

AUDIOTAPE

No matter how efficient your reception area is, and no matter how well your staff is trained to answer the telephone, you will often have to put callers on hold. Make that hold period work for you. Instead of silence or, worse yet, canned music, make a hold tape you can play while a caller is waiting. Use the time to promote a service or a special promotion. Keep the tape short. Make it lively and to the point. Stress benefits. Don't forget to thank the caller for his or her interest in your salon. And apologize for making the caller hold.

Change the tape often. Audiotapes are easy to make, and they are inexpensive, so you can adjust the message frequently. If you don't have a good speaking voice, try using members of your staff. Use a professional announcer if you have to, but make the tape sound professional.

Have two kinds of audio tape—a hold tape and an after-hours tape. Use the hold tape while you are open. Have an after-hours tape for when you are closed. Use much the same format for the after-hours tape as for the hold tape, but add information about your hours of operation, credit cards you accept, and other relevant information. And tell the caller what he or she should do with a statement like, "Call tomorrow for an appointment" or "Leave your name and telephone number and someone will get back to you as soon as possible." Don't ask for this, however, unless you really intend to call back. In most cases, this won't be necessary.

Write the script carefully, and record the audiotape from the script. Don't try to ad lib. Practice the delivery of the script before you commit the words to tape. Retape as often as necessary to get the message you want, in a way you want it delivered. Figure 14-7 shows a sample script for an audiotape.

Thank you for calling Tess's Tresses, where everyday is a celebration of beauty. Our receptionists are taking another call, but one will be with you as soon as possible. We offer a full line of beauty services, including haircutting, hairstyling, coloring, and permanent waving, as well as complete skin and body care, waxing, electrolysis, and nail care. This month we're having a special sale on manicures. Save 10 percent on acrylic nail application.

(repeat, if necessary)

Figure 14-7.   Sample hold tape script.

NEW CUSTOMER KITS

Prepare a welcome kit for new customers. Start building a good relationship right away. Put together a package containing a letter of welcome from you and your staff, your salon capabilities brochure, and a small gift of some type, perhaps an advertising specialty item. Make the package attractive. Gift wrap it in colorful paper. It should look like the present it is intended to be.

Give one of these welcome kits to each new client who comes into the salon. Handing him or her one of these packages is an excellent opportunity for you to spend a few minutes gathering the information you need for your customer database.

As suggested in Chapter 13, "Direct Marketing," you might also mail one of these welcome kits to new arrivals in the neighborhood. Check the real estate section of the newspaper for names and addresses of people who have just purchased homes in the area.

ENVELOPE STUFFERS

If you bill customers for services, you should also use a stuffer in every envelope. A stuffer is a small flyer that describes a product or service for sale, and it is most commonly included in envelopes with bills and invoices. Keep stuffers simple and to the point. For best results, make them in the form of a coupon that the client has to bring in for redemption.

YOUR CAR

Don't limit your promotional activity to the salon building. Make your car an extension of the salon. Reproduce your salon name and logo, along with address and telephone number, on your car. Make your car a moving billboard for your salon. If you don't want salon identification painted permanently on your car, have magnetic signboards made and attach them to the doors. That way, you can remove them when you don't want them on your car.

FREQUENT-CUSTOMER PROGRAMS

Take a tip from the airlines' frequent-flier award programs. Offer a free service after the purchase of a certain number of that service.

This approach can work well for services you are trying to build. For example, you could have a frequent-facial membership, wherein the client gets a sixth facial free after purchasing five facials.

PUBLIC RELATIONS

Continue promotions through your public relations efforts. Like other promotions, the aim of public relations is to influence attitudes among certain segments of the population. The difference is that those tools are concerned with influencing purchasing decisions for services and products, whereas public relations is concerned with influencing opinions about the business. The goal of public relations is to keep your salon in the public eye in a manner that makes it attractive and desirable.

As discussed in Chapter 9, Marketing Communications, positioning is an important concept in the success of your business. Public relations is the means you use to position your business as an entity, apart from the products and services you offer. It includes the means you use to establish and reinforce your image.

Public relations has another very important use: It is a vehicle for damage control. Sooner or later, while you are in business, something will go wrong. How you handle the aftermath can affect your image and your business greatly. Good public relations lets you minimize any bad effects.

There are many different public relations tools you can use. They are effective means of keeping your salon in front of customers and prospects, and, unlike advertising and direct marketing tools, can be very inexpensive. Like all other tools, however, your public relations efforts have to be planned. You can't approach these efforts haphazardly and expect to get any benefit. In fact, done improperly, there is the danger they can backfire on you and create the wrong impression of your salon. So be careful.

PUBLICITY

Publicity is a valuable public relations tool that serves as an adjunct to your other promotional efforts. The best part is that it is free. It is also very credible, because it is a third-party endorsement of your salon. That is, someone else is saying good things about you. You're not saying them about yourself. Publicity can be in the form of news coverage, press releases, or feature articles.

NEWS COVERAGE

Cultivate good relations with the local news media, including the newspapers, radio stations, and television stations that cover the area in which you operate. Get to know the various editors and reporters. They are always looking for good human interest items to use as fillers. Help them out. Let these people know when something is going to happen in your salon, especially if it's an unusual event—which you will have staged for its promotional value. This could be almost anything that you could think of. Make it a media event.

Look for the newsworthiness in anything that happens in your salon. Sometimes this takes some imagination. You might ask, What's newsworthy about a woman getting a haircut? One enterprising salon owner had a client come in to get her first haircut in more than 20 years. Her hair was six feet long. She had it cut on television. A local television station taped the cutting and showed it on that evening's news broadcast. The owner got a lot of free publicity.

PRESS RELEASES

Press releases are short news items that are prepared by businesses and sent to the media in hopes of publication. They are different from news coverage. When you get news coverage, the reporters visit your business and gather information for the story. With a press release, you write the story and send it to the press. To get news coverage requires an event that has unusual aspects to it. With a press release, there is a much wider latitude in the subject matter.

Newspapers, especially smaller local papers, are always looking for good, interesting, newsworthy items to print. Whenever you have something that may be newsworthy (for example, a new service being offered, an industry award that you've won, or even something as simple as a promotion for an employee), write a short press release and send it to the newspapers. If there are local magazines that service your area, send the releases to them, too. Don't forget to include the radio and television stations in the distribution list.

Keep the news releases short, simple, and factual. Answer the questions, who, what, where, when, why, and how. Put the most important facts down first and expand on them in following paragraphs. Include a glossy black-and-white photo if you have one available. Stick to the facts. Don't engage in puffery or self-aggrandizement. On the top of the release, provide your name and telephone number, so the editor can contact you for more information. Send the release to the news editor. Call up the newspaper and get his or her name (see Figure 14-8).

There is no guarantee that the newspapers or magazines will print your news release. They are under no obligation to do so. And don't insult the editors by pointing out that you advertise in the newspaper. That won't make any difference. If the item is newsworthy and fits their needs, and if it is reasonably well written and professionally presented, they will use it. It is important that the release be presented in a professional manner. This means it should be grammatically and stylistically correct and should be neatly typed double-spaced on one side of standard-size white paper. If you haven't the ability to write good, clear English sentences, by all means hire someone to write the releases for you.

PRESS RELEASE

Tess's Tresses
1615 W. Main St.
Doylestown, PA 18901

Telephone: (215)555-1000   **Contact:** Tess Truelove

For Release: Immediate   **Date:** February 20, 1995

NEW ELECTROLYSIS CENTER AT TESS'S TRESSES

Tess Truelove, owner and manager of the Doylestown-based salon, Tess's Tresses, announced today the opening of the area's most modern, up-to-date center for electrolysis.

The center, part of the salon's on-going expansion program, adds a new dimension to the removal of unwanted hair. Electrolysis is the only method that removes unwanted hair permanently.

The center is staffed by Catherine Hawkins and Sheila Robbins, both licensed electrologists, who bring years of experience to their profession. The center is open Tuesday through Saturday, from 8:30 am to 9 pm.

-end-

Figure 14-8. Example of a press release.

Either see your creative agency or check with your local high school or college English departments for a freelance writer.

FEATURE STORIES

A feature story is an expanded account of some subject within your area of expertise. It is longer than a press release, is usually illustrated, and is focused on a particular theme. It is the kind of thing that would appear in the Sunday magazine section instead of the society page. A feature story is also more exclusive than a press release. You send a press release to all relevant media. A feature story is normally written as an exclusive for one particular newspaper or magazine.

If you are an expert on a particular phase of the beauty business, or if you are trying to establish yourself as one, offer to write a feature story for the local newspaper or magazine. Give the paper or magazine exclusive rights to the story. Have a definite idea in mind when you approach the editor—for example, "Wrinkle control. Does it really work?"

Slant the story to appeal to the readers of the publication. Present data and ideas, and make the story benefit oriented. Use simple, direct language. As with the press release, answer the basic questions—who, what, where, when, why, and how. Verify all facts for accuracy. If you don't have the ability to write capably, it is perfectly acceptable to hire a professional to ghost write the story for you, as long as you supply all the facts and the general concept.

If you get a feature story placed in a publication, take advantage of it by getting reprints. Hand out reprints in the salon, or mail them to your customer list. Use the piece to demonstrate your expertise.

OTHER MEDIA EXPOSURE

If you operate in a relatively small market area, explore the possibility of having your own radio show or newspaper column on beauty care subjects. Take advantage of your expertise. Develop a format. Tape some sample broadcasts and present them to the radio station director, or write some sample columns and send them to the managing editor of the newspaper. However, unless you are a well-known and recognized expert, this approach will only work for small radio stations and newspapers. Media in major metropolitan areas usually already have similar shows.

PERSONAL APPEARANCES

Not all demonstrations have to be in your salon. Take the show on the road. You can get a lot of good public relations by speaking to local groups about beauty issues. This is a good way to demonstrate your expertise and to meet a lot of people.

Organizations are always looking for good, interesting speakers, especially those who will talk for free. These groups, like the local garden club, the Kiwanis, a church group, etc., usually hold regular meetings, and they need presenters to attract attendees. Get a list of organizations in your area and write a letter to the group president about your presentation.

Then put together a presentation. Keep it to an hour or less, and illustrate the talk with slides or overhead transparencies. If you can demonstrate a process, such as skin care, that's even better. Prepare handout materials you can leave with the audience. And don't forget to include your business card.

SPONSORSHIPS

Become a sponsor. Take your local girl's soccer team or Little League team under your wing. Provide hats and team shirts, and take advantage of the public relations value. Every time the team takes to the field, you get free publicity. And it doesn't come only from people watching the games. Remember, every relative of every team member is a potential client.

COMMUNITY SERVICE

Get involved in your community. Take part in community activities. Offer your services in charitable causes. For example, give a facial as a prize for the church bazaar. Or donate a makeover as a prize for your local PBS station fund raising.

Join the service organizations. They are excellent groups to work with for performing community service, as they usually have programs established. This is a good way to get involved. It is also a good way to network—to meet people and to become known in the community. In addition to keeping your name in front of the community, you'll also be giving something back to the community. But it is important to keep the focus of these activities on the help you're giving, not on what you'll get. Be careful not to give the perception that you're only doing these things for your benefit.

SUMMARY

- Sales promotion activities are oriented toward promoting services. Public relations activities are, in many cases, similar but are oriented toward promoting your business as an entity.
- Your staff can help with sales promotion and public relations activities. Solicit their suggestions and share successes with them.
- You undertake personal selling virtually every time you talk to people. This is the tool that provides the personal touch necessary to the salon business. Encourage your staff and your clients to spread the good word about your salon. Let everyone sell.
- Let your salon be a giant display case for your products and services. Make it distinctive. Choose your decor carefully, starting with the signs outside and extending through to the nonpublic areas. The ambience is also a big part of the decor.
- Utilize displays of all types. These can be window streamers, door stickers, posters, counter displays, and floor displays.
- Sales are promotional devices that build store traffic. You can reduce prices on certain services, offer a free or lower-priced service with the purchase of one at full price, or give products away with the purchase of a service.
- Take advantage of special events for holding sales. Holidays, anniversaries, and birthdays all have natural ties to business promotions. Develop a theme around the event and carry that theme in displays and advertisements.
- Open houses and demonstrations are good ways to introduce prospects to your services. Schedule them for a time you are normally not open. Make it a party atmosphere, with door prizes and refreshments.
- Make promotional deals with other businesses in your area, as long as they have some bearing on your field and are noncompetitive. For example, a tie-in with a bridal salon or flower shop could benefit both parties.
- Public relations is the tool to influence attitudes about your salon. Public relations can help position your salon in the marketplace. It is also a good tool for damage control, to limit the

after-effects of serious mishaps that occur in all businesses from time to time.

- Publicity is free, and it is credible. Try to get news coverage for your salon. Get to know media people—reporters and editors. Cultivate good relations with them.
- Send press releases to the media. Newspapers, especially in smaller markets, are always looking for good, interesting, newsworthy items to print. Keep news releases short, simple, and factual. Answer the basic questions—who, what, where, when, why, and how.
- Consider writing a feature story for one of the local publications. Remember the audience and the publication when you decide how to slant the story. If you place a feature story, make use of it by mailing reprints to your customers.
- Explore the possibility of having a radio show or writing a newspaper column about beauty care.
- Personal appearances may also be effective. Give talks to local organizations. Prepare a presentation and offer it to them.
- Get involved in community affairs. Network through membership in various service organizations. Provide community service.

Glossary/Index

Acceptance, 194. (*See also* Marketing Communications)

Account supervisor, 204. (*See also* Agencies, marketing communications)

Accounting and bookkeeping, 85–86, 97–98. (*See also* Computers)

Advertising, 4, 20, 178, 259–96. (*See also* Marketing Communications)
effectiveness, 263–67, 270, 285–86
media, 267–85
objectives, 261–63
overview, 259–61
print anatomy, 287–91, f12–10
radio anatomy, 291–94
specialties, 284–85

Advertisement, is a paid public notice designed to call attention to a product or service with the intent of persuading the people it reaches to form a favorable opinion of the item and to purchase and use it, 259

Advertiser identification, 290. (*See also* Advertising, print anatomy)

Advocacy marketing, 27–29

Agencies, marketing communications, 202–7
compensation, 203–4
finding, 208–9
functions, 203
relationship, 207–8
structure, 204–7, f9–4
types, 204

Aging, 8–9. (*See also* Environment, social)

Ambiance, is the feeling the client gets when he or she walks into the salon, 105–06

Analysis
clientele, 25–26
data, 5

Annual reports, detail the company's finances for the year and informs the stockholders of profits and losses, 319–20, f13–9

Art director, 206. (*See also* Agencies, marketing communications)

Audience, knowledge, 264. (*See also* Advertising, effectiveness)

Audience, target, 32–34, f2–1

Audiotape, 338–39

Awareness, 193–94. (*See also* Marketing Communications)

Bait and switch, 185

Body copy, is the main text of the document, 221, 289. (*See also* Design, copy)

Broadcast media, are those that utilize the airwaves to transmit their messages, 277–81. (*See also* Advertising)
radio, 277–79
television, 279–81

Brochures and catalogs, 312–14, f13–6

Budgeting, 76, 201–2

Build strategy, 75, f3–2. (*See also* Strategic Business Unit Theory)

Bulletin boards, 281–82. (*See also* Advertising, media)

Business data management and analysis, 85. (*See also* Computers)

Cable television, 280–81. (*See also* Broadcast media)

Calendar programs, 98. (*See also* Computers)

Captions, describe and embellish the contents of a photograph or illustration, 222. (*See also* Design, copy)

Cash and expense management, 140–43

Cash cows, 72, 74. (*See also* Strategic Business Unit Theory)

Cash flow management, is the difference between income and outgo, 141. (*See also* Cash and expense management)

Catalogs, brochures and, 312–14, f13–6

Causes, 27

CD-ROM players, is an input peripheral for the computer that takes data from a laser disk and inputs it into the computer, 94. (*See also* Computers)

Characteristics, social, 8–11
changing, f1–3

Chemicals, 14

Circulars, are simple printed sheets describing your services, 314–15, f13–7

Clientele, 7, 103

Clip art, are stock photos which provide an inexpensive alternative to illustrations, 232–34

Color, is the overall density of materials on the page and is a function of column widths, margins, gutters, and the amount of white space available, 216, 235–37. (*See also* Design)

Color xerography, 247. (*See also* Production, alternatives)

Communication, is an exchange of information, 174

    management, 86–88. (*See also* Computers)

    marketing, 5, 176–80, 191–210

    theory, 174–76

Community service, 345–46. (*See also* Public Relations)

Competency, means that the services and products you provide are of the highest quality, 22

Competition, 139–40, 159–62

Competitive intelligence, 32–34, 40–42

Competitors, 18–19

Compounds, 14

Computer, 5, 12, 211–12

    choosing, 99

    communications, 89

    equipment, 89–99

    input devices, 93–95

    output devices, 95

    proper use, 99–100

    software, 96–99

    uses, 81–88, f4–1

Computer printers, 247. (*See also* Production, alternatives)

Consideration, means that you treat everyone with respect, 22–23

Consistency, means that your customers know they can rely on you and your employees to do the job right every time they patronize your salon, 22–23

Consumer behavior, 138–39. (*See also* Demand)

Consumer Protection Agency, 16

Control, 298–99. (*See also* Direct marketing)

Cooperative advertising, 284. (*See also* Advertising, media)

Cooperative mailings, consist of stacks of small circulars from a number of companies, bundled together and mailed to occupants in various neighborhoods, 316

Copy writer, 206. (*See also* Agencies, marketing communications)

Copyrights, provide protection for creative works, such as books, magazine articles, musical compositions, photographs, and art works, 186–88

Cosmetology trade associations, f2–8. (*See also* Research)

Cost, marketing, 20, 136–37, 300

CPU, is the brain of the computer system, and is composed of a microprocessor that performs all of the analytical and computational functions, 90–91. (*See also* Computers)

Customer

    base, 21

    data record, 54–56

    kit, new, 340

    lists, 83–84. (*See also* Computers)

    satisfaction, 20–21

    service, 2–3, 20. (*See also* Marketing, mix)

    service records, 84, f4–3. (*See also* Computers)

Cycles, product, 3

Data analysis, 5, 57–58

Data storage devices, such as disk and floppy drives, are devices used for storing and accessing information, 92–93. (*See also* Computers)

Database management, programs organize and manage information, 82–83, 97. (*See also* Computers)

Day parts, 277–78. (*See also* Broadcast media)

Decor, 104–05

Demand, 137–39

Demographic data, describes the characteristics of the people that you want to make up your target audience, 29, 34–36, 138, 277

    sources, 35

Demonstrations, open houses and, 336. (*See also* Sales Promotion)

Design, 211–40

    color, 235–37

    considerations, 213–15, f10–1

    copy, 219–22, f10–5

    graphics, 230–35

    importance, 211

    layout, 215–19

    principles, 211–13

    size and shape, 237–38

    typography, 222–29

Desktop publishing programs, 98. (*See also* Computers)

Digital still cameras, 94–95. (*See also* Computers)

Digitizing tablets, 93–94. (*See also* Computers)

Direct mail marketing, is sending printed sales solicitations through the mail, 24

Direct marketing, is a means of reaching out to your target audience and delivering a message designed to bring the members of that audience into your salon, 4, 24, 178–79, 237–38, 297–325

and advertising comparison, 297–300
annual reports, 319–20
brochures and catalogs, 312–14
circulars, 314–15
cooperative mailings, 316
lists, 300–302
mailers, 302–10
measuring effectiveness, 323
newsletters, 316–19
sales letters, 310
technology, 322–23
telemarketing, 320–22
vehicles, 302
video mailings, 320

Direct structure, 291–92. (*See also* Advertising, radio anatomy)

Directories and programs, 282. (*See also* Advertising, media)

Displays, 329–32, f14–1, f14–2, f14–3, f14–4. (*See also* Sales Promotion)

Disposal, waste, 18

Distribution channel, is the route a product takes on its journey from the manufacturer to the end user, with a series of intermediaries in between, 151–55

availability, 155–56
retailer utility, 155

Duplicating, high-speed, 246–47. (*See also* Production, alternatives)

Ebbinghaus Forgetting Curve, 265–66, f12–3. (*See also* Advertising, effectiveness)

Economy, state of, 5

Economic conditions, 138. (*See also* Demand)

Electrolysis, is the only method of removing hair permanently, 118

Employee records, 85. (*See also* Computers)

Employment statistics, 7. (*See also* Environments, economic)

Envelope, 306, f13–2. (*See also* Mailers, direct, elements)
stuffers, 341. (*See also* Sales Promotion)

Environmental Protection Agency, is responsible for protecting the environment, 17–18

Environmental marketing, includes those measures you take that are in step with your customers' beliefs and that demonstrate your concern for the environment, 26

Environmentalism, 26

Environments, marketing, f2–1
competitive, 18–19, 42, f1–1
economic, 7–8, 42, f1–1
natural, 17–18, 42, f1–1
political, 13–17, 29, 42, f1–1
social, 8–12, 26, 42, f1–1
technological, 8, 12–13, 42, f1–1

EPA, 17–18. (*See also* Environmental Protection Agency)

Ethnic background, 8, 11

Expense management, 141–43

Expert panels, is a group of people you know and trust, that sit in a room and give opinions on the subject being researched, 52–53

External factors, 5

Facials, 119–20. (*See also* Skin and body care services)

Fashion trends, 5

FDA, 13–15. (*See also* Food and Drug Administration)

Feature story, is an expanded account of some subject within your area of expertise, 344

Federal Trade Commission, regulates commerce in the U.S. by enforcing laws that prevent unfair competitive practices, 14, 64, 182–83

Flights, 278–79. (*See also* Broadcast media)

Focus groups, offer in-depth observations of consumer opinions, 51

Food and Drug Administration, is the regulatory agency responsible for ensuring that products meet the standards of the Food, Drug and Cosmetic Act and that these products are both save and effective, 13–15, 64, 183

Forecasting, 5

Four P's, 2–4, 101, 133, 151, f1–1. (*See also* Marketing, mix)

Frequent customer programs, 341–42. (*See also* Sales Promotion)

Frequency, 265–67, 299–300. (*See also* Advertising, effectiveness and Direct marketing)

FTC, 14, 16. (*See also* Federal Trade Commission)

Fundamental principles, 43–44

Global economy, 7. (*See also* Environments, economic)

Goals, are a declaration of measurable accomplishment for your business as a whole, both in the short term and the long term, 43–44, 140
Government agencies, 13–14, 16–18, 63
Graphics, are the pictures that support the words, 87, 98, 230–35. (*See also* Computers)
  charts, diagrams, and tables, 234
  devices, 234–35
  effective use, 235
  illustrations, 232–34
  photographs, 213–32
GRAS, 14
Gravure, also called intaglio printing, is used for high-quality reproduction, 245. (*See also* Production, printing)
Grids and columns, 217–18. (*See also* Design, layout)

Hair removal services, 118
Hair services
  coloring, 115
  cutting, 112
  straightening, 115
  permanent waving, 114
  scalp treatments, 114–15
  shampooing, 111–12
  styling, 113
  wig sales and maintenance, 115–16
Hardware, refers to the computer system machinery, 89
Harvest strategy, 75, f3–2. (*See also* Strategic Business Unit Theory)
Hazardous waste, 17
Headlines, are short statements designed to attract readers' attention and entice them into reading the rest of the copy, 219. (*See also* Design, copy)
  functions, 287–88. (*See also* Advertising, print anatomy)
Hydrotherapy treatments, are services for cleansing and balancing internal body systems, 122. (*See also* Skin and body care services)

Illustrations, 291. (*See also* Advertising, print anatomy)
Image
  ambiance, 105–06
  clientele, 103
  customer satisfaction, 107–08
  decor, 104–05
  employee demeanor, 106–07
  establishing, 102–03
  importance of, 102
  location, 103
  name, 103–04
  services, 108–10

Income level, 7. (*See also* Environments, economic)
Information, is just the facts, the raw data, 65
  needs, 32–34
  sources, 58–65
"In-your-face" marketing, is a confrontational approach that some marketers use where the messages tend to be loud and raucous and focus more on style than substance, 29
Input devices, are those that let you put information into the computer, 89
Internal Revenue Service, 64
Inventory controls, 86. (*See also* Computers)
Inventory
  control, 168–70
  management, 162–67
Involvement device, is an artifact designed to increase the reader's involvement with the package and his or her attention to its contents, 309. (*See also* Mailer, direct)

Kerning, controls the space between pairs of letters and is used to give certain letter pairs a better appearance, 227–28. (*See also* Typography)
Keyboards, 93. (*See also* Computers)
Kickers, are short statements that introduce a headline, 221. (*See also* Design, copy)
Kit, new customer, 340. (*See also* Sales Promotion)
Knowledge, is the understanding that comes from analyzing the facts, 65

Layout, is the arrangement of the words, pictures, and other design elements on the page, 215
Leading, 227–28. (*See also* Typography)
Legal and ethical issues
  regulatory agencies, 181–84, f8–4
  truth in advertising, 184–86
Letter
  lift, 307–8, f13–3
  sales, 307, 310–12
Letterpress, the oldest form of printing, was developed by Gutenberg in the mid-1400s, 244–45. (*See also* Production, printing)
Lifestyle changes, 8
Lifestyle marketing, is nothing more than knowing and understanding how people live and how their lifestyles affect their buying habits, 25–26
Lists, direct marketing, 300–302. (*See also* Direct marketing)

Location, 103

Magazines, 272–74. (*See also* Print adver-
    tising)
Mailers, direct, 302–4
    elements, 306–10
Mailings, cooperative, 316
Makeup and cosmetic application services,
    123
Margins and gutters, 219. (*See also*
    Design, layout)
Market situation, 42–43
**Marketing, is that series of actions you
    take to develop your products and
    services, ensure their quality and
    value to the customer, set their
    prices, make them available, identify
    to whom you want to sell them,
    inform consumers of them, persuade
    prospects to come intoyour salon,
    satisfy clients' needs, and get them to
    come back, again and again, 1–2**
Marketing
    advocacy, 27–29
    communications, 5, 79, 176–80, 191–210
    costs, 20
    customer satisfaction, 20
    demand creation, 2
    demographics, 34–36
    description, 1–2
    direct mail, 24
    environments, 5–6, 42, f1–2
    importance, 2
    information, 4–5, 31–67
    "in-your-face", 29
    lifestyle, 25–26
    mass, 23
    micro, 23
    mix, 2–4, 25, 101
    niche, 23–24
    objective, 22
    plan, 19, 69–80 (*See also* Plan, market-
        ing)
    pricing, 20, 40
    principals, 20
    process, 2
    promotion, 20
    psychographic data, 36–40
    quality, 20
    research, 44–57
    telemarketing, 24–25
    trends, 20–29
Marketing communications, 191–210, f9–1
    advertising, 178, 259–96. (*See also*
        Advertising)
    agencies, 202–7
    budgets, 201–2
    direct marketing, 178–79
    elements, 191–92, f9–1

measuring effectiveness, 200–201
    objectives, 193–95, f9–2
    personal selling, 177–78
    public relations, 180
    sales promotion, 179–80
    strategy, 195–200
    tactics, 200
    tools, F8–2
**Marketing plan, grows from your overall
    business plan, and it provides you
    with a structure for conducting your
    marketing programs, 19, 69–80** (*See
    also* Plan, marketing)
**Mass marketing, is an approach that
    matches the view that the product is
    more important than the customer, 23**
Massage, body, 120–21. (*See also* Skin and
    body care services)
**Material Safety Data Sheets, also known
    as MSDs, help you track and product
    that might be classed as hazardous,
    164, f165**
Measurement and analysis, 76–77
Media director, 206. (*See also* Agencies,
    marketing communications)
Media knowledge, 264. (*See also* Advertis-
    ing, effectiveness)
**Merchant associations, are small, local
    groups, usually consisting of small
    retail and service business owners in
    a given area, 63**
Message, 197–200, f9–3. (*See also* Strategy,
    marketing)
    principles, 198
Mice and trackballs, 93. (*See also* Comput-
    ers)
**Micro marketing, puts more emphasis on
    the customer's needs and desires and
    less focus on the product, 23**
**Mission statement, clearly and concisely
    sets the parameters of your business
    and focuses your attention on the
    details that will help make your
    salon a success, 43**
Model releases, 188
**Modems, are devices that let your com-
    puter communicate with other com-
    puters by telephone, 96.** (*See also*
    Computers)
Monitors, 92. (*See also* Computers)
Multiculturalism, 8

Nail services, 116–17
Name, 103–04
Needs, information, 32–34
Networking, 87. (*See also* Computers)
Newsletters, 316–19, f13–8
Newspaper advertising, 269–72. (*See also*
    Print advertising)

Niche marketing, 23–24
Noise, an unwanted event that interferes with communication, can be physical or psychological, 175
Norms and values, 38

Objective, marketing, 22, 193–95, f9–2
Occupational Safety and Health Administration, is responsible for ensuring safety in the workplace, 17
Offer, 309–10, f13–4. (*See also* Mailer, direct)
Offset Lithography, is a transfer process that relies on the principle that oil and water don't mix, 245–46. (*See also* Production, printing)
Open houses and demonstrations, 336. (*See also* Sales Promotion)
OSHA, 17. (*See also* Occupational Safety and Health Administration)
Outdoor advertising, 281. (*See also* Advertising, media)
Output devices, are those devices that let you get information out of the computer, 89

Page color, 216–17. (*See also* Design, layout)
Paper, 251–54. (*See also* Production)
  characteristics, 253–54
  classifications, 252–53, f11–2
Patents, give the holders the right to keep others from making and selling similar items, 186–88
Personal appearances, 345. (*See also* Public Relations)
Personal computers, 5
Personal selling, 4, 177–78, 328–29. (*See also* Sales Promotion)
Persuasion, 194. (*See also* Marketing Communications)
Photo gallery, 338. (*See also* Sales Promotion)
Place, are the distribution channels for the products and the methods by which you get your products in the hands of the client, 2–4, 151–72, f1–1. (*See also* Marketing, mix)
  availability, 155–56
  distribution channel, 151–55
  retailer utility, 155
  retailing concepts, 156–70
Placemats, 283–84. (*See also* Advertising, media)
Plan, marketing
  budgeting, 76
  communications, 79
  measurement and analysis, 76–77
  mission and goals, 70–71
  objectives, 71
  process, 78
  Strategic Business Unit Theory, 72–76
  strategy and tactics, 71–76
  structure, 69–70, f3–1
Political Environment, 13–17. (*See also* Environment, political)
Population shifts, 5, 40–41
Positioning, 196–97. (*See also* Strategy, marketing)
Postage, 304–6
Postproduction phase, 243
Premium, is an artifact of some type that serves as an inducement to accept the offer in the direct mail package, 309. (*See also* Mailer, direct)
Preproduction phase, 242–43
Press releases, are short news items that are prepared by businesses and sent to the media in hopes of publication, 342
Price, is the amount of money the customer gives you in return for the value he or she receives, 2–4, 40, 133–49, f1–1, 7. (*See also* Marketing, mix)
  decision factors, 133–40, f6–1
  policies, 143–44
  raising, 144–46
Principals, marketing, 20
Print advertising, 268–77. (*See also* Advertising, media)
  magazines, 272–74
  newspapers, 269–72
  telephone directory, 274–77
Printers, are devices that let you produce hard copy from the information you've entered into the computer, 95. (*See also* Computers)
Printers, commercial, 254–55
Principles, fundamental, 43–44
Product, is the products and services you offer for sale, as well as your salon and yourself, 2–3, 101–31, f1–1. (*See also* Marketing, mix)
  choices, 127
  cycles, 3
  display, 170–71
  mix, 25
  private labeling, 127–28
  retail, 126–30
Production, 241–57
  alternatives, 246–48
  color, 249–51
  paper, 251–54
  photographs and graphics, 248–49
  printers, 254–55
  printing, 244–46
  process, 241–43, f11–1
  stages, 241

Production phase, 243
Production manager, 206. (*See also* Agencies, marketing communications)
Promotion, is marketing communications and the steps you take to inform and persuade your customers, 2–4, 20, 128–30, 139, 173–90, f1–1. (*See also* Marketing, mix)
  brochure, 307
  communication theory, 174–76
  legal and ethical issues, 180–86
  marketing communications, 176–80
  model and property releases, 188
  trademarks, patents, and copyrights, 186–88
Property releases, 188
Psychographic data, is the kind of data that tell you about consumer attitudes and what "hot buttons" you need to push to get response, 36–40, 65–66
Public relations, are those activities that promote your business more than services, 180, 327–28, 341–46
Public relations director, 206. (*See also* Agencies, marketing communications)
Publicity, 4, 341–44
  feature stories, 344
  news coverage, 342
  other exposure, 344
  press releases, 342–44, f14–8
Pull-Quotes, are short statements extracted from the main text and given prominence by setting them in a different typeface and placing them in the margin or in a box within a column, 221. (*See also* Design, copy)

Quality, 2–3, 20–21. (*See also* Marketing, mix)
Quick-print shops, 254–55

RAM, is random access memory that stores information, but can be changed, 91. (*See also* Computers)
Reach, 297–98. (*See also* Direct marketing)
Recession, 7–8
Records analysis, 53–57
Reference groups, 39
Reproduction, color, 249–51. (*See also* Production)
Research, 44–57
  associations & organizations, 60–63
  books & magazines, 59
  expert panels, 52–53
  focus groups, 51
  government, 63–65
  Government Printing Office, 60
    library, 46–47, 59
    newsletters, 59–60
    observation, 47–48
    records analysis, 53–57
    SCORE, 65
    surveys, 48–51
Research directory, 206. (*See also* Agencies, marketing communications)
Response mechanism, 290–91. (*See also* Advertising, print anatomy)
Retail concepts
  competition, 159–62
  inventory control, 168–70
  inventory management, 162–67
  strategies, 156–57
  supplier relationships, 157–59
Retail inventory management, 147–48
Retail sales and services, 124–30
  area, 170–71
  pricing, 146–48
Retailer utility, 155
Retailing, is the selling of products and accessories related to your salon services, 125
Role theory, 38
ROM, is read-only memory that stores information, but it cannot be modified, 91

Sales, 333. (*See also* Sales Promotion)
Sales promotion, covers all the things you do to sell your services, 4, 124, 179–80, 194–95, 327–41
Sales transaction, 135
Sales slip, 53–54, f2–6
Salon, 329. (*See also* Sales Promotion)
SBA, 64
SBU, 72–76, f3–2
Scanners, are devices that translate images, such as photographs and drawings, into digital information that can be handled by the computer, 94. (*See also* Computers)
Scheduling and appointments, 85. (*See also* Computers)
SCORE, the Service Corps of Retired Executives, is a volunteer counseling group who donate time to provide advice and guidance to small business owners, 65. (*See also* Research)
Securities and Exchange Commission, 319. (*See also* Annual reports)
Self-image, 38
Service, customer, 21
Services, salon, 110–24
  categories, 111
Sidebars, perform the same function as pull-quotes but are longer blocks of copy, 221. (*See also* Design, copy)

Signals, are the symbols that carry the information, such as the spoken or written words, 175

Silk-screen printing, 247–48. (*See also* Production, alternatives)

SIMMs, are single in-line memory modules which contain RAM memory, 91

Skin and body care services, 119–22

Slice-of-life structure, 292–94. (*See also* Advertising, radio anatomy)

Small Business Administration, 64

Social characteristics, 8–11

Software, refers to the programs, or instructions that tell the computer machinery what to do, 89

Special events, 333, 335, f14–5. (*See also* Sales Promotion)

Specialized software packages, 98. (*See also* Computers)

Sponsorships, 345. (*See also* Public Relations)

Spreadsheet programs, 97. (*See also* Computers)

Social class, 38–39

Strategic Business Unit Theory, 72–76

Strategy, marketing, is the basic play of action you take to achieve your business objectives, 195–200

Subheads, are short transition statements than can guide the reader from the headline to the body copy or can be inserted within the body copy to introduce new thoughts, 220, 289. (*See also* Design, copy)

Surveys, 48–51

Tactics, are the methods you use to achieve your objectives, 200

Tag line, is a piece of copy used at the end of the ad, summarizes the main idea of the ad and reinforces the major benefit, 289–90. (*See also* Advertising, print anatomy)

Technology advancements, 5, 12–13, 322–23

Telemarketing, is a form of direct marketing where potential customers are contacted by telephone, 24–25, 320–22

Telephone directory advertising, 274–77. (*See also* Print advertising)

Three C's, 22–23

Tie-in promotions, 336–37. (*See also* Sales Promotion)

Tracking, controls the overall spacing between letters, 227–28. (*See also* Typography)

Trade associations, are organizations established to serve the collective needs of member businesses in a given industry, 61

Trademarks, identify a product or service and distinguishes it from other similar products or services, generally in the form of words, symbols, or pictures, 186–88

Traffic flow, 40–41

Transaction, sales, 135 (*See also* Price)

Trends (*See also* Environment, social)
business, 25
family, 11–12
fashion, 5
marketing, 20–29

Typography, is the treatment of the words on the page, 222–29. (*See also* Design)
alignment and column width, 229, f10
effective type use, 229
fonts, 222–24
letter and line spacing, 227–28
size and case, 226–27
styles, 224–26

Utility software packages, 99. (*See also* Computers)

Value, 21

Video, 87. (*See also* Computers)
mailings, 320. (*See also* Direct marketing)
tapes, 338. (*See also* Sales Promotion)

Virus protection programs, 98. (*See also* Computers)

Volatile organic compounds, also referred to as VOCs, are the vapors released into the atmosphere when products made with petroleum-based solvents are used, 17, 126

Voltage spike protectors, prevents damage and loss of information on your computer from voltage surges coming through electric power lines, 96. (*See also* Computers)

Waste
disposal, 18
hazardous, 17

Waxing, 118

Word of mouth, 267–68. (*See also* Advertising, media)

Word processing, programs let you write and edit documents, 86–87, 97, (*See also* Computers)

Wraps and packs, 121–22. (*See also* Skin and body care services)

Yellow Pages, 274–75. (*See also* Print advertising)

Zoning laws, 16

NOTES

NOTES

NOTES

NOTES

NOTES

NOTES

NOTES

NOTES

NOTES

NOTES

NOTES

NOTES

NOTES

NOTES

NOTES

Style.
Savvy.
Solutions.

every month.
SalonOvations

SalonOvations is a professional and personal magazine designed with you in mind. Each issue delivers great features on personal growth and on-target stories about the beauty business. Get helpful hints from industry pros on starting your own salon business and how to satisfy your clients. Plus, you'll get pages of colorful photos of the latest trends in haircutting, styling and coloring.

All this at a great price of ~~12~~ **15** issues for only $19.95 a year! **3 FREE issues** - Save over 40%

(price subject to change)